A Mere Grain of Sand

The extraordinary story of Britain's
most remarkable spiritual healer

Ray & Gillian Brown

with

Paul Dickson

Tagman

www.tagman-press.com

A Mere Grain of Sand

First published in Gt Britain in hardback and paperback in July 2004 by Tagman Worldwide Ltd in The Tagman Press imprint.

Tagman Worldwide Ltd
Lovemore House, 5 Caley Close, Sweet Briar Estate
Norwich NR3 2BU, England UK
Tel: 0845 644 4186
Fax: 0845 644 4187
www.tagman-press.com
email: editorial@tagman-press.com

Acknowledgements: The authors and publisher are grateful for the permissions granted by *Psychic News* and *News of the World* to reproduce the items from their publications which appear between pages 110 and 111.

ISBN
Hardback 1-903571-48-0
Paperback 1-903571-47-2

A CIP catalogue record for this book is available from the British Library

Edited by Jenny Smith
Text & Cover Design by e-Digital, London
Illustrations, line drawings & diagrams by Matt Willis
Authors' photographs by Haydn Jones and Paul Dickson's photograph by Created Images Ltd
Printed by: Barnwells, Aylsham, Norfolk

Tagman

Dedicated in gratitude to our dear friend Paul
who has brought so much wisdom
and love into our lives.

CONTENTS

Part Three
Paul of Tarsus

Part Four
Testimonies

Publisher's Preface

by Anthony Grey

When is Ray Brown not Ray Brown? When he is St Paul!

This conundrum and its answer sums up succinctly, the momentous central claim outlined in this extraordinary book: that St Paul who died nearly 2000 years ago is still effectively alive today and through Britain's leading spiritual healer, Ray Brown, provides modern evidence that all humanity survives physical death.

This almost daily exchange of personalities between two men sharing the same body – a seemingly simple changeover which I have frequently witnessed myself – has potentially profound implications for our scientific and spiritual understanding of the reality in which we live. But can or should we believe the explanation offered by the book's authors?

It is important to say at the outset that some facts of the story are not contestable. Ray Brown has been a trance medium for 37 years and he obviously allows his body to be occupied by a remarkable 'spiritual surgeon' for up to seven hours each working day. During nearly four decades, that surgeon has indisputably healed thousands of people who conventional medicine could not help, including myself.

The work continues to be carried out at regular makeshift clinics up and down Britain and at similar venues during trips to Africa, Asia and Europe. The healer quietly insists he is Paul of Tarsus, who after a dramatic conversion to the faith on a road to Damascus some two thousand years ago became a main founder of one of the world's most influential religions, Christianity. Today he says he prefers to sum up his spiritual philosophy simply in the following words: 'I am just Paul, a servant of God, a mere grain of sand in a vast desert, so being one grain of sand I am part of the whole.' He chose part of that quotation as the title of this volume.

'A likely story, where is the proof ?' is the natural and understandably sceptical response to all this, especially among those who have not personally benefited from Paul's healing ability. But even among those who do benefit there are also doubters as to their benefactor's real identity.

Outright and undeniable proof of the whole concept is of course not available - but the circumstantial evidence of the story told in this book is in my view deeply compelling. Most significantly for me the healing is not of a 'magical' or miraculous kind. Paul asserts he is carrying out practical surgical operations, employing an advanced form of our own medical science. He says he is doing this with the direct assistance of teams of skilled, trained surgeons and doctors who are operating simultaneously with him in the spiritual dimension on every individual case he tackles. Where necessary he guides their surgical instruments and lasers which are equally invisible to us. They are able to succeed where our best medical professionals fail, he says, because knowledge of medical science in that spiritual dimension is about 100 years in advance of our own. He does not however claim to be able to cure everybody who seeks his help.

During those many years of his healing work Ray has also frequently given over his body to Paul at other times so that he can speak at seminars and workshops and provide a more comprehensive understanding about those spiritual dimensions. Effectively Paul is pursuing a two-fold mission: delivering updated teachings about the totality of our existence and the best ways for us to tackle it, while almost daily healing the sick or easing their suffering.

In essence, Paul of Tarsus, if that is who he is, has for nearly four decades been tirelessly pursuing a travelling mission of teaching and healing that is very similar to that carried out by the man he first persecuted then served so selflessly until his execution nearly two thousand years ago. One big difference between the two is that after his death, Jesus of Nazareth showed himself physically resurrected from the dimension of Spirit in his own body while Paul of Tarsus says he makes use of another's body to demonstrate the same truth. However, he no longer describes his teachings as Christian; he says our deeply troubled world today desperately needs one single spiritual teaching – and his, he maintains is the most basic.

He confirms that re-incarnation back to Earth is possible - yet advises against it since individuals coming back from the realm of Spirit are hampering our progress. Also he says karma is worked out in the spiritual dimensions, not on Earth.

To those who might be sceptical about this whole extraordinary story, after knowing Ray and Gillian and Paul for seven years I feel moved to point out how much courage and self-sacrifice is required from Ray each working day. It took quite a few years of training for him to learn how to become a trance medium after he sensed and realised it was his destiny to do such extraordinary and potentially alarming work. However much Ray makes light of it, it can not be easy to vacate your body for many hours each day to 'go under an anaesthetic' somewhere else as Ray likes disarmingly to put it. Paul says that in fact Ray was selected for the unique role from many other potential candidates whilst still in his mother's womb – in the same manner, I seem to recall, as some prophets of the Old Testament are said to have been chosen!

No other trance medium anywhere in the world apparently is known to spend up to seven hours each day away from his body. To do this obviously requires a massive trust on Ray's part. Gillian's crucial support role in all this to-ing and fro-ing and the constant travelling and nurturing which she organises for Ray and Paul, is in my view equally heroic. I personally regard it as a great privilege to know all three of them as friends - and to assist them in bringing their amazing story together in this book so that it might be offered to the general public at last for wider consumption.

I have become its publisher because I have personally benefited from Paul's spiritual surgery skills since 1997. Following two arthroscopy operations for a very painful cartilage problem in my right knee, which caused me constant exhausting pain, a conventional surgeon advised me in that year as a last resort to have a wedge-shaped chunk of bone chopped out from my lower leg. I had already been told running and tennis were things of the past and that I should take lifts not stairs and always use a car instead of walking. Learning of Ray Brown's existence a few days before the operation I drove from London to consult him quickly at Fir Tree Lodge near Lutterworth and on examining the knee Paul said immediately: 'Don't have the operation, I will fix it.' And he did, sorting out displaced nerves and tendons on the spot and eventually 'inserting some material' in the joint to cushion the area where the cartilage had been worn away completely by excessive devotion over the years to playing football, rugby, squash, tennis and skiing. Paul has topped up this 'material' regularly ever since and the repair was so successful I was able to resume playing tennis and cricket and, under Paul's supervision, to fulfil a lifetime's ambition and complete the London Marathon for the first time in the year 2000. Paul told me the 'material' used in my knee was made inside my body and I said that sounded a bit like modern stem cell therapy. 'We've been working on stem cell research for over 70 years,' he replied quietly.

So I personally have no difficulty now accepting Paul's contention about his true identity, although as a former foreign correspondent with Reuters I sometimes wonder what my former editors might have said if I had filed a news report claiming to have interviewed St Paul, nearly 2000 years after he was beheaded on the orders of the Roman Emperor Nero!

I accept his claim without reservation mainly because over the past seven years I have come to know a very intelligent, warm, compassionate and dedicated individual who is both light-hearted and at the same time deeply serious and earnest in his approach to his work. He speaks with seemingly equal authority and integrity about his advanced knowledge of medicine and his past life originally as Saul, then later as Paul the

Apostle or Paul of Tarsus. So it would be totally inconsistent with all that I know of him for him to speak anything but the truth on the matter of who he really is. I have recommended many friends and acquaintances with health problems to consult Ray and Paul over the past seven years and for all these reasons The Tagman Press will be offering copies of this book to leading representatives of the medical professions in Britain, including the British Medical Association and the Royal College of Surgeons and trusting that some of them will be open-minded enough to investigate further.

Three medical professionals have already endorsed the value of the work being done by Ray and Gillian Brown and Paul. Dr. Andrew Powell, the writer of the following Foreword urges that Paul's work be scientifically evaluated to provide a platform for further research and study; Walter Fisher who writes one of the Testimonies in Part Four is an experienced Norwegian neuro-surgeon who explains why he preferred to undergo a 'spiritual operation' by Paul for a slipped disc in his neck rather than be treated by one of his own professional colleagues; and a General Practitioner based in Liverpool has often referred her patients to Paul for treatment and sometimes taken medical students to Paul's clinic to watch him at work.

So, clearly one of Paul's chief ambitions which is to demonstrate that his work as a spiritual surgeon can be an important complementary support to our current mainstream medicine, is already being achieved on a modest scale. Overall, this narrative and Ray's life's work, I feel sure, take medical science and our understanding of the science of spirituality to new frontiers. I am convinced that both this book and Ray and Gillian's work with Paul when more widely known and understood, will prove to be of historic importance in both spheres and will draw greater attention to the larger aspects of Paul's mission in the wider world.

Foreword

by Dr. Andrew Powell

MA, MRCP, FRC Psych

Throughout my years working as a consultant in the Health Service I have had a deep concern with the nature of the healing process, which influences my work as a psychiatrist and medical psychotherapist.

As well as publishing a number of papers in this field, I undertook practical studies at the College of Healing and joined the Scientific and Medical Network, an international body of scientists, doctors and other health professionals who are concerned with widening and extending our understanding of scientific research and knowledge to include the spiritual dimension.

As a member of the Royal College of Physicians and Royal College of Psychiatrists, I regard the mind/body connection as crucial. Indeed, I believe that our understanding of the psyche-soma will hold the key to developments in medicine in the 21st century.

My contact with Ray Brown followed from a television documentary in which his healing practice was described. I have spent a number of days observing his clinical work at first hand.

Working under the guidance of his higher spiritual source, Ray Brown as 'Paul' then saw and treated up to 30 patients each day. The majority of patients suffered from severe musculo-skeletal disorders, many with prolapsed intervertebral discs and chronic sciatica. Some had failed to improve, or had deteriorated after surgical interventions.

There were also a number of patients with a diverse range of problems, from multiple sclerosis and Parkinson's Disease, through to inflammatory bowel disease, cancer and other multi-system disorders.

The clinic is run on a professional basis, with the administration competently managed by Gillian Brown. After a brief history is taken in note form at consultation, 'Paul' works with unwavering concentration. He is courteous and respectful in all his consultations and demonstrates remarkable clinical acumen, especially in the field of back disorders.

I personally saw a number of patients who attended with an established history of severe medical problems which remained untouched by a range of physical treatments. Most responded immediately and with demonstrable success to the healing intervention, so that back pain, which had profoundly restricted movement, for example, was entirely or substantially relieved. I am not able to comment personally on long-term follow-up, but I am told that the majority of these patients remain well.

The technique used involves physical touch and the manipulation of joints and soft tissues. However, this is not to be confused with osteopathic or chiropractic manipulations as the bony structures are not handled in any way that gives rise to the risk of injury or other trauma. There may be some discomfort but the client is warned of this.

On the few occasions when articles of clothing needed to be removed, the patient was chaperoned and towels were placed over the patient appropriately.

These interventions differ from the more usual practice in spiritual healing of working without body contact. Also importantly, Ray Brown is a trance medium working in trance as 'Paul'.

However, it should be emphasised that during his clinical work as 'Paul', he is entirely alert and fully conscious, taking the term in its usual sense, so that patients have the experience of being seen by a competent and experienced clinical practitioner. 'Paul' also discussed at length with me his understanding of pathology and the basis of neuromuscular disorders so that we could see in what ways his ideas are similar to, and different from, current medical understanding. It is noteworthy in this regard that 'Paul' wishes to share his thinking with medical practitioners so as to help build a bridge between physical and spiritual medicine. Finally 'Paul' did not offer any advice that conflicted with the patient's medical practitioner and where doubt existed, he suggested that the patient consult their own doctor.

From the point of view of those many people clearly seeking healing and physical relief from pain and distress, the work that Ray and Gillian Brown are doing impressed me as being of great value and I do not doubt that they are entirely conscientious and sincere in their therapeutic approach.

Because patients are evidently coming from far afield and in some cases need treatment on consecutive days, the immediate aim is to provide a larger centre with residential accommodation for overnight stays. Such an endeavour is coming at a time when links between healers and the medical profession are beginning to take root. There is now academic and research-based evidence that healing works (see 'Healing Research' Volume I by Dr Daniel Benor, Southfield MI: Vision Publications 2001, ISBN 1-88678-11-2, describing over 150 controlled studies of healing, of which more than half demonstrated significant positive effects).

In my view, the work of healers such as Ray Brown should be readily amenable to objective scientific evaluation and this will provide a further important platform for research and study.

Introduction

by Paul Dickson

A Mere Grain of Sand is in many different respects a story that could indeed grace a Hollywood blockbuster. Primarily of course it offers an answer to the great age-old question of whether there is an afterlife beyond our present physical existence. Yet in essence it is also the down-to-earth tale of three people Ray Brown, his wife Gillian and Paul, the spiritual surgeon who works through Ray.

In the pages which follow, Ray, Gillian and Paul tell their own interlocked stories in their own words with only a little help from me in organisation and presentation. So perhaps it might help if I first explain where I come in.

I met Ray, Gillian and Paul in November 2001, when I went to their surgery for treatment in a very basic community hall in Bury St Edmunds. I was also simultaneously researching a feature on Ray Brown for the local Suffolk Journal magazine. This was my first brush with a spiritual surgeon. I was feeling quite apprehensive and was armed with a fair dose of scepticism.

I had travelled to Bury St Edmunds with a friend of a friend, Lynn – a lady in her seventies. She was in considerable pain from a hip replacement operation that had gone wrong. I had a bad back and various old rugby injuries that needed attention. Lynn and I agreed to swap notes on our experiences.

I was almost overwhelmed by the positive vibes that were emanating from the very ordinary room that was being used as a surgery. Gillian and her mother, Connie formed the reception committee, and took personal details and information on my physical complaints. A cup of tea was offered and I settled back to wait for my appointment with Paul.

Files were displayed full of testimonials from satisfied patients along with press cuttings, most notably from the *News of the World* in 1998. Paul had successfully healed Associate Editor Phil Taylor's back. He'd also come to the rescue of the actor Sir John Mills, who had a very bad back condition that was preventing him from going on stage. Facsimiles of these newspaper articles are shown among this book's illustrations.

Paul saw Lynn before me. He quickly ran his hands over the affected areas and asked Lynn to take a few steps. She said she was walking more easily and Paul told her to come back the following month.

Then it was my turn. I sat face to face with Paul. We discussed my condition. It was just like being at a doctor's surgery. Here seemingly was a well-spoken, knowledgeable surgeon with a faintly Middle Eastern accent, assessing my problems.

But no, this was Ray Brown, a former brickie and dockyard worker with no medical training, and I was just about to let him loose on my body – or was this Ray Brown?

Paul sat me on the consulting couch and began prodding my back. Things started going pop. These were my nerves being put back in place. Soon my session was over and I was asked to come back the following month.

I returned twice for healing and each time my back felt better. I felt taller and more relaxed. At the end of my first session I had witnessed the transformation between Paul and Ray. Paul rubbed his eyes briefly and gone was the urbane doctor and before me was an ordinary bloke from the South Coast.

There was definitely something extraordinary happening, it couldn't just be a clever act. The change between Paul and Ray was striking. The healing also seemed to be working.

Paul's healing can result in residual discomfort and special ointment is supplied to rub on affected areas. If the pain doesn't go, Gillian can arrange for Paul to do absent healing.

Lynn remained in some pain after her third consultation and asked for some special healing, which she was told would happen in the middle of the night. 'I woke up and sensed a presence in the room', she told me. 'Then my leg was moved around the bed. It was an incredible experience.'

Sadly Paul was unable to heal Lynn. Her joints were too worn out and she went for another conventional hip replacement operation. I was impressed by this honesty. This was no charlatan taking money from helpless people, but a caring medical practitioner.

I was hooked. I wanted to find out more. What does Paul do when he works through Ray? Why was Ray chosen to host Paul? Why had Ray had such a difficult life and how did he survive all his terrible accidents? Why did Gillian leave her family to follow Paul? What happens 'on the other side' – in the spirit world?

My curiosity led to my agreeing to help write this book in which these and many more questions are answered. Outside perspectives are provided by testimonies I was given by people whom Paul has healed and interviews I recorded with friends of Ray and Gillian who have helped them along this special path which they are treading. Ray and Gillian's stories are narrated in their own words based on edited, recorded interviews with them. I simply set the scene at the start of each chapter with a few words of my own which appear in italics.

Paul's story is also drawn together from interviews and his lectures in which he always explains that he is the spirit of the early Christian leader, Paul of Tarsus, who was beheaded in Rome during the reign of Emperor Nero. He says he is the same man who famously was converted to Christianity following a vision on the road to Damascus. After his death, he says he chose to train as a doctor in the spirit dimension and was later selected to return to Earth to heal and also to teach and increase our understanding of the spirit world. In addition to his new teachings and explanations of the spiritual dimension, Paul also explains his reasons for working through Ray and Gillian.

In one of our early interview sessions, when I was talking to Gillian, I was suddenly aware that Ray was staring at me. But in fact this was not Ray! Paul had arrived unexpected and unannounced in Ray's body. I felt very uncomfortable as he continued to stare very intently at me. It felt as if he was reading my mind. Afterwards Ray and Gillian told me smilingly he was just checking that I was up to the job!

Paul, I can only say I trust that I have been able to do justice in these pages to you and this whole extraordinary and fascinating story.

Part One

Raymond Brown

Chapter 1

Beginnings

Ray Brown was born in Birmingham on May 4, 1946 to parents Ivor and Marcia Brown. His elder brother Peter was born four years earlier. The family moved to a little community on an old RAF base at Atherstone-on-Stour, just south of Stratford-upon-Avon, when he was two. Ray's violent father left for another woman when he was five. Ray contracted tuberculosis soon after he went to school and did not have a formal education until he was 10. He began to have out-of-body experiences after he was diagnosed with tuberculosis. Marcia met another partner, Bob. They moved to Portsmouth for Ray's health, when he was seven, and lived in a house paid for by Ivor out of a substantial sum of money he won on the football pools.

My Dad was a policeman in Birmingham, before I was born. He was quite a good boxer and used to box for the Midlands Police Force. I think he was beaten up badly during the course of his job and spent a lot of time in hospital. He might have had a nervous breakdown but I have never been able to get to the bottom of that.

He definitely had a violent streak. When he lost his marbles he really did lose them and went frantic. I can remember him coming home drunk one night when I was very young. He hit Mum and dragged her round the house by her hair. He also slapped my brother Peter, but left me alone. I suppose I was too small a target.

I screamed the place down telling him to stop. Mum took a few hidings from him but never used to talk much about it.

Dad became a storeman after he left the police. He was a hard working bloke and did not get home until 7pm. Mum used to prepare his bath for him in an old fashioned tin bath. She went across to the communal boiler house on the camp where a big copper urn was used to boil water for several families. Mum carried Dad's bath water home in a bucket. During the summer he would have his bath outside. Then we would hop into his water after he was finished and have a swill down!

There was an old Native American on the camp, called Gertie. I have a picture of her pushing me in a pram.

My brother was on his way to catch the bus to school and one of the buttons had come off his braces. Gertie saw him and said, 'I'll sew it back on for you, boy.' She took him back to her house, stitched a new button on, tucked him in and sent him off to school.

Later on that day Peter wanted to go to the toilet but couldn't as she had sewn the button to his trousers and his shirt. My brother laughs about that now. I don't know how she came to be living at Atherstone, but she had obviously married an Englishman.

Dad was the self-appointed tough guy in the community. Once a cow became stuck on a fence. It had tried to jump the gate. The poor cow's udders were being ripped by the barbed wire on the fence and its legs were hanging over either side. The farmer didn't know what to do.

Instead of waiting for help, Dad said, 'I'll get her off.' He took hold of two hooves and lifted the animal up. The cow managed to free itself from the fence, kicked out, smacked him in the mouth and knocked him to the ground!

He still did a lot of boxing, probably semi-professionally and was a great boxing fan. One good memory I have, is sitting on his knee with my brother, listening to a Don Cockel and Rocky Marciano fight on the radio. Dad did all the boxing moves as he followed the action. A motorbike accident finished his boxing career. The chain came off the bike and virtually sliced the calf off one of his legs.

Another good example of his violent nature was the time that Peter and I 'borrowed' his bike.

Peter said to Mum: 'Can we play with dad's bike?' He was about 6ft 3in, so his saddle was miles up! I sat on the child seat and my brother got on a big boulder and climbed onto the main seat. Peter's feet just dangled nowhere near the pedals.

We went flying off and Peter couldn't reach the brakes. A bird was sitting on the path and wouldn't move. As we hurtled towards it, Peter just abandoned ship and jumped off. I was left hanging on as the bike careered down a hill. Eventually it toppled over in a field right into the path of a tractor.

I grazed all my arms and my back and was screaming the place down, but with the noise of the tractor nobody could hear me. The tractor's plough mangled the bike and fortunately missed me.

We ran away and left the bike. Mum came out and said: 'Your Dad will be after you for this.' She put the bike, or bits of it, behind the shed.

Dad was sleeping and was planning to go to the pub later. Peter thought we are in trouble here, and said: 'If Dad catches us he is going to kill us, so to get out of the way we will climb the big tree near the house.' The tree is still there, but the house has long gone.

Peter helped me up the tree and we sat there shaking. I could hear Dad talking to Mum. He said: 'I am off to the pub.' She replied: 'You don't need to go to the pub today do you?' She was trying everything to stop him finding the damaged bike.

Anyway, he went to get the bike and screamed out when he saw it. You could tell he was not very happy. He shouted: 'I'll kill them, I'll kill them,' along with lots of unprintable words!

He called out our names, but we hid in the tree. After a couple of hours he said: 'Come on my boys, I won't hurt you.' He knew we were around but did not know where. Because his voice was calm, my brother thought that he was over it and said: 'I think we can go down now.'

But he was not over it. Dad lashed out with his belt and buckle across my brother's head, neck and back. Of course I was lashed as well because I was part of it. I kept trying to blame Peter but it did not work! We spent two days in our room. That is how bad my dad was, he was a big violent man.

He left home when I was five. I know very little about it, but he won money on the pools, and disappeared off the scene. Mum told me that he met another lady in London.

I went to see him in London when I was seven. I was put on a train in Portsmouth. We had moved to Portsmouth, because it was better for my tuberculosis, and Dad had given Mum the money to buy a house.

Dad met me at Waterloo Station. We went to the sweet shop that he had bought with his girlfriend.

Dad was always spoiling for a fight. He once took me to a pay phone outside the sweet shop. This man came along. He was shouting at Dad and obviously knew him. Dad was on the phone talking to Mum and said: 'Just hold on a moment my dear there is a small problem.'

He turned to me and said: 'Stay there son,' and went out. I heard muffled sounds. They shouted at each other, as the man pulled his coat off. That was Dad's favourite trick: 'Go on get your coat off'. Then once the coat was over his opponent's shoulders, he would let rip and hit him.

He knocked this man onto the pavement, came back in and said: 'Well

I have solved that small problem.'

I probably only went up to London twice. It faded after that. Peter did not want to go and I think Dad got a lot of hassle from the woman he was living with so stopped having us up there.

Much later, around 1968, I tried tracing him, but did not get anywhere. So he must have died. The last I heard was that he had moved to Australia but that could have been my Mum's way of making me forget him. The only thing he gave me was a temper and a lot of good hidings.

Mum was a tiny little thing. She was the type of person who would always help other people and would never hurt a fly, well not intentionally! Mum had her own religious beliefs and did not think that you had to go to church to be godly and walk the path.

I think there was Romany blood in the family as she had an olive skin. She also had great musical talent and played the violin. Mum enjoyed playing jazzy type music as well as classical. When I was ill in bed she would practice. She always practiced when her partner Bob was out.

Mum met Bob Black after Dad left. When he was at home he did not like her to play. So when the house was quiet and she had done her housework, she used to get the violin out and practiced for up to three hours.

There is a particular piece of music, which I still love, called 'Romanza'. She played that a lot. Everybody on the camp would open their windows and listen to her music.

Mum called me Jack not Ray. I was known as Jack, because when I was tiny, I knocked out my front baby teeth. I had no teeth in the front for a while. As the saying goes, Jack Sprat could eat no fat. So because I could not chew anything, I was given Jack as a nickname and it stuck.

Everyone in the family knew me as Jack and it is only in recent years with Gillian that the family has actually started calling me Ray again!

Bob Black was in the Army when we were at Atherstone-on-Stour, but when he was discharged he became a fitter for De Havilland, the aircraft manufacturer. He probably met Mum down at the local pub. We used to go there on Sundays. All the kids would be in the garden. Bob moved in permanently sometime before we went to Portsmouth, because my eldest half-sister was born at Stratford-upon-Avon.

To begin with Bob must have just stayed with us when he was off duty from the Army base at Long Marsden. Dad visited one night and sparked off an assault by Bob on our home, armed with a rifle! I do not think Dad would have stayed over had he known about Bob, but Mum was probably too scared to tell him.

Somehow Bob heard that Dad was in the house. I do not know what went through his mind, but anyway he got drunk. The story goes that he knocked out the guard in the sentry box at the barracks and took his rifle with fixed bayonet. Then he rode over to our house on his bike, no doubt getting more and more wound up.

Dad had gone to bed with Mum. Peter and I were not asleep. We were talking and messing about with our torches. Suddenly we heard this awful crash and splintering of wood.

We shot out of bed and ran to Mum's room. Bob was outside swearing and cursing. His bayonet was stuck through the door and he was prising it open. I saw Dad's bum disappearing out of the bedroom window, trousers in hand!

Bob charged in and searched the house. It ended up with Mum, Peter and myself lined up against a wall. Bob was shouting at Mum and waving the rifle at us. My grandmother lived next door and could hear all the commotion. She marched into the house holding a large, cast-iron frying pan, hit Bob on the head and knocked him out.

Bob was discharged from the Army in disgrace, but the incident did not deter Mum as their relationship blossomed.

He definitely was not living with us when I contracted TB, because I was at home with Mum on my own a lot.

I have some recollection of being at school. I can visualize the schoolhouse and playground along with Mrs Bulbeck, our teacher. The doctor came to school to do the TB test. My test was positive and I was sent home.

I went to Stratford-upon-Avon Memorial Hospital and was there for a long time. When I came out, the District Nurse visited every day to give me injections; in fact I had daily injections until I was 10. I watched for her car until it approached across the old runway. Then I would think: 'Right, it's time to leave or hide somewhere.'

I never left the house, but normally hid under the bed. She knew exactly where I was. The needles were in a carrying case in her little black bag. I listened as she flicked the lid off and asked Mum for some boiling water. The needles were prepared in the water, then when she was ready, she would call out: 'Where is he, I wonder where he is?'

On one occasion I went under the bed and got stuck half way. Actually it was quite convenient for the nurse as my bottom was sticking out. She entered the room and said: 'Gotcha!'

I kicked my legs about, but she still managed to hit the spot! They were huge needles for such a small kid. In those days they were just one size and nine times out of ten the nurse sharpened them herself. So you can imagine.....

There was no education for me at home or when I was in hospital. I used to go potato picking with Mum. I would be tucked up next to a straw bale as she went to work. Mum used to do four plots and some-times I chipped in with half a plot.

I had a little white terrier called Spot to keep me company. I used to go everywhere on the camp with him. But one day he followed another dog into a field. The other dog started chasing the cows and Mr Bishop, the farmer, took a pot shot at both dogs and killed Spot. The other dog lived to fight another day, but that was the end of my Spot.

My out-of-body experiences started at night when we were still at Atherstone-on-Stour. I did not take much notice of the first one because I thought it was a dream. But when the next one happened I told my Mum, because it was quite scary. She just calmed me down and said it was my TB.

I think she spoke to the nurse about it and she said it was the result of the trauma caused by falling ill and leaving school. Of course it carried on. Unfortunately I cannot remember what it actually felt like in the early stages. But when I got a bit older, I was more aware of what was happening. I felt my body lift, then suddenly I was looking down at it from above the bed.

It was a very peaceful experience. It is like you are there but you are not! It is a weird sensation that is very difficult to explain. Once I was used to it, I would stand in the room next to my body in the bed. Then I started walking about the house. The next morning I would remember what I had seen, but it would seem just like a dream. I would tell Mum what I had seen her do in the kitchen. There would be a look of shock on her face. So that made me wonder what was going on.

At one stage I came out of my body every night. Paul told Gillian that the reason for doing it was to make the transition between Paul and myself easy. The worst part of going into trance is the fear of handing over your body to someone else.

Paul wanted the transition to be as smooth as possible, so that is why he lifted me in and out a lot. I became used to leaving my body for periods of time. The best time to do it is in the sleep state, because you can leave your body for long periods, without doing any harm to yourself.

Over the years Mum started threatening to take me to the doctor, if I did not stop talking about my experiences. She did not like it at all. Mum would say: 'I have had enough of this, Jack. I have had enough of your messing about.' She thought that the only way to understand it was to think that I was getting out of bed and going downstairs, hiding somewhere and listening to conversations. But I used to tell her that I had seen her making Bob's sandwiches. I would tell her what the ingredients were. It used to freak her out!

By the time I was 15 and growing up, the out-of-body experiences began to disturb me. I asked Mum if I was mentally ill. She said: 'I don't know. I think I am going to have to take you to see a psychiatrist.' I suppose it upset her a lot. Fortunately she talked to Ron and Marjorie Wells about my problems. We were living with them at the time in Portsmouth.

Ron and Marjorie were members of the Christopher West Healing Group. This was a spiritual healing group. They understood straight away what was happening to me and asked Mum if they could take me along to one of the meetings. George Jones, the leader of the group had a spirit called Dr Hoist who came through and told me that a spirit would work through me, and that I had to sit to prepare myself; but more on that later.

The out-of-body experiences stopped that night.

Chapter 2

Early Years In Portsmouth

Ivor Brown used his pools win money to buy the family a house in Portsmouth, which was thought to be a better area to live for Ray's health. Marcia, Bob, Peter, Ray and new half sister Helen moved to Portsmouth when Ray was seven. Treatment continued for his TB and Ray stayed away from school until he was 10. A second half-sister, Diane, was born in Portsmouth. Meanwhile Bob began an affair with a canteen woman at the De Havilland factory. In 1959, he announced that he was going to sell the family home and look for a new property. He moved Marcia and the children up to Wallsend (Tyneside) to live with his relatives, on the pretext that they needed somewhere to stay, while he looked for a house. Then Bob promptly ran off with the canteen woman and the proceeds of the house sale. After six months in Wallsend, Marcia and the children returned to Portsmouth and stayed with her sister Jean. Marcia spotted an advert in a paper offering lodgings, and moved the family to Ron and Marjorie Wells' house. However, Bob returned to live with them again and the family moved to New Road. Bob's violent nature was often directed at Ray and Peter and successive beatings eventually spurred Ray into studying judo and karate so that he could protect himself. When Ray was 17, a row over his bike developed into a fight which was to become a turning point in both their lives.

Life at home with Bob was quite difficult. In the early days, Peter and I used to get a slap around the ear at least once a day and a good hiding once a week. He really ignored us after our half-sisters were born, but always gave us lots of verbal abuse. Diane, my second sister was born in St Mary's Hospital, Portsmouth.

As far as Bob was concerned, when he got in from work, you would either have to be in bed or out of sight. If you answered him back he would hit you. You were not allowed to say 'but'. He would threaten you and say: 'I'll butt you'. Then he would come over and hit you.

Peter and I had to learn to please him to avoid his wrath. If he came in and said: 'I want fish and chips' - we would have to go and get them. He would not drive to get them. We would have to walk. Of course by the time we returned, the fish and chips were stone cold. So he would hit us for that and would hit us again if we answered back.

If he'd had a bad day at work, he would round on us in the evening. Peter and I were always banished from the TV room. We had a black and white 12-inch TV. Bob and Mum watched the TV and we were sent outside to play. But my sisters could go in and sit on his lap and watch the programmes with them. He segregated the family.

I ended up hating him because I was battered every time I did anything – right or wrong. He had this attitude that he was the man of the house and you would do as you were told and that was that.

Sadly I can only remember the bad things about Bob. When I was about 14, he had an old Vauxhall Vanguard that would not start in the morning. He would get Peter and I up at 6am to push-start it down the road. It was like pushing a tank and he would get really angry if we could not get it going. He would call us weaklings and all sorts of names.

My brother began to rebel when he was seventeen. One day he decided enough was enough, went down to the Army careers office, and joined up.

Peter was in the Army for over 10 years and travelled the world. He was based in British Honduras, Jamaica and Germany. When Peter went, Bob's verbal abuse was focussed on me.

He was quite a heavy drinker. On Friday nights he would go out for a quick one. But Saturday night and Sunday lunchtime were his main drinking times. He was always paralytic on Saturday nights. That was when he was at his worst.

I kept out of his way when he had been drinking. He never laid a hand on Mum. No matter what he put her through, he really seemed to love her. They never married, because Mum did not get round to divorcing Dad.

We never had much money. Every Monday, Mum would go to the local pawnshop and pawn something so that she had money to last us through until Bob gave her the housekeeping on Friday. The same things always went in; a lot of people used to do it.

She joined a clothing club and bought blankets and sheets, but never opened them. They would go in and out of the pawnshop on a regular basis! Quite often she would get the extra money just to ensure that Bob could have his tobacco.

She was a very caring person, a typical housewife. Mum was always put down by the men she was with and was never allowed to flourish. She never worked other than seasonal harvesting jobs when I was a baby, but did a little bit of cleaning for some people when we were together in Portsmouth. Mum had a weak heart, which prevented her from doing too much.

I went to the clinic in Portsmouth and had my last check-up when I was 10. Successfully cleared of TB, I returned to school at the end of my last junior year. Not being a 'scholar', I ended up in a Secondary Modern School and could not cope. Nothing was done to help me. They did not really have special needs education in those days. So I was just put in the D class, D for Dunce!

Most of the kids in my class either had health problems or were just dunces like me. There were children with epilepsy who, because they had fits and took time to recover, never managed to get a clear run at school. If they had a fit in class, the teacher would come over and stick a ruler in their mouth. They would stay in the class until the fit was over. There wasn't anywhere to go and lie down and recover, not like today. They just had to sit back in their chair and wait until it was all over. People with no academic ability were sent outside to do gardening to fill in the day.

I could not even do my two times table when I went back to school. It was difficult to get my head round arithmetic because I had lost so much time. They were teaching fractions and decimals and I thought, what are these things?

Because I did not really have a clue what I was doing, the teachers tended to lose interest. If I was given an exam paper, I would just push it aside and say: 'I cannot do that. I do not even know what you are talking about!'

I was no good in science classes because I was not able to read. In English, the teacher would write things on the blackboard and because I did not even understand what he or she was saying, I would lose interest, and end up getting the blackboard rubber thrown at me for not listening.

I was regularly sent to the headmaster for not concentrating. The only place that I could get on was in the woodwork class or metalwork. Mind you my work was fairly rough and ready because I could not use a ruler properly!

Over the years, I gradually began to understand how to use a ruler and read it properly. But even though I learnt to read a bit, poor spelling held back my development. I was told that the only job I was likely to get was road sweeping! But I managed to pass a test for an apprenticeship.

I spent a day at Wadham Stringers' car workshop in Southsea and had to clean up a piece of metal ready for spraying. I handled the tools well, but I failed the written exam. Anyway I was lucky because they took me on. My practical skills must have been enough for them.

But long before Wadham Stringers, my Mum, half-sisters and I spent six months living with Bob's relatives in Wallsend on Tyneside.

As I said before, Bob worked at De Havilland's aircraft factory as a fitter and began having an affair with a woman who served in the canteen. He left us for the first time to live with her for about eight weeks.

Mum was taken to hospital with heart problems just after Bob moved out. She had valvular heart disease and was quite sick. My grandmother came down from Birmingham to look after my sisters and me and let Peter know that Bob had moved out.

Peter was given leave from the Army and went to see Mum in hospital to tell her about Bob. He also let the hospital know what had happened so that the doctors and nurses could keep an eye on her.

He found out where Bob's girlfriend lived and went round to confront him. Peter 'duffed' him up a bit and left! Bob returned home when Mum came out of hospital. He told her that he had finished with his girlfriend and suggested that we should start afresh, sell the house, and move away.

Mum fell for this. The house was sold and we headed north to Wallsend and lived in a flat that had been found by Bob's Geordie relatives. His family were really good to us. Then one day Bob told Mum that he needed to go back to Portsmouth to tie up some unfinished business.

Bob did not come back. He married his girlfriend using Mum's money and left us virtually penniless in Wallsend. We stayed there for six months before returning to Portsmouth to live temporarily with Mum's sister, Jean.

Mum found us lodgings with Ron and Marjorie Wells who, as I described in the last chapter, introduced me to the Christopher West Healing Group. I'll say more about that later. Meanwhile like a bad penny, Bob came back on the scene again soon after my fifteenth birthday. He found out that we were in Portsmouth and visited Mum. She decided to give him another chance. So we moved out of Ron and Marjorie's to a property in New Road. There was no money left, Bob had spent the proceeds of the house sale on his girlfriend.

By now I was at Wadham Stringers and needed a bike to get to work. I bought one on HP. It costs seven shillings and sixpence a week. Bob had to act as guarantor, because I was still under-age.

I also had a Saturday job in a local bakery. At the end of the day they gave me doughnuts and allowed me to choose a loaf. One day I took a cottage loaf. I really liked the top bit, which was crispy. But when I arrived home, Bob said that he wanted the top of the loaf. I refused to give it to him and an argument began.

This time it was much worse than usual. I gave Bob a bit of lip and he launched himself at me. I was trapped between the cooker and the wall as Bob pounded me mercilessly. Mum had to step between us because she was frightened that he would kill me.

My ribs were badly damaged. I could not go to work for three weeks. I had had enough of Bob's violence so decided to take up judo to protect myself. I studied judo and karate and became a black belt in both disciplines, but had to give up after my accident in Portsmouth dockyard (see Chapter Four). I was just about to represent Portsmouth at judo at that time, but it was not to be.

My relationship with Bob did not improve until the day I managed to get the better of him in a fight. I was seventeen and was becoming quite a martial arts expert. We had a big row about my bike. One morning his car would not start, so he took the bike to get to work without asking me. He told Mum to tell me that I had to walk or get the bus.

When I arrived home from work, the bike was back, but the handlebars were bent because he had hung his heavy tool bag there. I was livid. We had a row. I lost my temper and hit him. Bob swiped back. Then I threw him. He had to go hospital to get treatment. After that we managed to get on better. But by now I had met Helen Thorn and I asked her to marry me at the tender age of seventeen.

Chapter 3

A Medium-in-Waiting

Ron and Marjorie Wells introduced Ray to the 70-strong Christopher West Healing Group (CWHG). The group was led by an outstanding medium called George Jones who had two main Spirit guides, Chang Liu and Doctor Hoist. Chang Liu was a philosopher, who also specialised in physical manifestations. Dr Hoist was a Spirit doctor. He was the Spirit guide who told Ray that he had to sit in a circle to prepare himself for trance so that another spirit doctor could work through him. The CWHG did not give Ray the chance to sit for trance, as George Jones' mediumship was entirely focussed on the work of his Spirit guides. Ray went to a healing demonstration by Harry Edwards, the nationally-renowned spiritual healer, at Portsmouth Guildhall. He was selected from the ranks of the CWHG to assist Mr Edwards. This was a great honour for Ray, who was the youngest member of the group. The dramatic success of Mr Edwards' healing technique on a wheelchair-bound woman, who was able to walk after her healing session, convinced Ray that he was pursuing the correct path. So, unable to develop as he wished with CWHG, Ray searched high and low for a circle that would welcome him. He was turned away from many groups because he was too young. Eventually, two members of the CWHG, Dorothy and Ted Brown offered to help Ray and he began sitting with them but Ray was unconvinced by Ted's mediumship and fell out with him. Dorothy, however, continued to sit inconclusively for him with other friends. Meanwhile Ray, at the age of seventeen, embarked on a disastrous marriage with Helen Thorn, a woman eleven years older than him for reasons he now finds difficult to explain. These troubled times were to lead to the dramatic appearance in his life of a highly valued Indian spirit guide who is still with Ray today.

I was really glad Ron and Marjorie Wells took me along to the Christopher West Healing Group. The leader, George Jones was a brilliant medium. Two spirit guides came through him, Chang Liu who was a philosopher and Dr Hoist who was a Spirit doctor.

It was Dr Hoist who gave me vital information that I would be doing full time healing and that a Spirit doctor would join me. He said that I had to sit and train for trance. Healing in trance was a bit unusual for the spiritualist world of the 1960s. I realised then that I had been chosen for something very different.

George Jones, with Dr Hoist working through him, chose the healers for each patient and asked them to place their hands on the affected areas. The healing was done by the laying on of hands.

We were allowing the power of healing to pass through our bodies without them being taken over. This is what is known as spiritual healing. Paul is quite different – he is a spiritual doctor and carries out surgical operations through me.

There was no mention of doctors being with the group, we understood we were simply using the power of healing. In hindsight, I suppose that doctors must have been working with us but we were not aware of it.

The biggest event I attended with the group was a healing demonstration by Harry Edwards in Portsmouth Guildhall. Around 80 healers were there. We stood at the back of the stage.

Harry worked at the front of the stage and called me forward to help him heal a wheelchair-bound woman's knees. He asked me to put my hands on her knees while he worked on her spine. I felt this was a great honour for me, as I was the youngest healer there.

When he finished he said to me: 'OK you can go now, let go.' So I walked away. Then he said to the woman: 'You can walk now.' I believe she replied: 'I cannot walk, I cannot walk.' He calmly said: 'Yes you can.' Mr Edwards took hold of her hands. They walked across the stage and she climbed down the steps into the audience.

This was very impressive as the woman had been in the wheelchair for about four years. The famous Harry Edwards always managed to finish his demonstrations with a grand finale! The experience had a profound effect on me. I had played my part in some wonderful healing. It confirmed that I was on the right path. I never sat for trance with George Jones, but just went along to assist at healing evenings. George never gave me the opportunity to sit with him to train for trance, because his mediumship was entirely focused on the work of his spirit guides.

George also held intriguing evenings. I used to say to Ron Wells: 'What do you mean by special evenings?' He would reply: 'You would not understand.' This was not good enough. I said: 'I am in the healing group, what is the difference, why cannot I come along?' He agreed to ask George and I was allowed to join in and witnessed some incredible occurrences.

George went into a trance and Chang Liu, his other spirit guide gave philosophical talks. He also did 'apports' - producing physical phenomena out of thin air.

Chang Liu created roses, mainly for women who were lonely. He rubbed his hands and out dropped a stem. The next thing you saw was a rose in his hands.

One evening there was a lady there who was not very well. Dr Hoist said to her: 'There is a surprise for you tonight. But you will have to wait until Chang Liu arrives.'

Chang Liu came through and asked her to sit in front of him. He said: 'I believe that there is something that you have always wanted.' 'Oh yes' she said. 'Before I pop off and Spirit takes me away from here, I would like a real rosary.' Chang Liu asked: 'What do you mean by a real one?' She replied: 'An old one. I cannot get hold of one now.'

He said: 'That is not a problem. I can get you one.' He rubbed his hands and suddenly a cross dropped out followed by all the beads. He said: 'There you are, straight from Spirit,' and handed her a rosary. She passed on about a month later.

On another occasion, near Christmas, Chang Liu said: 'I want you to get a recording tape, wrap it up, seal it, sign across every seal and hand it to me.'

The group duly brought a new tape, still in its wrapping, to the next meeting. We sealed it in a package and signed it as instructed. Chang Liu came through and asked for the tape. He said: 'Right, I want you to give it to anyone in the room.'

It was given to a vicar who was at the meeting. He was told to bring it back next week. Then Chang Liu said: 'There will be a special Christmas message on the tape from spirit for everyone in the room.'

The vicar brought it back the next week. We checked that the seals had not been broken, opened the package, played it on the tape recorder and listened to Chang Liu and Dr Hoist's Christmas message!

George Jones was an amazing medium. Physical mediumship was at its height of popularity in the 1960s. It has died off now. I think that the world of spirit – or Spirit as we say - feels that this style of proof that the spirit dimension exists is not necessary any more.

I learnt a lot with George Jones, but I had to find a group that would sit for me and help my development. Because I was so young, people told me to come back after I had more experience and was married with children. They did not like trance mediums in the 1960s. Clairvoyance was the big thing at most circles. I always thought: "Why bother with clairvoyance, when you can have a direct experience through trance mediumship?" The trouble was, I needed a special circle as I had by now realised I was being trained for a very unusual task.

Maybe sitting around and waiting was a lesson for me. It slowed me down and tested me to see if I really did want to become a trance medium. In the early days I was not really sure if I wanted it or not.

Paul's motto has always been: 'If you really want something you will work for it. Because if you do not work for it, it's not worth having.'

During my search for a circle, I met a woman called Mrs Homer. She had converted her front room into a chapel. The walls were all black and she had black curtains which were closed for ectoplasmic demonstrations.

She played the organ at the beginning of a sitting and sang terribly. One day, I was there with a mate and she cried out: 'Bow your heads, God is coming through the window!' My mate suddenly went over the seat and fell onto the floor.

She asked what was going on and he piped up: 'God's boot has just caught me on the back of the head.' Needless to say we were thrown out and I never returned.

I began to get worried. How could I develop without the help of a circle? To speed up the process, perhaps Spirit decided that I should get married. I would have my own place and could run a circle there.

This must have been the reason, because I cannot remember otherwise why on earth I married Helen Thorn!

I think we met in a park near where she lived in Eastleigh. Somehow we started talking, and then she said: 'Oh, I'll be here next week at the same time if you want to come along.' That is how it started. Helen was eleven years older than me. I was seventeen when we met and only seventeen and a half when we married.

I can understand why Mum nearly had a fit when I said I was going to marry her. Although Mum gave me love, there was no stability at home because of Bob's aggressive nature. Helen gave me, what I thought at the time was love, and a safe home away from Bob.

I sort of fell in love. But it did not last long, because once we were married, she became very possessive. Helen was jealous when I went to see Mum and hated me going out anywhere by myself. I was with her for seven years. It was not a happy marriage.

On the day we married, the taxi driver who took me to the Registry Office said to me en route: 'I have already taken your wife to the Registry Office. I have had a good look at her and if I were you I would jump out now!' I should have taken his advice. Life with Helen was a nightmare. I had to lie about everything as she was so jealous.

At the beginning I was able to keep up with judo, but on competition days I had to pretend that I was at work at Wadham Stringer's. A mate at work used to say: 'OK Ray, if she rings I will cover for you.' If she asked where the money was for the overtime, I had to tell another lie. The things I used to do to get round her. It was crazy!

Helen would not let me stay away overnight for judo competitions. She would come out with: 'I know where you are going, you are off to meet another woman.' I felt that I was being stifled; it was no way to live my life.

She'd had a very strict upbringing and treated me like her parents had treated her. Her father fought in the First World War as a gunner in the Horse Artillery. His attitude was very Victorian and her mother was also very, very Victorian.

Helen was living with her parents when we met and they insisted that she came home every night by 9pm. This was the 1960s when we were all supposed to be into free love. But Helen, a 28 year-old adult, had to be home by 9pm – incredible!

I stopped going to the Christopher West Healing Group soon after we married, because she created such a fuss about it. She was all sweetness and light about me going, but when I came back there would always be a terrible row. She would say: 'Why did you go when you know I did not want you to go?'

I thought: 'This is madness. There is no point.' If I had an argument or heavy discussion with her, I paid for it three days later. Without any warning she would hit me in the mouth in bed, for daring to start an argument. She was a strange woman.

Our marriage should not have gone ahead but who knows, my life might have been entirely different if Helen and I had not been together. Maybe it was all part of Spirit's plan for me, part of my test. But it is also possible I was just a vulnerable 17 year-old who allowed himself to be led towards disaster!

My search for a development circle was solved when Ted and Dorothy Brown, both members of the Christopher West Healing Group, offered to run a circle with friends at their house.

I told Helen that I had to go and sit at the Brown's house and she said: 'There is no need to do that, you can have it here.' I replied: 'No I have arranged it in Ted and Dorothy's house, so I will go there.'

Of course she turned on me and said: 'No, you are having it here.' I knew then that there was no point in arguing because she would not let me go out. Helen very rarely joined in the circle. She normally went off to the kitchen, but was no doubt happy that I was safely within her sight.

There are some good sitters and some bad ones and Ted was a bad one. He had a Chinese guide and spoke in a funny high-pitched Chinese voice. He would waffle on and hold an audience without actually doing it for a purpose. I was there for a purpose, sitting to train for trance. I could not take the rubbish that he pumped out. If it was truly Spirit, it would have been presented differently.

Ted was only in a light trance, if it was trance at all. It is possible that he was just putting on an act. At best, he was controlling the guide, rather than the guide controlling him. We used to sit in the dark and Ted always said in his funny Chinese voice: 'When the big hand gets to the twelve and the small hand gets to nine it is time for me to leave.'

He asked us to check the time, but we could not see the clock in the dark. If there had been a spirit guide with Ted, he would have known what time to leave without looking at our clock.

I tired of Ted's performance and one night I said: 'Well if you are a spirit you should know what time to leave. You should not need us to tell you.' Ted never came back after that, but Dorothy and a couple of her friends continued to sit with me.

Most of the people I met in the Christopher West Healing Group were all nice people. But of course there were egos floating around the group and Ted had one of them.

The circle continued with Dorothy's help, but there would be breaks every now and then. I was beginning to get bored because nothing was happening.

I sat on and off for nearly four years waiting to go into trance. Then one night, soon after my 21st birthday I said to the group: 'This is going to be my last night. I have had enough. I could still be waiting here in another 20 years.'

They all understood. I sat down and suddenly, it was as if a hammer had struck the back of my head. It happened as quickly as that.

I sat down and closed my eyes to go into a state of meditation. I felt my eyes go 'boom, boom, boom'. Lights were flashing in front of my closed eyes. Afterwards, the group said that they saw nothing move, but I felt as if my eyes were going berserk.

Suddenly I had gone and a being I've known ever since as Waters Running arrived.

Chapter 4

The late 1960s and early '70s

If you mention 1966 to most people they will remember it as the year England won the Football World Cup and the Beatles released 'Revolver'. But for Ray 1966 was a year of profound change. He became 21, twins Julia and Adrian were born and Paul and Waters Running appeared in his life for the first time. He completed his apprenticeship at Wadham Stringer's and moved to a job on a local building site before becoming a crane driver in Portsmouth Naval dockyard. Ray continued to sit with his home circle and had an unforgettable and potentially dangerous visit from an entity calling himself Geronimo. Fast forward to 1971. Tragedy struck in April when his mother, Marcia was killed outright in a car accident. Bob died a few days later. If this was not enough, his wife Helen spat on his mother's hearse, a bizarre and for Ray, an unforgivable response to the tragedy.

When Waters Running came through he (or I!) started dancing round the room. I was aware that I was there, but still thought that I was sitting in my chair. Waters Running who is an Apache Indian, looks after my life force when I 'leave' and Paul takes over my body.

On that first evening, I knew that I was talking but I could not hear myself. There was a brief pause when I felt that I was slumped on the table. I think that was the change over between Waters Running and Paul being in possession of my body.

When Paul first came through, he announced himself as Doctor Andrew Portlock. It was a far deeper sensation than with Waters Running. Paul did not reveal his true identity until much later, and it was not until the 1990s that he explained his background and spiritual mission in public. Paul had a heavier control over me than Waters Running. Of course when

I came out of the trance everybody said there you are, it has happened.

From that first night I insisted that whenever Paul wanted to talk to me that he did it through other people. The reason for this was that I did not want to listen to anything in my head.

If I do hear Paul talking to me in my head he will only be joking around. He will come out with some quick phrase. As a result I do not have any real dialogue with him. I dare say that he listens to me, but there is no regular two-way communication.

To start with I was worried how it might affect me. I thought that I would be diagnosed as being mentally ill and put on pills and special treatment. That frightened me a lot in the early years.

Of course now I fully understand what is happening to me. When we are doing clinics, my day is planned. I know what I am going to do and I just let it happen. I do not even think about Paul coming through until the time comes. I think: 'This is the time to do it,' and Paul arrives.

I do the job, then get on with my life. After all these years I have met Gillian and I want time with her. I have someone who loves me and want to spend as much time as I can with her before my life has gone.

I have always tried to keep the two elements of my life completely separate. That is why there has not been a great deal of dialogue with Paul, but there has been a lot of trust.

My home circle continued. Waters Running and Paul came through and talked to those present. There was one occasion when Helen invited some young people she had met and did not tell me in advance.

It turned out to be a really bad evening for me. I went into trance, but instead of Waters Running coming through before Paul, I was taken over by Geronimo, the Native American Indian chief.

He was chanting, singing and dancing. As he was singing one of the new people started to shout out football results. The spirit became very angry. I was sitting opposite the person who was shouting out the football scores. I guess I weighed about eleven stone at the time, but I was very fit from my judo training and my work at the dockyard.

The man opposite was quite big, well over fourteen and a half stone. Geronimo (I) stood up, grabbed him by the throat, pulled him over the top of the table, threw him against the wall, then left.

When Geronimo left, he came out through my stomach. Normally spirits come in and out over my head. I could not move for four days. I was black and blue from my groin to my chest.

That evening really taught everyone in the room that you should always take care over who you invite into a physical circle. It was Helen's fault; she invited people who were not spiritually attuned. So of course we had the inevitable row and she blamed me for going into trance.

Paul always managed to get me into trouble in the early days. Helen would send me off to do the shopping at the new Sainsbury's. Off I went on my bicycle, but would come home with no shopping because Paul had taken me over to go and sit and study medical books in the local library.

He did this quite a few times. I think he was so desperate to find out about today's society.

I can remember going into the library and coming out again. Nothing made sense. I thought: 'What am I doing in here?' Then I would get on my bike, panic about the shopping and pedal like mad to get to Sainsbury's. Of course, it was always shut by then and I had to go back to face the music and have another row.

The only good thing to come out of my first marriage was the twins, Julia and Adrian who were born in 1966.

Taking the children to see Mum was a nightmare. Helen always wanted to go to her parents for Sunday lunch. This was the only day that I could take them to see my mother, because I worked most Saturdays.

There would always be a big row if I insisted on taking the children with me to see Mum. It created a lot of problems and held me back from working with Paul.

Meanwhile I completed my apprenticeship at Wadham Stringer's. My mates started teasing me about all the money they were earning on building sites. So I left Wadham's and got a job at a local firm in Waterlooville. They were building council houses. I basically went along as the tea boy.

I progressed to digging manholes and a bit of bricking, but the job dried up. Then I saw an advert for trainee crane drivers at Portsmouth dockyard, applied for a job and was taken on. First of all I was taught to be a grease monkey, greasing all the cranes. It was good fun. I climbed cranes that were up to 200 feet high.

After about three months I was employed as a stoker working on the steam cranes. I shovelled coal into the boiler to keep the pressure up. This allowed the driver to move the crane about. Then I was taught to drive the cranes. I learnt how to work steam and hydraulic cranes as well as the huge gantry crane.

The gantry crane ran along tracks with a long boom that came out to hang over a ship in the dry dock or alongside. The crane had two drivers. One drove the top cab that moved the crane along the track and put the booms into position. The main cab operated the lift mechanism. I had my first major accident on the gantry crane, but more of that later.

Mum had her silly little ways. I remember going down to her house and she proudly announced: 'I have bought a new cooker from the Gas Board, son.' 'But your old cooker was all right Mum,' was my response.

She replied: 'Ah, but it is only 30 shillings a week (£1.50) and they have given free saucepans with it.' Mum had bought a cooker for a free set of saucepans!

She was very small. I used to pick her up with one arm, when I arrived at her house and lift her off the floor. She used to beat my back and say: 'Put me down, put me down you big ox.'

The last time I saw her alive was late March 1971, about two weeks before the car crash. I always took her a bar of chocolate or flowers, so she would remember that I had been. We had a good day, a nice chat, but it did not last long because Helen was soon on the phone asking where I was.

I was probably only there for about two hours. I remember Mum saying: 'Are you sure you cannot stay for dinner?' 'No,' I replied, 'I have to get back home.' That was it. The next time I saw her was at the scene of the accident.

My half-sister Helen had started work a couple of weeks before. She had just received her first wage packet and Bob and Mum decided to take her out to celebrate at a pub in Hambledon. My grandmother and other half-sister Diane were also in the car.

At 10 o'clock that night there was a knock on the door. Immediately Helen started making a fuss. 'Who is that knocking on the door at this time of night, blah blah blah...'

I opened the door and two policemen were standing there. They said: 'Are you Mr Ray Brown?' 'Yes', I replied. 'I am very sorry, but we have to inform you that there has been a terrible accident involving your parents. We want you to come to the scene.'

Of course Helen started ranting at the police. 'What are you doing taking my husband out of the house at this time of the night to see her.' I said:

'Listen it is my Mum. Mum and Bob have been in a terrible accident.' She ranted on: 'You do not care about me and the kids.' So I just turned to the policeman and said: 'Come on let's go.'

I shut the front door and from that moment everything went in slow motion. I cannot remember much about the ride in the police car. It was almost as if my brain had switched off.

We arrived at the scene of the accident. There was a Landrover with a horsebox off to one side, with Bob's car in the middle of the road. Mum was lying on the ground covered up but her legs were twitching.

Bob was still in the driver's seat. They were busy trying to cut him out. My sisters were missing. My grandmother had been taken away in an ambulance straight away. They found one sister in the ditch and the other was over a fence. The impact had shot her out through the window.

Helen had a broken back and Diane had a fractured skull and lacerations, but both of them made a full recovery. Although Helen still has problems with her back.

I watched them remove Bob from the car, then they picked up Mum and put her in an ambulance. They stopped me from seeing her. But the police asked if I wanted to go to the hospital.

I was taken to the hospital where Mum was pronounced dead on arrival. My brother, Peter, met me there. He was married and lived not far from us in Portsmouth.

Bob had the steering wheel in his chest. They had to do an eight-hour operation on him. The police were hovering around because they wanted a blood test to see if he had been drinking.

There was a big argument with the doctors. They refused to take the blood sample as Bob was in such a critical condition.

Bob and Mum had been travelling down a country road from Waterlooville to Hambledon. There is a hump-backed bridge just before Hambledon. The Landrover was coming the other way towing a horse trailer. The driver was messing about with his girlfriend. His parents were in front in another car. He was showing off and tried to overtake his parents.

He hit the hump-backed bridge and met Bob coming from the other direction. It was a head on collision. Mum went through the windscreen straight away. Nobody in the car was wearing a seatbelt. It was long before the law came in requiring people to belt up. The Landrover driver broke an arm and a leg and his girlfriend suffered lacerations. He was charged with careless driving.

When we were in the hospital, Peter decided to go and see how the other driver was faring. We found his ward and he was lying there with his leg in traction. My brother said: 'Hi, I am the son of the other people.' He started to rant and rave. Peter said: 'Just hang on a minute, it was your fault.'

He denied this and shouted at us. Peter tried to calm him down and said: 'Look, the police have already told me that it was your fault so do not rant and rave at us. I have come to see how you are.'

The Landrover driver swore at Peter, who lost his temper and began tugging at the wires of the leg support system. A priest, who was at the far end of the ward, flew towards us, grabbed my brother and said: 'Please calm down, please calm down sir. God will sort everything out.'

Peter shouted: 'Bollocks to God. I'll sort it out myself. I'll strangle the bleeder!' He had really lost it, so I pulled him away from the bed and managed to get him out of the ward.

Mum was buried on April 28 and Bob died the same day. My uncle came down from Birmingham for the funeral and was wearing a black armband on a white shirt. I went with him to the hospital to see Bob.

Bob's head was the size of a pumpkin. His head was so swollen that we could not see his eyes. There were just two black holes. The medical staff did not know how he was still alive. He must have noticed the black armband and thought that he was the only one alive. Tears started running down his face.

We went off to the funeral and when we returned, they told us that Bob had passed away. He must have thought that there was not much point in carrying on.

Because Bob died after the car crash, there was not an inquest into the cause of his death. But it was different for Mum. It was a nightmare going to the coroner's court and seeing Mum in the coffin. They put her behind a screen and I had to walk in and formally identify her in front of the coroner.

The top of her head had been sliced off in the accident. It had been put back in place. There was dried blood on her face, ears and eyes. She looked a terrible mess. I nearly passed out with the emotion of it. My brother helped me keep it together.

We gathered at Mum's house for her funeral. The hearse arrived with her coffin. Then Helen completely flipped. She said: ' I am not going to this funeral. I do not believe that they should be buried together as they were never married.'

Then she spat on the hearse.

Chapter 5

Dockyard Disaster

Ray managed somehow to get through both funerals. Bob was buried on Ray's birthday May 4, 1971. His marriage staggered on, with Helen becoming obstructive about Ray paying Marcia's funeral costs. Ray went back to work at Portsmouth dockyard after a period of compassionate leave. But soon after his return he fell over 100 feet from his crane to the dockside below. Amazingly Ray survived the fall and was taken to hospital where X-rays showed that he had broken his neck. Overnight whilst Ray lay in the hospital bed, a spiritual operation was performed by Paul. Much to the surprised horror of Ray's medical team, he then climbed out of bed in the early hours of the morning to go to the loo. A further x-ray showed that Ray only had a hairline fracture. To the amazement of the medical staff, Ray was discharged and returned home. Helen continued to oppose Ray meeting Marcia's funeral expenses, so Ray's brother Peter came to the house and gave her 'a piece of his mind'. Helen took offence and left the matrimonial home, taking the twins with her. Ray decided he liked the peace and quiet so went to a solicitor to begin divorce proceedings. This led to a very acrimonious divorce case. Helen falsely accused Ray of sexually abusing the twins and, although the accusations were absolutely groundless, she managed to keep the children away from Ray for the next seven years.

When Helen spat at Mum's hearse I wanted to grab her by the throat and strangle her. But she turned round and went back indoors. I just climbed into the car and set off with the family for Mum's funeral.

Helen also went on and on about Bob being buried in the same grave as Mum, saying it was a sin because they had never been married. Bob's funeral soon followed on my birthday.

There was no money to pay for the funerals as Bob and Mum had died virtually penniless. The bill was about £700. Peter offered to pay the lion's share and I was left with around £200 to find. Helen did not want me to pay it although it was my money coming from my earnings. She gave me hell every time I went to the undertakers to make a payment.

In addition, my mother's death had a big effect on my spiritual development. I went through a phase of questioning how such a terrible event could have happened and I deliberately turned my back on the spirit world.

I went back to work on a Monday morning after my compassionate leave and was put on the gantry crane that required two drivers. I was given the first driver's position and a mate, Paul Groves was given the upper position. Paul had not arrived for work so I climbed up to my position without thinking about whether the electricity was on.

My cab was 90 feet up. When I reached there I noticed that the lights were off in Paul's cab. For some reason I must have thought that he had switched them off. So I decided to climb up to put his lights on.

The ladder had enclosed safety rails all the way up except for the last section, which was completely open. Near the top, I grabbed hold of the handrail to pull myself onto the gantry. The handrail came away in my hand. I fell back and went over the top of the guardrail and fell onto the first gantry, then rolled underneath the railings and fell to the ground.

I fell around 120 feet, but fortunately my fall was broken on the first gantry. I landed sideways. My head did not hit the ground, but my right shoulder and hip took the impact. Amazingly I stood up and walked towards the switchgear to put on the electricity. Somehow my brain was telling me to make the switch. Incredibly I had no immediate recollection of falling from the crane.

My right arm was hanging loose. So I placed it against the switch and pushed. My shoulder had been dislocated. Pushing the switch made it go back into place, then I passed out from the pain and fell face down into a deep puddle.

Other dockyard workers just stood and watched me drowning, as they had been sent a memo a couple of days before which stated that if someone had an accident, they should not be moved! My first job of the day had been to remove the brow from a Leander class frigate that was about to leave harbour. Fortunately one of the ship's officers had seen me fall and he rushed off the ship to remove me from the puddle. I would probably have drowned if he had not moved so quickly.

I woke up in Portsmouth dockyard surgery where the naval doctor said that I needed to go to hospital. So, they took me to what was then called the Royal Hospital, near the dockyard in the centre of town.

They did X-rays and other tests and decided that I had broken my neck. My upper body and neck were put in a cage, balanced with weights and pulleys. I was told that I would have surgery the next day.

The dockyard notified Helen and she came down with the children to see me. While they were sitting round the bed, I suddenly had an out-of-body experience, just like when I was a child.

I remember looking down and seeing myself in bed surrounded by Helen, Adrian and Julia. But this time it was different, my entire body was engulfed by what seemed to be multi-coloured bubbles of light. It was like a Ready Brek glow!

Soon I was back in my body and opened my eyes. It was dark outside and the ward lights were on. It felt as if I had only been out of my body for a few minutes, but I realised that several hours must have passed. Incredibly, the pain had gone from my neck.

Because I had no pain, I decided to get up to go to the toilet and started to unbuckle the cage. This created havoc on the ward. The nurses rushed up to me and said that because I had moved, I would have to have another X-ray to see if there was more damage.

I went off for the second X-ray and was brought back into the ward. The consultant gave me a right old rollicking for taking the cage off and told me how I could have done serious damage to myself.

Then he looked at the X-ray. He went away to get some more doctors for a second opinion. I asked: 'Well, what has happened?' He replied 'We are not sure. We will let you know.'

The consultant came back an hour and a half later and said: 'It appears that your neck is not broken. The first X-ray must have been faulty, because all we can see is a hairline fracture. In fact we cannot even be sure that it is a fracture. It looks as if someone has placed a hair on the X-ray. You definitely do not have a broken neck, but we will send you home with a collar on as a precaution.'

My shoulder was strapped up. There were no broken bones there either, although it was really painful. It should have been smashed to pieces because it took the full impact of the fall.

I returned home but things there went from bad to worse. I was paying £7 a month to the undertakers and phoned them to ask if I could delay payments for a while until I was able to go back to work. As soon as I put the phone down Helen started going on again about the funeral expenses. So out of desperation I called Peter and told him that there was no way I could pay off my debt, as Helen was making such a fuss about it.

Peter said: 'Who is the man in this house, you or her?' I replied: 'Me of course, but you want to come and live with her for a while.'

He offered to pay the bill to help out, then came to see us and told Helen: 'I think what you are doing is out of order. In fact, if you walked out of his life you would be doing him a favour.'

She replied: 'Right I am going back to my mother's. I am taking the kids and you will never see them again.'

I quickly decided that I did not want her back. So I went to see a solicitor and he advised me to change the locks on the house. Then he sent a letter to her saying that I was divorcing her on the grounds of her unreasonable behaviour.

Helen's solicitor replied saying that she wanted a reconciliation. I did not want to go down this route, but my solicitor said that I had to make the effort. He told me to take her to a restaurant and have a meal. But as I did not want the meeting to work, I decided to take her to the local chip shop!

Of course this had the desired effect and Helen began shouting at me and even tried to pull my hair out. Then she said: 'I am definitely going to make sure that you never see your kids again.'

I went back to the solicitor, told him that the reconciliation had not worked and he began the divorce proceedings. When we went to court, the judge decided that I only had to pay 50 pence maintenance per child every month until further notice, because I was off work, receiving sick pay.

Now this really angered Helen. She went absolutely mad in the courtroom and was ordered outside by the judge. When Helen returned, she dropped her bombshell. She told the judge that she did not want me to have access to the children because I had interfered with them sexually.

This was probably the worst thing she could have done to me. The judge was left with no choice and would not allow access until psychiatric reports had been made. Her accusations were utterly groundless, but it greatly added to the stress that I was going through at the time.

The interviews with the psychiatrists were a complete nightmare. I went back to court and said to the judge: 'I have not done anything to my children, but I withdraw the request for access, because I cannot cope with any more interviews. My children will be able to speak for themselves when they are older and then the truth will come out.'

I did not see the twins for seven years. One Christmas, soon after the divorce was finalised, I took presents for the children, hoping that Helen would let me talk to them. I knocked on the door. She took the presents from me, would not let me in the house and as I walked away, threw the gifts into the street.

I get on with Adrian and Julia really well now, but they know what I think about their mother. When she passed over a couple of years ago, I told them that I could not feel any grief because of the way she had behaved when Mum and Bob died. Helen received from me what she gave to my mother – no pity. She died a very sad and bitter woman.

The divorce came through in 1973, but by then, thanks to all the added stress of Helen's abuse accusation, I had suffered a complete mental breakdown. I became an in-patient at St James' Hospital, Eastney where I met Sally a fellow patient, who was to become my second wife. It was Sally who helped me reconnect with Paul.

Chapter 6

New Marriage and New Circles

After they had recovered and left St James' Hospital, Ray and Sally soon moved in together. One night at home Paul materialised in front of Sally who promptly passed out! Fortunately Sally's Aunt Janet was experienced in spiritual matters and Ray began sitting with her and Sally's parents. Paul performed his only operation with a knife in this circle. But the group split up when Paul, who was still calling himself Andrew Portlock, revealed for the first time that his true identity was Paul of Tarsus, St Paul the Apostle. Sally's family could not accept this new, extraordinary development. During the 1970s, Ray met Jeanne Lambourne. She hosted a circle at her home where Paul carried out some spiritual operations. Ray and Sally married in 1977. Their first child, Sophie was born in 1979. Ray had been working for the building firm, M.J. Clancy, but wanting to work closer to home, went back to Portsmouth dockyard around the time of Sophie's birth.

The added pressures of the divorce caused my mental breakdown. I could not stop myself from crying. I could not sleep and I could not think anything through properly.

I went to my doctor to get help and he said that I had to go into hospital where I could get full medical attention for my condition. I ended up at the mental hospital, St James' Hospital, Eastney.

Initially I was put on the isolation ward (ICU). This is a secure area where you are assessed. I had a lot of problems in there, because I found it very difficult being mixed with people that were very ill mentally.

I remember one female patient who talked incessantly and a man who threw balls off the snooker table. This really affected me badly and I became very aggressive. I picked fights in my desperation to get out of the ICU.

Of course all the medical staff did was drag me into a padded cell and fill me with 'calming' drugs. I spent four days in the cell. Then when they thought my behaviour was more acceptable, I was discharged from the ICU and was put on the Harold Pink Ward. That was where I met Sally.

Sally was in hospital following a nervous breakdown at university. She had just lost her grandfather and had worshipped the ground he walked on. This and the pressure of her university work caused the problem.

The Harold Pink Ward was for people who had had light nervous breakdowns. Mind you I was still sent to the therapy room. The therapist said to the group: 'We all have to imagine that we are candles.' I thought: 'Imagine we are candles! How do you do that?'

Of course people began putting their hands on their head and some waved their hands and arms around as if their bodies were flickering. I just fell on the floor.

The therapist said: 'Raymond what on earth do you think you are doing?' I told her that I had melted! That was the end of the session for me. I was thrown out. I ended up in woodwork and made bird tables. This helped me, because I could switch off when I was working.

Sally and I met up at night. We were allowed to leave the hospital after the therapy sessions had ended for the day. I was not on any medication and she did not take hers. We popped across the road to the nearest pub.

We clicked and when I was allowed to leave, Sally decided she did not want to lose touch with me. She discharged herself and left the hospital at the same time. I found a flat in Southsea and we moved in together.

Sally gave me the stability I needed after the trauma of my Mum's death, the crane accident and the divorce.

I left the dockyard after the accident to work as a crane driver at Camber Quay, loading and unloading the ships that came into the port. My breakdown finished that job, but when I came out of hospital I managed to get fixed up with British Crane Hire.

I was with them for some time. Then I decided to go back onto the building sites, qualified as a bricklayer and went to work for M.J. Clancy.

My dealings with the spirit world had been on the back burner, to say the least, since my mother's death. But one night, soon after we moved into the flat, Paul materialised in front of Sally and recommenced my spiritual development.

I was sitting on the settee drinking a glass of shandy and Sally was making my corned beef sandwiches. She turned round to say something and saw Paul standing next to me. Sally promptly passed out with fright!

I had no idea what was going on, as I could not see anything. Sally recovered, did not tell me what had happened and just finished the sandwiches. When I came home from work the next day, her Aunt Janet was waiting to talk to me. Sally was nowhere to be seen. Janet said: 'Sally is a bit frightened and does not want to come home because of the weird things that happened here last night.'

I said: 'What do you mean, the weird things that happened here last night? I was just sitting here having a beer and she passed out while she was making my sandwiches.' 'Well she told us that you had a strange man standing beside you. Can you shed any light on this?' I replied: 'Yes I can. That was my guide.' I told Janet my story. Fortunately she knew a lot about spiritualism. Once again Spirit had linked me with someone sympathetic to my need to develop.

Sally came back and Janet began a circle for me at her house. Paul started coming through again, but still called himself Andrew Portlock. Sally did not join the circle, but her Mum and Dad, Margaret and Ken became involved.

Paul began by healing the family. The first operation that he did was on Janet's daughter, Kay. Janet, Ken and Margaret had been questioning him about the mechanics of his surgical work and why he did not use knives. So I reckon to shut them up he came through one night and announced that he would show that his surgery could be done with knives.

Kay had cartilage and arthritic problems in her knee and agreed to have the operation. Ken went off to the chemist to get antiseptic bandages to prepare for Paul's surgery.

At the beginning of the next circle, Paul came through and went to the kitchen. He came back with a knife and promptly began to operate on Kay's knee. Blood gushed everywhere and all Kay felt was a 'funny sensation'.

After the operation, he bandaged Kay's knee and told her that it would be healed the next day and that there would be no scar. The next morning Kay rang up very excited and told me that she felt fine. Her Mum came with her to our flat. We took the bandages off and there was no scar.

Paul trained Ken to go into trance so that he could do healing with his own spiritual doctor. Ken's doctor was called Patrick O'Brien and came through with a broad Irish accent. It was only a light trance, because Ken did not have the same experience as me.

Dr O'Brien was one of Paul's team in Spirit who had decided that he would like to come down and work on the Earth plane. Paul, as you will read later, has a large number of spirit doctors who help him perform operations when he is working through me.

Sometimes during that period other guides came through me to talk. On one occasion, a spirit called Athelstane arrived. He asked Ken to make up a drink from his (Athelstane's) time. It was a very strange concoction, definitely from another era. Anyway we managed to work out that he was the Anglo-Saxon King Athelstane. He only came once.

This particular circle came to an end after we moved to a flat at Leigh Park. It was further for everyone to travel. But the parting of the ways came when Paul revealed who he was. Sally's family could not accept this, so the circle split up.

In the mid 1970s, my cousin introduced me to Jeanne Lambourne, a lady who was very interested in spiritualism. I went to her development circle for a couple of years. Paul performed his first major neck operation in her house. Jeanne explains in detail what happened in the text of her testimonial in Part Four.

Sally and I decided to get married in 1977. She was a very bright girl, with far more qualifications than me! Sally had won a scholarship to a private school and did really well at 'O' and 'A' level. She was planning to become an Air Traffic Controller in the RAF, but all that went on hold after she had the nervous breakdown. She worked as a solicitor's secretary until the birth of our first child, Sophie on 17 June 1979.

My work for M.J. Clancy took me away from home and I would quite often end up in places like Eastbourne and Farnborough. I really wanted a job close to home, so when I saw an advert for dockyard workers, I decided to go back to Portsmouth naval base.

They were advertising for people to work nightshift on submarines or be trained as submarine painters. My service record had been good up to my fall from the crane, so it was quite easy to get myself hired. In hindsight my return to the dockyard was not exactly the smartest move of my life. In fact it set me up for some more near-death experiences.

Chapter 7

More Dockyard Disasters

In December 1979 and May 1980, Ray had two more near-fatal accidents in Portsmouth dockyard. The first accident was followed by a serious car crash during which he was only badly bruised. In the second accident Paul intervened dramatically to save Ray's life and preserve him for the healing work that they are continuing to do together to this day.

December 1979 was a memorable month. I had an accident in the dockyard and a potentially fatal car crash on the same day!

I was doing a nightshift job painting submarine keel boxes. I was very slim at the time and was able to wriggle in and out of the narrow spaces wearing breathing apparatus. Another member of the team stayed topside to ensure that my air supply was not snagged.

Anyway I had painted half the keel box the night before. But because it was just before Christmas when the dockyard closed down, I came back the next day during daylight hours to finish it off.

Somehow my airline managed to get on top of an open hatch. Then somebody slammed down the hatch cover and cut off my air supply. I must have been about 100 yards up the keelbox from my access point and had been painting some time, so the toxic fumes from the paint had built up in the confined space.

I quickly realised that my air supply had been cut off and decided to get out. The space was so narrow that I had to crawl backwards to escape. My mate realised that there was something up because I tugged on the airline. He began shouting up the keelbox at me and could see me scrambling backwards. After a couple of minutes, I had to take the mask off because I had no air left.

The toxic fumes hit me immediately, burning my eyes and the back of my throat. I could hardly breathe. I managed to get my legs half out of the keelbox access point, then promptly passed out. Fortunately my mate had raised the alarm. Several people were on hand to pull me out and took me to the dockyard surgery where I came round.

There was a big investigation following the accident, but they never found out who had closed the hatch on my air supply. The hose had been cut in half. There was air pouring out of one end, but nothing to me!

I felt quite groggy, so the doctor decided to send me home. I climbed into my little blue Skoda and set off. On the way I saw that my petrol was low and called into a filling station.

The petrol fumes must have topped me up, because I began feeling very rough. I drove off and for some reason forgot to put on my seat belt. I drove round a corner near Bedhampton Crossing and noticed that the railway crossing gates were closed. Then I passed out.

The car went out of control and hit the first car coming from the opposite direction. It shunted me back across the road. By that time I had been thrown out of the car.

I came out through the driver's door, but my ankle was trapped underneath the clutch pedal. I was dragged along the ground. The car behind me slammed into the passenger's side and spun my car round. I was being swung around like a rag doll.

Then finally the car turned into the path of another vehicle which hit the Skoda head on. It was a miracle that I was not run over. I was told that my head was inches away from the Skoda's back wheel. I have no idea how the other cars missed me.

I came out of my body during the crash and floated above the car and saw the whole accident unfold. It all happened in seconds, but it seemed like hours.

As the dust settled, people rushed over to free my leg from the clutch pedal. If I had been wearing a seat belt, the steering wheel would have speared me through the chest. The car had been compacted by the three blows and resembled a cube!

I tried to get up and was spitting out lots of blood. But the onlookers forced me back to the ground, convinced that I was badly injured.

Meanwhile the ambulance arrived and they strapped me onto a stretcher and took me to hospital. Of course the police wanted to do a blood test to see if I had been drinking.

They took my blood away to be analysed. Then I had X-rays. There were no serious injuries, only a cut in the roof of my mouth, a split lip and bumps, bruises and 'road rash'.

I was discharged the following day, which happened to be Christmas Eve. I remembered that my toolbox was in the car boot and went to Wadham Stringer's in Bedhampton where the car was being held.

I walked in and my conversation with one of the mechanics went like this.

'I have come to get the toolbox out of my car.'

'Which car?'

'It was a Skoda, brought in yesterday.'

'Oh right, when are they burying the chap that was in the car?'

'They are not burying anyone because I was the driver.'

'You have to be joking. You mean to say that you got out of that and you are still walking.'

'Well here I am!'

'Well you go and have a look at that car and tell me how you got out. By the way, take a crowbar with you because you'll need it to get your toolbox out.'

In those days Skodas had the boot in front and the engine at the back. I was totally amazed when I saw the car. The toolbox had fused with the boot, which had been pushed back into the driver's seat. The roof and sides had collapsed inwards and the steering wheel was through the seat. That is why the mechanic was convinced that I was dead.

The police came to see me and told me that they were going to prosecute me because the blood test had shown that I had alcohol in my body and was over the limit.

I protested and said that I had not had a drop to drink, and explained about the accident but didn't think that the paint had included alcohol, so was not able to use that in my defence.

The police explained that I was only six milligrams over the limit and that if they had pulled me up under normal circumstances, they would have stopped me from driving and just sent me home. But an accident was different. So I went to court and lost my licence.

I started cycling to work. To begin with I went to Bedhampton railway station and caught a train to make the journey easier. As soon as I was fit enough I pedalled the seven miles there and back.

One morning I was on the train and a fellow passenger said to me: 'Were you around just before Christmas when that maniac in a Skoda caused a pile up? He ran into one car, another car knocked into him, then he started heading towards me on my bike. I had to jump off into a garden to get out of the way.' Well, I owned up to being 'that idiot.' His immediate response was: 'Bloody maniac.' Then I explained what had happened and found that he worked at the dockyard and knew a lot of people on the paint squad. We met every day on the train, but after a while I decided it was time to save some money, replaced my bike with a racing version and cycled to the dockyard.

There were no long-term effects from the accident, but the next incident in May 1980 was to have more complicated results.

I was working on the same submarine. We had finished off the keel boxes and had moved into the ballast tanks. On the day of my next accident I was painting in the forward main ballast tanks. To get in, I had to squeeze through an opening that was no wider than my shoulders.

Another mate and I were doing touch up work on the day shift. The main painting had been done and we were going in after the welders to make sure that all the surfaces were covered with paint called tankalene.

We normally wore air-fed respirators to do the work, but for some reason they were not working so they gave us masks with air filters. We were only allowed to paint in a confined space for a maximum of 15 minutes before having a break. So the plan was for two people to work together, one having a rest and keeping an eye on the time, while the other worked.

The chap who was working with me had to go to the dentist and went to the paint shop foreman and said that I would need a relief.

The relief had not arrived when the time came for him to go to the dentist. But he said that he would ring the office to get someone down. So I went into the ballast tank, planning to come out in 15 minutes. Unfortunately I lost track of time. My relief never turned up and I ended up staying in the ballast tank for five hours.

I was breathing in pure toxic fumes from the paint after 30 minutes. Apparently I ripped the mask off and splashed the paint everywhere. I was covered in silver paint from head to foot when they got me out of the tank.

Eventually someone raised the alarm. But because I was so far gone they could not coax me out of the tank. Burning a hole in the side was not an option because of the build up of toxic fumes. They would have blown up the submarine.

Somehow they had to get me out under my own steam. They tried all sorts of things to get me out. They even got one of my friends to shout down that he had raped my wife. But I ignored everything and hung onto a bar singing 'Just One Cornetto'!

In the end they angered me enough to get me moving. I stuck my arms out of the access hole and I was pulled onto the deck. My lungs collapsed with the first breath of fresh air. I was given emergency treatment on the quayside, then they flew me by helicopter to the Royal Naval Hospital at Haslar.

Haslar decided they could not deal with me, so I was returned to Portsmouth and was taken to St Mary's Hospital heart and lung ward. I was put in an oxygen tent and lay there for what seemed like a long time.

Paul had a hand in getting me out of the tank. Because they were struggling to get me to move, he intervened, took over my body and put my hands through the hatch. Everyone was amazed that I managed to get out. They really thought that I was past help and would die in the submarine. They did lots of tests on me in hospital and found that the industrial alcohol in the paint had narrowed all my arteries.

Eventually the Admiralty paid me compensation and gave me a certificate to say that the accident had given me three per cent brain damage. My union, the Transport & General Workers, took up my case and gave me a solicitor. The foreman was given a rocket. They admitted liability from day one, but it took six long years for the money to come through.

Chapter 8

Undertaking, Building and Healing

Ray recovered from the ballast tank incident, left the dockyard and began working for a firm of undertakers. Meanwhile he was reunited with his twins after a gap of seven years. Then Alistair, Ray's fourth child was born in 1981. After this, the marriage with Sally went steadily downhill. Ray moved from undertaking back to the building trade. The nature of his job prevented him from attending regular healing circles until he met Pat Cowen in 1985. Her house became Paul's first regular surgery.

I was in St Mary's Hospital, Portsmouth for 19 weeks after the ballast tank incident. Then I had about six months on the sick list. I went back to the dockyard on light duties, but the solicitors who were handling my case advised me to leave and get a completely different job. So, I took a job with an undertaker, driving the hearse and working as a pallbearer.

Around that time I managed to get back in contact with my twins, Julia and Adrian. Julia was 13 and was developing into a bit of a wild child. Helen was taken to court because of Julia's behaviour. She was totally out of control, so begrudgingly her mother asked me to help out.

I had to attend the juvenile court with Julia who was sent off to a place called Red Hatch for six months to calm down! The trauma brought us back together again and I have remained in contact with Adrian and Julia ever since. Julia has had some fairly rocky relationships, a bit like me really, but she has managed to develop a good career as a financial adviser.

We lived close to a tampax factory when I was getting to know the twins again. I remember Adrian turning round to me and saying: 'They make lovely cars in there Dad.'

I burst out laughing and said: 'I think that you had better have a chat with your mother.' Obviously he did not know what I was going on about. We just had a laugh over it and still joke about it now.

I worked with the undertaker for two years and of course had several unusual experiences! The owner was about the same size as me, so I had to wear his big crombie coat. The only problem was that I had to wear his hat as well. His head was size eight and a half and mine was only six and a quarter. I put paper in the hat to keep it off my ears. I looked a bit of a mess, as my arms were shorter than his were.

The business had a reputation for being the place in Portsmouth to look after your funeral. The cars were old Princesses. They were bought at auction and had once been part of the Royal Family's fleet. The boss used to walk in front of the car. He was a bit of a show-off and walked miles at funerals.

One day when I was driving, I got bored crawling along behind him, and began bumping the back of his knees, to try and get him to speed up. He ended up nearly running. Of course he hopped into the car and told me off and I promised to slow down – until the next time!

Then there was the early funeral at the crematorium. We used to stand outside waiting for the mourners to come out. But I soon became bored and went for a wander around the Garden of Remembrance. I spotted a clump of mushrooms and decided to pick them.

I took off my oversize hat and used it as a basket. I put one load of mushrooms in the car's glove compartment and was half way through gathering another consignment when the crematorium doors opened and the mourners filed out. I quickly put on my hat, mushrooms and all. As my boss walked past me accompanying the mourners, he said out of the side of his mouth: 'Take that bloody hat off.' I did as I was told and all the mushrooms fell out.

This went down like a ton of bricks. We climbed back into the car and he was telling me what an idiot I was then asked: 'Where is the flower list?' I said: 'In the glove...' and stopped when I realised what would happen. He opened the glove compartment and out fell more mushrooms. I was taken off funerals for about six weeks as punishment, but that did not worry me. It was quite funny really!

Then at another funeral I fell into a grave. The boss always put two short pallbearers at the front and two taller men at the back. As usual, being on the short side, I was leading the way. We walked quite a distance through the cemetery in the pouring rain. When we reached the graveside I had to turn round and clamber onto the boards over the grave. They were covered up, so I could not be sure of my footing.

As I started moving backwards, the boards parted and I fell into the grave. The coffin came down on top of me. Again the punishment was another six weeks off funerals. The boss did not see the funny side, but it was a pure accident.

* * * * *

Sally and I had our second child Alistair in 1981. Our marriage started to go downhill after his birth. Sally had a bit of a drink problem, but the alcohol progressively took her over. She was also spending beyond our means and was putting us into a lot of debt.

At one stage I had to take her to St James's Hospital where she spent time in the alcoholics' ward drying out. Our marriage staggered on, but it became more and more stressful, as her drinking got out of control.

I went back to the building trade after my undertaking experience. First of all, I worked for Bridgewater Brothers from Littlehampton. They were laying a big pipeline through Leigh Park where I lived so I could walk to work. That was an eight-month contract. I built all the manholes and pumphouses.

After that I did a lot of travelling with them. I bought a Sherpa van to carry my tools. I was with them for a couple of years, then I got a job with M.J. Clancy from London, doing more manhole work, initially on a job near Petersfield.

That is where I worked with some Irishmen and had several amazing experiences, some of which are not suitable for this book! One night I was called out about two o'clock in the morning by the police as I had the keys to the site office. They said that there had been an explosion and could I tell them what was going on?

When we arrived at the site, I noticed that the drying shed had disappeared. The police said: 'So that is what is scattered all over the field?' They had also called out John Calvey, the foreman, who arrived at roughly the same time as me. He used to pay our two Irish workers subsistence so that they could get somewhere to sleep. But the lads spent the money on drink and slept in the drying shed.

Propane gas bottles outside the shed fuelled the drier, which dried our wet clothes. Apparently the lads had put the drier on and then disappeared down the pub. The wind had blown out the flame but the propane gas continued to pump into the shed.

They returned worse for wear and one of them kicked the door open with a lit cigarette in his hand. A huge explosion blew them out of the building. One lost his leg and the other one was very seriously injured.

Initially the police could not find them, as the force of the explosion had thrown them into the field. John Calvey said: 'It is an awful thing to happen to the boys. Go into the office and put the kettle on, we will have a cup of tea.'

I took one look at the office and realised that we were not going to get a cup of tea, went back to John and said: 'We can't put on the kettle John, the explosion has blown off the back of the office and the kettle has gone flying with it!'

* * * * *

During the early 1980s my spiritual development went on hold again because I was working away from home so much. When I was on a long contract in Eastbourne, I put an advert in the local paper asking any local healing or development circles to get in touch with me. I still could not write very well so had to get someone to do the advert for me.

Soon after the advert appeared I was hard at work down a new man-hole and John Calvey came along waving a perfumed letter. He said: 'Look at this, Ray's got a bit on the side!'

The lads passed it around and had a good sniff and laugh at my expense. The letter was from a 'posh' woman inviting me to her circle in Eastbourne.

I did not have a car then but John said: 'You can take my van if you're going to meet this bird.' They all thought I was going on a date and had no idea what I was really up to.

The house was set in its own grounds. I went down the long drive and rang the bell. The door was answered by a butler who let in this scruffy builder in a pair of old jeans and a blue hat!

I put five pounds in a collecting bowl and then sat around waiting for the lady of the house to appear. She made a grand entrance all dolled up in a big flowing dress.

My visit only lasted about 10 minutes. She asked me: 'What do you do Ray?' I replied: 'I go into trance. I am a trance medium.' She said, 'Oh, we do not have trance mediums here, you will have to leave.' I took my fiver out of the dish and left. She wanted a clairvoyant and was not interested in trance mediumship.

By 1985 I was fully involved in a weekly healing circle at the home of Pat Cowen in Widley, just to the north of Portsmouth. I met Pat through her husband, who had suffered a heart attack. I went up to the house so that Paul could do some healing on him. Pat found out that I was a bricklayer and builder and asked me to do some slabbing in her garden. Then she said that she had some friends who needed healing and her home developed into my first regular clinic as Pat describes in her testimony in Part Four.

I moved on from M.J. Clancy to a temporary job with Dyer & Butler. I worked for them as foreman at the Bargate in Southampton. Adrian, my son, was working with me as a pipelayer.

One day I sent him off to a nearby shop to get me a couple of their apple turnovers. When he returned, he said: 'I'm sorry Dad there were no apple turnovers, so I bought you two pasties.'

The site agent was sitting next to me and thought that this was very funny. A few days later, Adrian asked if anyone wanted anything from the shop. The site agent piped up: 'Yes, when you go there, get me two apple turnovers and if you cannot get them, get me a tin of emulsion paint!'

My son left the job soon after. He could not handle working with me. Adrian stayed in the building trade and has worked his way up to site carpenter.

Once the Dyer & Butler contract ended I moved to Southern Groundworks, who offered me home-based work. I stayed with them until I moved to Needham Market in 1990 to become a full-time healer.

Gary Crichton, who was to become a good friend of mine, owned the firm with his father. I started off with them as site foreman then was promoted to site manager.

My compensation money for the dockyard accident finally came through from the Admiralty in 1986. But rather than make life easier, this heralded a period of further turmoil in my life – which included another divorce - and a failed suicide attempt.

Chapter 9

Divorce, Attempted Suicide and a New Start

Ray finally received his compensation from the Admiralty in 1986 and paid off all his and Sally's debts. However, their marriage was falling apart and in 1988 Ray left. He and Sally divorced, but the trauma of it all drove Ray to try and commit suicide. On a more positive note, his old friend, Jeanne Lambourne, introduced him to new contacts in Dagenham and Bognor where Paul began doing small clinics. It was at Bognor that Ray met a lady called Rebecca who invited him to Needham Market in Suffolk. The plan was that Ray would attempt to become a full-time healer.

I received £28,000 in compensation for the ballast tank accident from the Admiralty in 1986. Sally and I went to see our solicitor about the payment. He took me to one side and said: 'Please do not take offence at what I am going to say. I would advise against your wife getting hold of your money. Would you like us to secure the payment and make sure nothing happens to it?' Of course, like an idiot I replied: 'No, I trust her.'

But he was right. Once the money had gone, she had no more interest in me than flying round the moon. I paid off all the debts that had accumulated after the ballast tank accident. We had 14 county court judgements to clear. Sally had run up big credit card bills. Then there was all the new furniture that she had bought for the house. We were paying small monthly amounts as a result of the county court judgements, but the compensation wiped out all our debt.

The court gave me a letter of satisfaction to show that I had no debts and my name was removed from the record. This helped me to get a mortgage. I decided to buy our house from the council, put down a big deposit and went to a financial adviser who sorted out the mortgage.

Sally and I stayed together for two more years. One of the more unusual incidents towards the end of our marriage was the time I hit a vicar. I went to our local church to see my children get their Girl's Brigade and Boy's Brigade certificates at a special service.

I was late getting there because I had been working, so sat at the back. Two youths in front of me were swearing and showing off. I told them to be quiet but they ignored me.

They came from another church in Waterlooville. Brigade groups from three local churches had combined for the special service. The lads were probably friends of people that were there but were completely out of order. The churchwarden should have removed them but he seemed reluctant to confront the youths.

The vicar began praying and the lads continued to play up. I had had enough so tapped one of them on the shoulder and asked them to be quiet. The lad turned to his mate and said: 'Four eyes wants us to shut up. Have you got an answer for that.' They turned round, looked at me, started swearing again and said: 'You make us shut up if you think you are good enough.'

I replied: 'Oh I'm good enough all right.' I asked them one more time to keep quiet. But they swore again. So I decided that I had had enough and leapt over the pew, grabbed them by the hair and smacked their heads together. Then I dragged the pair out of the church.

Once we were outside, I hit one of them and shoved the Bible down the other's mouth, because he was still swearing at me. Then I hit him as well. My glasses were knocked off in the struggle. But before I could do anything, the lads stepped on the glasses deliberately. That put me at a disadvantage. I could not see a thing without my glasses and was hitting out at everyone who came near me.

The girlfriend of one of the youths started shouting at me. She took off one of her stiletto-heeled shoes and whacked me in the centre of my forehead. I still have the deep mark of the wound there to this day.

Blood began spurting out down my face. That really got me going. I was very angry and pushed her to the ground. Then someone tapped me on the shoulder, so I swung round and lashed out. It was the vicar and he ended up flat on his back! My children, who had been watching, ran back into the church to tell Sally that I had just floored the vicar! So she disappeared with them. She did not want anything to do with it.

I was really sorry that I had hit the vicar and went back the next day to apologise. But he was extremely understanding and even offered to pay for a new pair of glasses.

Sally gradually whittled away the rest of the compensation. I became more and more tired of her antics. When I came home one day and found her in a compromising position with another man and a woman, I decided that enough was enough.

I left our house with what I could carry and moved in with my Aunt Jean. Sally actually had the nerve to divorce me on the grounds of mental and physical cruelty.

As a result a big depression really hit me. Sally was in a big mess. The pressure of her misery and alcoholism along with worrying about the kids got to me in a big way – and this time drove me to try and take my life.

I had lost my house, lost my kids again, and had a wife that really wanted me dead anyway. She actually played around with suicide herself, slitting her wrists several times when she was drunk.

Each time she slit her wrists the kids phoned and screamed that there was blood everywhere. My uncle and I went round, tidied up the house and drove her to hospital. Sally would say: 'I will go in there and get myself sorted out.' Of course all she did was discharge herself the next day. It drove me crazy.

Worn out by it all, I went to see her and said: 'I am fed up with this. You do not really want to kill yourself, otherwise you would make a damned good job of it. I am the one who ought to top himself.'

She said that I would not do that, but I shouted back: 'Oh, yes I will. I feel like doing it right now.' I picked up a handful of pills from the bathroom, took a can of her beer to wash them down, and walked out of the house. The pills soon took effect and I decided to jump off a bridge into the washout that runs through the middle of Leigh Park. In my confused state, I must have thought this would speed up the process.

I jumped off the bridge, but instead of hitting the water, landed on the bank. 'Well,' I thought. 'That wasn't any bloody good! I can't even kill myself!'

I managed to get back to my aunt's house and collapsed outside the front door. Uncle Tony phoned Sally to find out what had been going on. She told him about the pills, so he took me to hospital where they pumped me out.

When I came round I said: 'What the hell did you do that for, I want to be dead?' That is when they decided I should see a psychiatrist. An ambulance took me to see him, but I was feeling very rough and was rushed back to the hospital where I was diagnosed with pneumonia and pleurisy.

I was in there for about 10 days. Sally kept pestering me and said that she felt sorry for me. She offered to pick me up and arrived steaming drunk in her Reliant Robin. We turned a corner too quickly and the car toppled over onto its roof – just like the scene in Mr Bean!

Sally would not leave me alone and kept phoning in the middle of the night. I did not know what to do. My aunt tried really hard to cheer me up and get me fixed up with dates. She made me join a singles club. I used to call it 'meals on wheels'. That is all that it was. You would take a woman out for a meal and at the end she would say: 'On yer bike!'

Even when my hair was black, I had grey in my beard. My aunt decided that I needed to tidy myself up a bit for one of my dates. She said: 'I will go over to the chemist and buy some stuff that you can wash into your beard to blacken it.' She presented me with this bottle, not realising that it was hair dye: 'All you have to do,' she said 'Is put it on your beard when you have a bath and just wash it off afterwards.'

I put the colouring on my beard, had a bath, washed it off and lay back for a soak. When I stood up, my whole body was black from the neck downwards! I had to wear a polo neck jumper for about six weeks until the marks had vanished.

By now I was working as a site manager for Southern Groundworks. The 'blue loo' escapade is probably the funniest but the most dangerous incident of my final years as a builder. I was working at the Memorial Hospital in Bognor Regis. We were building a new operating theatre and hydrotherapy pool. There were portaloos on site, which we called blue loos.

One morning I went to the loo and the lads thought that it would be funny to lock me in. The loo was standing on a pallet. Not only did they lock me in, but they also decided that it would make an even bigger joke if they picked up the pallet and loo with a forklift. As soon as it was in the air, the loo fell off the pallet, crashed to the ground and split open. I was covered in blue chemicals. Fortunately the portaloo had just been put on site, so it was fresh! It took months for me to get rid of the chemical stains from my skin. Luckily it missed my eyes. I sacked the forklift truck driver because of his stupidity.

*   *   *   *   *   *

I did not know what to do with Sally who continued to harass me. On New Year's Eve 1988, I felt really down and decided to call my old friend Jeanne Lambourne for a chat.

About a year before, Jeanne had arranged for a friend from Dagenham, called Ken Parr, to be treated at Pat Cowen's. Ken had such a bad back, that he arrived in an ambulance. Paul worked on him and Ken managed to walk out of the house. Ken thought it was a miracle.

Jeanne realised that I needed to get away from Portsmouth and took me up to Dagenham to visit her friends Charlie, Irene and Ken. I agreed to do a little clinic for them. Jeanne writes about this in her testimony in Part Four.

Paul did healing on Charlie and Irene and their daughter who was suffering from depression after her husband, who was a Post Office electrician, had been killed in an accident at work. I began going up there regularly and stayed with Ken, who suggested that I put a plate out to collect donations for Paul's surgery.

Jeanne also introduced me to a chap called Billy Smith who lived near Bognor Regis. He came from Bognor to Pat Cowen's every week, then invited me to his house to do a fortnightly clinic. I charged five pounds to cover my petrol.

That is where I met a lady called Rebecca from Needham Market near Ipswich. In 1990, she invited me to stay with her so that I could get completely away from Sally, and also make a go of full-time healing.

I told my boss, Gary Crichton, what I was going to do. He said that my job would be kept open if the move did not work out. Little did I know that I was going to meet Gillian and that my work as a healer was about to blossom in a way that I could never have imagined.

Part Two

Gillian Brown

Chapter 10

Gillian's Spiritual Awakening

Gillian Brown was born in London. Her father left home when she was three and died when she was seven. Her mother, Connie remarried. Gillian's grandmother Jessie, had spiritual gifts and used to read cards for friends and family. Terry Sitton, Gillian's first husband, came into her life when she was 13. Gillian was nineteen when they ran away to get married. Their first son, John, was born the year after and son number two, Colin, a couple of years later. The Sitton family moved to Bury St Edmunds and when Gillian became very stressed over a house move, her grandmother did her first reading for her. This led to Jessie's spirit guide, Chan, visiting Gillian to give her some healing. Her father's spirit visited the Sitton household next, but a malevolent spirit, which terrorised Gillian every night, took his place. She managed to get help from a Cambridge-based healer called Ed, whose spirit guide protected her. Gillian began healing in Ed's circle.

I was born in North London on October 20, 1945. We lived in Tufnell Park Road, Holloway in a council flat. My father was there for the first few years but I do not really remember him. He was an entertainer, a ventriloquist, and a bit of a flirt. He used to flirt with a lot of other women and my mother had a difficult time with him. He left us when I was three. My mother had to work, and a neighbour called Rita, who lived along our balcony, looked after me.

Mum met my stepfather, Arthur, when I was about seven. Dad died soon after Mum met Arthur. He had diabetes and died because his mother spoilt him with the wrong food.

I went to Grafton Road Primary School and then to Archway

Comprehensive. My first Saturday job was in a hairdresser's shop, just down the road from where we lived. I loved that because I met a lot of people. I washed the customers' hair and was the general dogsbody!

One of my best friends was Iris George, the sister of Charlie George, who played for Arsenal. I watched him play football in our playground. She used to say: 'He is going to be a famous footballer.' We laughed about it because he always said that he would!

When I was 13, she said that a scrumptious boy had moved in near her and that I should go and meet him. By chance we bumped into him outside the Gaumont Cinema. She said: 'There is that Terry Sitton' and that was it! It was love at first sight. Terry was determined to marry me from the start.

I studied for my 'A' levels at school and did RSA typing and Pitman shorthand courses. I really wanted to be a hairdresser, but I was advised that I should become a secretary.

When I was nineteen, Terry and I married against Mum and Arthur's wishes. We ran away together and my grandma said that we could move in with her in Finsbury Road. She did not want us to live in rented accommodation. My grandfather and grandmother tuned and built pianos and had a big factory. Within a year my first son, John, was born.

After his birth, we moved to our first flat in Arcadia Gardens, Palmers Green. Then my grandma, Jessie, heard that Vitality Bulbs were setting up a factory in Bury St Edmunds. She knew the boss very well and helped Terry to get a job with them. Vitality Bulbs were really good to us and organised a house in Salmon Walk in the Suffolk town.

Grandma had spiritual gifts and was the sort of person that everyone came to with their troubles. She read tea leaves and ordinary playing cards. Mum had three sisters and they were always asking grandma: 'Mum, can you tell us this? Mum can you tell us that?'

Grandad did not want her to go to spiritualist churches or circles. But she knew early pioneers of the spiritualist movement like Edward Fricker and Harry Edwards.

She was a brilliant home medium. She told my mother that she would meet Arthur and also told her that I would be married twice.

When friends or family came to her with problems, she would say: 'Come on, let us help you out.' As she lay out the cards, she chattered away to her guide, Chan.

He talked to her in her head. She would often say: 'Oh, stop it Chan' because she could hear him speaking in Chinese. She was overshadowed by Chan but was still in control - quite an amazing woman.

My second son, Colin, was born in Salmon Walk. Then we moved to Bright Close. We had heard about council houses being built and applied for an exchange. The borough council gave us a new house. Eventually we bought the house from the council and around 1975 decided to move. We had a lot of problems selling the house and I was getting into a very nervous state.

Mum came to visit and said: 'Give me your ring.' She took it home with her, so that my grandma could do a psychometry reading. Grandma described the house that we would move to and told me that her guide, Chan, would visit me.

I did not understand what she meant. I had never seen Chan, so how could he visit? She said: 'He is coming to you tonight. He will arrive at about 10 o'clock.' I said to Terry: 'Grandma reckons that Chan is going to visit me. She said that I am not to be afraid and that I have to talk to him.'

Terry looked at me as if I was mad. He was more sceptical than me. His father, who had died when he was quite young, was an atheist and had indoctrinated Terry with his beliefs.

I went to our bedroom at 10pm to wait for Chan, shut the door, and made sure all the windows were closed as well. Suddenly an amazing breeze came to my right hand side. I was enveloped in a wonderful vortex of vibration that went through my body. My eyes were shut tight. I was petrified!

'Oh, this is healing' I thought. Grandma had told me that he was going to give me healing to help my depression. I said: 'Hello Chan.' The more I spoke to him, the stronger the wonderful feeling became. Then the breeze disappeared to my left.

I went to see Terry and said: 'I have just had the most amazing experience.' He said: 'Really?' 'Honestly, I feel absolutely fantastic.' I told him what had happened and he admitted that I looked good. He was amazed how different I was, because I had been in such a state.

I went back upstairs to try and make the feeling return, thinking that I had possibly done it myself. Nothing happened, so I arranged to go and see my grandma to tell her what had happened.

She was pleased and said: 'Right, I will get the cards out.' This was the first time that she had read cards for me. She told me lots of things about our new house and said: 'Oh, your father is going to visit you.'

I thought: 'Mum will not be very pleased about that!' She never encouraged me to talk about him, as it had been such a bad marriage. He was taboo in our house.

A few days later I woke up in the middle of the night. The light was going on and off and something was touching me on my left arm. It really terrified me.

Terry was fast asleep and I thought: 'I wonder if it is my father?' I spoke in my mind and my left arm went up and down as if to say 'get out of bed'.

As I climbed out of bed, a vortex of energy took hold of my hand. I was very frightened, but kept thinking that this must be my dad. He took me downstairs and I could see in the dark! My hand was guided to a pen and a piece of paper.

I sat at the kitchen table and said: 'Do you want me to write?' Flap, flap, flap went my hand. He moved my hand and wrote ROY, my dad's name. The energy disappeared and I raced upstairs, woke Terry and told him what had happened.

These initial experiences were a gentle way to bring me into spiritualism, as I was unaware of all the work ahead of me.

I decided to get some information from my father that only Mum would know. So I asked her to give his RAF number to Linda, my assistant, at work. My friend could then check that I had been given the correct number.

Dad arrived the next night at 1 a.m. I asked him to give me his RAF number and suggested a code. I would tap my hand up and down and when I came to the right number he would move my hand to the side.

I managed to get six numbers doing two numbers a night. Linda verified that they were correct the following day. On the fourth night I started to get the number, but it did not seem to work well. Then I saw a light on the wall.

I thought: 'He is trying to show me something now' but it did not go further than that. I went to sleep and was woken at 3 a.m.

My hand was flapping sideways and up and down. He seemed very excited. I tried to communicate, thinking that it was my father. The flapping continued and because it got so strong I said: 'If you are my father, come through my husband.'

I put my hand on Terry's chest and he was taken over! He woke up, leapt on me and tried to seduce me. It was very scary. I knew it was not Terry and screamed at him to get off. It really frightened me because I knew that this spirit could not be my father.

Suddenly Terry spoke and said: 'My God, what happened to me?' I thought: 'This is terrible.' I tried to cut the communication off. But every night the spirit returned.

Grandma told me to get incense and burn sulphur in the bedroom, but this did not help. Sulphur was supposed to drive malevolent spirits away.

Then the spirit started visiting me at work. I would be typing away and would suddenly lose control of my hands. He was making an absolute nuisance of himself.

I went to Cambridge Spiritualist Church to see if they could help. The medium came to me in the church. Now this was a new experience, as I had never been given a message before.

The medium said: 'You are woken up at night. Now I would not mind waking you up!' I thought: 'What a cheek, I have come here for help and I am in distress.'

The medium continued: 'You are a natural medium. You are going to join the spiritualist movement and have your own church. There is a lot of work ahead of you. I see a church spire over your head. You are going to do healing.'

A man called Ed, who ran a healing group and was in the church that night, offered to help me. He said that he would give me healing and would find out who was connecting to me.

He put his hands over my head and as he did this, my body was pulled to the left, but the power through his hands was guiding me to the right. Ed said: 'Do not worry, just relax. You have an unenlightened spirit with you. He is not your father. He has a very big ego and he is saying to me

'I am a healer, I am a healer.' I had been taken over by the malevolent spirit, because I had let my experiences go to my head.

After the healing, Ed said: 'You do not have anyone protecting you at the moment, because you do not know anything about spiritualism. This spirit has been watching your communication with your father. He now has a stronger link than your father's. You need protection. You have to come to this church and learn what it is all about. We will introduce you to healing. Meanwhile I want you to think of my guide, Red Cloud, who will protect you. Imagine a big cloak like a blanket coming over you.'

The next weekend I decided to go and see my mother at her caravan at East Mersea. Mum said: 'He will not find you here. I will be really angry if he comes into this caravan.' That shows how little we knew about Spirit at the time!

That night I had a terrible dream. I thought: 'That is not me.' I woke up with a jolt and thought: 'He is here.' I felt him. He used to come from my feet. It was like black treacle flowing over my body starting at my feet. Then I remembered what Ed had told me and thought about Red Cloud's blanket. Suddenly the treacle feeling went.

Ed continued to give me healing every week, and gradually with his and Red Cloud's help the malevolent spirit disappeared. I was ready to join Ed's circle and work as a healer.

Chapter 11

Healing, Rescue Work and Meeting Ray

Gillian started healing in Ed's circle. Then in 1975, after a meeting in Horringer, near Bury St Edmunds, she became involved in setting up and running Bury St Edmunds Spiritualist Church. She was closely involved for the next 15 years. Healing and development circles were held at home, with many famous mediums visiting the Sitton household. Terry discovered that he was also a natural medium and began doing rescue work after terrifying banging noises were heard in the house. Gillian trained as an aromatherapist and combined this with healing. She developed RSI and was off work for a year. In addition she had terrible earache for six months. In May 1990, a friend told her about a psychic surgeon called Ray Brown who had moved into the area and suggested that she should see him. Gillian and Terry after some hesitation, decided to meet Ray Brown.

I began to do healing in Ed's circle and soon felt as if I was going out of my body. Ed told me that I was going into trance. This was an area I knew nothing about.

He told me that they did not go into trance at his healing group and that I would have to find a circle to help develop my skills. There did not seem to be any activity in the Bury area, but I found a medium in Cambridge called Eileen Ison who let me sit in her circle.

Nothing ever happened to me at her circle. I just sat there! Then I heard about a spiritualist meeting that was going to be held at Horringer village hall near Bury St Edmunds. I decided to go to the meeting, not thinking that it might involve me in helping form a spiritualist church.

Just before I went to this meeting my stepfather, Arthur became ill. Grandma told Mum about a spirit called Dr Evans who came through Mrs Sampson, a medium in North London.

My Stepdad and Mum went to see Mrs Sampson who in trance said: 'Your daughter must come to see me because she is a natural medium and is going to be a healer and will have a doctor working through her. She is also going to help run a church.' My Stepdad was quite sceptical, but he told Mum who actually forgot to tell me!

There was a clairvoyance demonstration at the Horringer meeting. I sat with a group of people who said that they would like to set up a church and needed a secretary. There were about six of us. Bernard Cohen, who became the first President, asked me to help him.

I said: 'Yes, I will be the secretary.' Our first meeting was on October 4, 1977 in Horringer village hall. Then we moved to a Quaker hall. One by one the founding group drifted away and I was the only one left.

New people joined and I kept on as secretary, working for the church for 15 years. Towards the end I became President. I met lots of mediums and used to arrange big spiritualist demonstrations in Bury St Edmunds.

I also went at least three times a year to Arthur Findlay College, the spiritualist centre in Essex, and had many meetings with the famous medium Gordon Higginson.

He confirmed everything that I had been told about my spiritual gifts. I was frightened about going into a full trance because of my previous experiences with the unenlightened spirit, so only went into overshadow, a light trance.

I started my own circles at home. Terry, although he did not want to get fully involved, was happy to sit and help out. We used to help other mediums develop. Paul Lambillion, a local clairvoyant and healing medium, came round to our house quite often. I also ran a healing circle at the church.

One weekend, the healer Stephen Turoff came to do a transfiguration. A transfiguration takes place when the spirit guides or the spirits who want to communicate with the people in the room transfigure their face over the medium. The medium does this over a red light.

There were about 30 people in my lounge for this meeting. My neighbours used to get fed up with me because of the number of cars parked in the street.

Stephen began sitting and was right in the middle of his transfiguration, when a loud banging started. Colin was sitting behind me and said: 'Oh Mum, that noise is coming from my bedroom.' I agreed and tried to calm him down by saying: 'It will be all right, don't worry, it will be all right.'

Needless to say, I was getting really worried. Stephen Turoff turned round and said: 'What on earth is that noise?' The banging seemed to be all over the house. Colin was really frightened when he went to bed and would not turn off the lights. He had a very sleepless night.

A couple of weeks later he came down in the morning and said: 'Mum, someone knocked me on the nose in the night. I heard them say in my head: 'You have to go to London, you have to get a job in London!' He did as he was told, went to live in London and found a job with Everest Double Glazing.

Soon after the Stephen Turoff evening, we were sitting with a medium called John Parker. We heard more loud banging. It was very frightening. Terry bravely climbed the stairs to investigate. As soon as he went upstairs the banging stopped. Then when he rejoined us it started again.

John Parker said: 'Terry, this noise is with you. You are a medium and because you are holding back, not doing anything, just sitting for others, the energy is dissipating in the house. They are trying to tell you that you must sit.'

We started sitting for Terry. He went into a trance state and brought through lost spirits. This is called rescue work. Terry had to go through the sudden death experience with the lost spirit to encourage them to enter the spirit world. When death is very traumatic, some spirits get lost and do not accept that they are dead, so cannot pass through to the spirit world.

Terry had the most amazing experiences. I remember that he helped a World War II pilot, a boxer and a child caught in a fire. The child in the fire really upset him and put him off doing the work.

Ray has done rescue work as well. He helped Dr John, an American pilot. He came through reading the altimeter on his plane and flew the plane while the rest of the crew bailed out. He finally bailed out, but the Germans shot him in the legs on the way down and bayoneted him as he landed.

He kept saying: 'I cannot feel my legs. I cannot feel my legs.' Paul looked after him. He was cleansed, which means that his physical vibrations were taken away, so that he could progress to the light and pass on. John then trained in Spirit as a doctor and now works with Paul.

I never really trained as a healer it just came naturally. Ivor James, who was a psychic artist, told me: 'You do not learn to heal, you just do healing. Lay on your hands and it will happen. Anyone can do healing. If you want to do it and help people then get on with it.'

Everyone can do healing to some extent. It just depends on whether you want to take the time to help others. When you heal, you feel a vibration through your hands. If you sincerely want to be a healer, Spirit will draw close and will heal through you. Spirit want new healing channels. They might not make themselves known, but someone will be there to help.

I decided that I would like to do aromatherapy and combine it with healing. So, I went to the London School of Aromatherapy and qualified. Sadly as a result of the combination of work, healing and aromatherapy I developed repetitive strain injury (RSI). In the end it was so bad that I was typing with just one finger. I was away from work for a whole year.

While I was on the sick list, I had a sitting with Paul Lambillion. His guide, Hartstar, told me that in a previous life I had been a dancer in the temples in Mesopotamia and used to oil bodies. That was why I was drawn to oils and massage.

He also said: 'You are going to meet somebody and do professional healing with this person. You are going to do healing yourself and you are going to earn money healing.' I thought, I do not want to do that. I just want to develop my aromatherapy skills because I found it so interesting.

In May 1990, I heard about Ray from John Tarrant, one of the healers at the church. He said that he was going to see Ray Brown at Audrey and Eric Tyers' bungalow. He kept telling me how wonderful he was but I was not interested.

I was not impressed by this so-called psychic surgery and did not believe in it. I had seen Stephen Turoff do some psychic surgery work. It seemed very weird and was causing quite a stir in the spiritualist movement.

Stephen actually cut skin with a knife. I did not feel comfortable with this development.

John Tarrant told me that Ray's work was very different to that of Stephen Turoff. So because of the RSI and also a terrible earache that I had had for a long time, I decided to go and see Ray with Terry.

Ray was wearing very thick glasses and was dressed in an old tatty jumper with dirty-looking shoes. He looked very scruffy. I thought: 'He cannot be a medium, for God's sake. He is a right shabby so-and-so. What sort of evening is this going to be!' All the mediums I had known were very smart.

Anyway we sat in a circle and Waters Running came through. He started laughing and joking and I thought it was a load of rubbish. I turned to him and said: 'Excuse me friend, what is your purpose in being here?' I had been in the movement for so long and was used to quiet or very spiritual experiences, nothing like this.

Waters Running said: 'I come here to make people laugh.' I was still unimpressed, because he had this funny voice and kept laughing. He sounded very peculiar to me, very deep and guttural. At the time I did not know that his deep voice was a result of the plague that had killed him.

I said to Terry: 'What a load of rubbish.' But we sat there for a bit longer. Then Paul came through. It was such a shock. The transformation from Ray to Waters Running and finally Paul was incredible.

He had a beautiful soft-spoken voice. I told him about my ear, not about my hands. Paul worked on the nerves in my jaw and ears, which were very inflamed with tension and stress. Paul said: 'I know you have pain in your hands.'

I replied: 'I do not want you to touch my hands. I have had physiotherapy on these hands for a year. They are very painful and I am only just beginning to feel as though I can cope with them.'

He said: 'No, let me see your hands' and began working on them. One of my thumbs was particularly bad and he told me that it was sitting out of joint, and proceeded to put it back in. I was amazed.

Before we went home, I asked Ray who was looking after him, because he looked like a bedraggled old tramp. He said that nobody was and that he had moved to Suffolk to see if he could make a go of it as a professional healer.

Ray said that Audrey and Eric, and Rebecca, the lady he was lodging with, were helping him get going. I asked Ray if he would like to do a demonstration at our church. So we set a date. My earache disappeared that night.

Chapter 12

New Start

Gillian was drawn closer and closer to Paul and his work. The medium, Paul Lambillion did an auric drawing, which confirmed that she was going to pursue a full-time healing career. Gillian consequently began organising Ray's clinics and went all over England with him doing demonstrations at spiritualist churches. Because of this a rift appeared in Gillian and Terry's marriage. After she went on two healing trips to Kenya with Ray, who nearly drowned in a diving accident on the second visit, Terry gave Gillian an ultimatum: choose between him or Ray and Paul. Gillian decided to stay with Ray and Paul. She kept the house and Ray moved into the back bedroom. Their life together, to begin with, was a business arrangement.

Ray came to our church for the healing demonstration. Paul Lambillion had told me about a woman called Fiona Nichols who had a bad back problem. She was going to fly abroad in a few days and really needed help because she was in agony.

I told him to get Fiona to come along to the demonstration, as I was sure that Paul could help her. Paul worked on her nerves and disc. When he finished she said: 'I feel great' and walked round the church.

At that time, Paul did not warn people that in the days following treatment, they might have some problems due to the work on their inflamed and swollen nerves. On the next day Fiona phoned and said: 'This man is a fraud. He is no good. He has wrecked my back. I am in agony.'

I told her to come back and see him again but she refused. Paul Lambillion heard about it and said that Ray must be stopped because he was dangerous.

Paul said: 'Get Fiona to come back because I can help her. She will have this pain afterwards but it will calm down. Get her to come back to me.'

She did not come back and cancelled her flight. But her back did calm down and she was much improved. I think she went for healing to Paul Lambillion and said that he had fixed the problem. Anyway the whole of the church went against me, including Paul Lambillion, because I was involved with someone who they thought was no good.

This upset me tremendously because I knew Ray was a good medium. I watched him do his work, which was improving all the time.

Terry and I began going regularly to circles with Paul at Rebecca's house in Needham Market. After a couple of visits Paul said he had a spirit doctor called Barbara Lane who wanted to work with me. 'She is my assistant in Spirit and I need to place her with you.'

I thought: 'Wonderful, at last it is going to start. I will be working with Terry.' It did not occur to me that I would work with Ray. I thought that I would be the healer and would work with Terry. Paul continued to help my RSI, which improved. I also took my son John for healing on his shoulder.

I argued with Paul because I did not understand his teachings. His teachings about the levels in the spirit dimension and progression of the spirit were very different to anything I had heard before.

Everything I had learnt about spiritualism had seemed to conflict, but here was someone who was simply explaining what happens to you after you die.

It took some time for me to accept Paul's arguments, because I had been visiting Arthur Findlay College for 15 years and listened to deep-trance mediums and witnessed transfiguration. I had seen ectoplasm come out of Gordon Higginson's mouth and stomach and watched spirits form in front of me and speak to people in the room.

In the spiritualist church, there were lots of different views. I used to sit in church and think: 'Well, I accept now that Spirit exists. I accept that you live after you die, but I do not want to go any deeper because it becomes more confused.' Paul made everything so simple and straight-forward. I thought: 'This is it. This man talks so much sense.'

One night Paul explained that he was going to bring Barbara Lane through me. He told me to relax but I was afraid because of my experiences with the malevolent spirit.

Paul said that the guide would just overshadow me and that I would be fully aware of what was going on. Barbara arrived and spoke. Her presence was very strong and made me very uneasy. Paul realised I was worried and promised that she would never come through so strongly again. He just wanted me to know that she was there.

I do not bring her through very often. But Barbara does work with me. When Paul is doing surgery on patients he uses my hands as well. He knows Barbara is there, although she does not take me over. I feel her with me and I know where to place my hands. It is a very strange experience. I just act automatically.

Soon I started feeling drawn towards Paul. The feeling came from my solar plexus. It was as if I had fallen in love with him. I thought: 'Oh my God, this is not right.'

His big brown eyes looked right through me. I just knew that he knew what I was thinking and became really embarrassed. This wonderful feeling of love towards Paul flowed through me. But I thought: 'You have got to pull yourself together, you cannot fall in love with a spirit.' I definitely had not fallen in love with Ray. It was crazy!

I was still off sick from work at the Greene King brewery. It had been a full year and a letter came from the company saying that I was going to be put on half pay. This sent me into a terrible depression. I had no idea how Terry and I would be able to cope.

Then the phone rang and this voice said: 'It is me.' 'Who is me?' was my immediate response. 'It is me, Paul.' Well this completely blew my mind. I had never spoken to a spirit on the telephone. Apparently he had been pestering Ray to make the call! He asked why I was crying and I explained about my pay problems. Then Paul said: 'Do not worry, because I am going to earn enough money for us all.'

I still thought that this would include Terry and that the three of us would work together. I started doing Ray's paperwork and wrote to spiritualist churches to get bookings for him. We also began a clinic at our house.

Not long after Paul's phone call, a friend of mine, Christine, said she was having a special evening and wanted me to take a number from a hat – Paul Lambillion was going to do auric drawings based on these numbers.

Terry and I went along. Paul Lambillion produced the drawings and said: 'I must do number six first.' He did not know to whom the drawings related and just worked with the numbers.

Paul Lambillion continued: 'This person is going to be so busy travelling all over the country doing healing. They have the most amazing healing gift.'

I thought: 'He is not talking about me. He must be talking about Ray and Paul.' Terry was sitting next to me and whispered that Paul Lambillion was talking about Ray. His face dropped when he realised what this would mean.

Paul Lambillion said: 'Where is this person I am talking about?' I piped up: 'It is me, Paul.' He replied: 'Oh yes, thank you very much' and carried on to the next drawing. He knew that he had just sanctioned what I was doing with Ray. He had also reiterated everything that his guide Hartstar had told me during my sitting with him at his home.

Ray, Paul and I were soon working at regular clinics in King's Lynn, Wisbech and London and travelled all over England to do demonstrations at spiritualist churches.

Then in late 1991, we were invited to go to Mombassa in Kenya by a lady called Sylvia McFarlane who had seen us in *Psychic News*. She had a healing centre built specially for us. We went out there for two weeks.

We stayed on the coast at Diani Reef, which is the main tourist area. We healed ex-pats and locals and had a very successful visit including some lectures by Paul.

When we returned from Africa, my relationship with Terry began to deteriorate. I was out of the house more than I was there. It was not fair on him.

Ray and I were invited to go out to Kenya again in May 1992. Terry did not want me to go, but I wanted to do the work.

This visit did not go very well because Sylvia said we were too commercially minded. The truth was we needed to raise the money to cover our air fare.

Ray nearly drowned in a diving accident and contracted salmonella poisoning just before we flew home. I will let Ray explain.

> During our first trip to Kenya, Paul had done some healing on one of the instructors at the Diani diving school. Gillian told him that I was keen on diving. When we returned, he offered me a day's diving.
>
> We were only diving to 18 metres, what they call a shallow dive. But the experienced female diver who was supposed to be looking after me, came over the top of me and as she went past, caught my breathing apparatus with her fins.

It flipped out of my mouth, flew over my head and became tangled in my tank. I was desperately trying to get it back and she was below me unaware that there was a problem.

I began gulping water. The diving instructor looked up and saw me. By then my body was arching backwards. I could see the surface but thought I was going to die.

The instructor shot up, grabbed my jacket, inflated it and I flew to the surface. The instructor hit me on the chest, which made me choke. Then I was hauled into the boat.

When we got back to our accommodation, I was sick and must have brought up half the Indian Ocean!

We also had a free day trip to an island off the coast of Tanzania. This was instead of payment, because so many of our patients could not afford to give us money.

I ate some crab cooked by the local villagers, but unfortunately it must have been undercooked in dirty water. Salmonella takes four to five days to incubate. I fell ill when we returned to Bury St Edmunds and was taken straight to hospital where I stayed for a week.

They refused to discharge me unless I had someone to look after me. At the time I was living by myself in a flat. So Gillian and Terry had a discussion and, reluctantly on Terry's part, they agreed to allow me to move into their house until I was back on my feet.

When I was fully recovered, Terry told me to go, so I moved back to the flat. Then Gillian and I began travelling again.

I'll let Gillian explain what happened next.

Terry was very unhappy with our situation. I think Ray staying with us had been the last straw. He confronted me and said: 'It is Paul or me.'

I am not sure whether his actual words were Paul or Ray Brown, but it was decision time.

'It is going to have to be Paul' was my reply. I knew I had to be with Paul. Everything I had experienced in my life had led to this work.

It was mutually agreed between Terry and me that because of the clinic in the house it would be best for me to keep the house and pay him half of the value, and it was also agreed that he take our car and some furniture. Ray moved in as a lodger in the back bedroom. There was absolutely nothing between Ray and me at that time. Initially we had a working relationship.

A lot of people in Bury St Edmunds Spiritualist Church went against me after my split with Terry. I realised that my work with Ray and Paul was going to take me away a lot. I would not be able to commit myself to the church as much as in the past, so I resigned. Sadly after fifteen years of devoted service, the committee voted against my Honorary Life Membership, and that really hurt me.

But at least Ray, Paul and I were now free to concentrate on full-time healing.

Chapter 13

Travel, Marriage and New Challenges

Ray and Gillian were very busy from 1992 to 1994 running new clinics and developing a partnership with the Rainbow Enlightenment Foundation. Sadly plans to open a healing centre with the Rainbow Enlightenment Foundation floundered, but fulfilling visits were made to Israel in 1992 and Japan in 1993. Ray nearly had another terrible car accident when he had a stress attack just before flying off to Africa for the third and last time. Fortunately Waters Running and Paul ensured that Ray cheated death yet again! A successful visit to Africa was marred this time by Gillian's health problems; again Paul came to the rescue. Ray and Gillian returned from Africa in the summer of 1994 and split from the Rainbow Enlightenment Foundation. Then in May 1995 they married in Bury St Edmunds. Ray begins this chapter by explaining how their healing mission developed around this time.

New clinics came and went. We worked in Hainault and Hersham, which we kept going for a couple of years. Then we moved onto Broadstairs and also took on a clinic at Wimbledon Spiritualist Church, which we still do to this day. We stopped going to King's Lynn and Wisbech and started up in Flitwick in Bedfordshire, then Tring in Hertfordshire, and Coventry.

We visited Frankfurt in Germany and cured a Professor Steinstrup of prostate cancer. He was so thrilled that he went to the German Congress and announced the success. But the police threatened to arrest us if we did any more work in the country. Spiritual healing is against the law there.

Paul wanted us to set up a healing centre in England, where he could do more complicated surgery and have a base for lecturing and teaching.

We met Jane and David Bandy who ran the Rainbow Enlightenment Foundation. They had seen us at a demonstration and invited us to run a clinic at their base in Steppingley, Bedfordshire. They also offered massage with local aromatherapists to complement our work.

Soon the Bandys started to talk about developing a healing centre with us. This fitted in very well with Paul's vision. Because we were so busy doing our clinics, we agreed that they would handle the money and negotiations to purchase a property.

We met a lady called Caroline after a large demonstration at Wimbledon Spiritualist Church. She was very interested in helping us and offered to donate a substantial sum of money to help us to start the healing centre. Caroline agreed to pass the money to the Rainbow Enlightenment Foundation. She even started a little clinic at her home in Richmond.

Jane and David Bandy told us that they were thinking of going on holiday to Israel. We had never been there and thought it would be good to reintroduce Paul to the part of the world that he had travelled in, so we agreed to go on holiday with them.

We landed in Tel Aviv and spent a night there, then picked up our coach tour. The first stop was the Dead Sea where we had a day floating around in the water. After that it was up to the Golan Heights. We visited all the holy places in Jerusalem including the Stations of the Cross.

Paul did not come through until we went to where Jesus was supposed to have given the Sermon on the Mount. Gillian kept saying to me: 'Is Paul here? Is Paul here?'

I did feel him around me, but he had gone by the time we walked into the chapel that is built on the site of the Sermon on the Mount.

Paul took me over as we came out of the church and led Gillian down the slope and said: 'This is the where it would have happened.' Paul said a prayer and then let me back!

The Sea of Galilee stretched out before us. When we spoke, our voices echoed. We were sitting in a natural amphitheatre.

Next on the list was the place where John the Baptist delivered his sermons. Paul disagreed totally with the location and said that it was further downstream. Paul liked Masada and came through when I was filming the site. Masada is a large fortress that was built by King Herod. It was a final Jewish stronghold. They managed to keep the Romans out for about a year.

The Romans built a ramp up to the fortress using slave labour. As Roman soldiers neared the fort, the surviving defenders decided that they would not be taken alive. They selected a priest to kill them all and then the priest committed suicide leaving nobody for the Romans to capture.

The capture of Masada happened after his time, but he was obviously moved by this significant event in his people's history.

Gillian and I became a lot closer on this trip. I was definitely drawn towards her. Having time off together helped us get to know each other better.

I will let Gillian explain.

> Ray had to have somebody to look after him. I thought that he was very scruffy when we first met. I did my best to smarten him up. We grew together very slowly. The crunch came when we stayed at a kibbutz. They only had a double room and Ray refused to sleep on the floor! There was no great romance. It just happened. Our love for each other has grown over the years. We complement each other really well and do everything together. Now back to Ray again:

Plans for the new centre started moving quickly after we returned from Israel. We found a fabulous mansion in Poddington. It had a lot of potential, but it came at a pretty price: £750,000.

I thought it was a risk and would have been happier with another property which was not as large and had outbuildings that could have been converted in time. It was going to cost £300,000, which was a more manageable price.

The Bandys were convinced that they could make the bigger house work. Meanwhile during the summer of 1993 we were invited to go to Japan. Derek Robinson, President of Wimbledon Spiritualist Church had received a request from Japan for a visit from a healer with special qualities. He asked us to go and we jumped at the chance to see the Far East.

I was becoming more and more concerned about progress with the healing centre and phoned David Bandy from Japan and asked him not to put the deposit on and to wait until I got back, but David was convinced that we would get all the money to buy the property. He said that he would be able to find backers and pressed ahead. Sadly the deal fell through, we lost our deposit and the dream of opening a healing centre was temporarily put on hold.

We had a great visit to Japan, despite our worries back home. We did healing demonstrations combined with clairvoyance from Jill Hay and Alan Law. The Japanese were absolutely crazy about Paul's healing. They could not get enough! Our Japanese hosts funded the whole trip. Every move was photographed. We were given six books of photographs when we left.

Our hosts made us very welcome but we could not get used to the raw food! We lived on jam sandwiches. One of our hosts ran a sandwich company and offered a great selection of jam sandwiches.

I remember pleading at a railway station: 'For goodness sake, get me some chocolate.' A seventy pence bar of UK chocolate cost about five pounds at the station, but it was worth it.

Then we went to a Chinese restaurant and I thought we might get some ordinary food, but it was Japanese Chinese. There was no rice. Everything was fishy and raw. I found out that I was eating jellyfish. It was like chewing an elastic band!

We stayed in a tiny room in one hotel. I thought that we had been given a single bed but it was a double. I said there was no way we could both sleep in it. So we took two rooms.

We visited a Shinto shrine; a lot people were meditating in the lovely gardens. It was a wonderfully peaceful experience.

Our relationship with the Bandys changed after the deal fell through. They did our bookings for Flitwick. We had patients from 10 a.m. through until 7 p.m. or 8 p.m. I found it very hard going. We were contributing money from every patient at Flitwick to the Rainbow Enlightenment Foundation and had to cope with overbooking.

The Flitwick clinic staggered on until July 1994. We were just about to go out to Africa for the third and last time, when our dealings with the Rainbow Enlightenment Foundation caused me to have a stress attack, with near fatal consequences.

The Foundation wanted all of our clinics to be run under the Foundation umbrella. The plan was for us to give them five pounds a patient. We were then charging only £15 for a consultation. We had run with this arrangement at Flitwick, but were not happy to expand it to our other clinics.

Matters came to a head when Jill Ricketts, who helped out at the Flitwick clinic, offered to host a small clinic at her house in Tring. Unfortunately Jane Bandy did not take kindly to this and stopped her from helping out at Flitwick. Paul was very angry with this and we had a big row with the Bandys.

Paul told them that what they were doing was not spiritual and they had to sort things out. A row flared up and Paul said: 'I come here to heal the sick. I do not come here to be abused. I feel that you are abusing me and Spirit. As from today, this has to stop.'

We drove home to Bury St Edmunds because of all the upset. We had planned to stay the night with the Bandys, then head on to our clinic at Edgware on the following day. This was our final day's work before we flew to Africa.

I went off during the evening to fill up the car with petrol, but promptly passed out at the wheel soon after leaving home. My foot slipped off the throttle and the car cruised across the road and mounted the pavement.

Waters Running took hold of me. Then Paul drove the car back. He is hopeless behind the wheel. He screeched into the drive and nearly put the car through the garage door!

Over to Gillian again:

> I thought: 'What on earth is going on? That was quick, he could not have been to the garage.'
>
> Paul staggered in and said that he had taken over Ray: 'You have to get Ray upstairs and onto the bed. I do not know what has happened to him. I must have a look at him.' He went up the stairs on all fours, with me dragging him. Ray looked very strange. Paul lay down and I said: 'I will have to get a doctor.' 'No, do not get a doctor. I will go into Spirit and will look at him,' replied Paul. So Paul disappeared. Ray returned and said: 'What is the matter

with me?' I said: 'Just lay back, the spirit doctors are looking at you to see what has happened.'

As he relaxed on the bed, Paul returned and said that he was worried. He thought that Ray had had a stress attack and that we should get him checked out as soon as possible. I had to get him to hospital.

I went downstairs to get Ray a glass of water. He climbed out of bed to follow me and collapsed. I dialled 999 and an ambulance came very quickly. The hospital did tests just in case he had had a heart attack.

I phoned the Bandys to say that there was no way we could go and see them after our Edgware visit, because Ray was in hospital. That was the last time I spoke to them. They thought that I was just making excuses. Our Flitwick clinic was finished.

Ray can explain what happened in hospital:

The doctor said that I would not be able to fly to Africa. He was worried that I might have had a heart attack. I told him that I was going to leave hospital the next day because I had to go to Africa.

Gillian's Mum and Stepdad sat with me in hospital. I told them that I was going to let Paul through. I asked them to ask him if I had had a heart attack, or just a stress attack.

Paul told them that it was a stress attack. I told the doctor that I was leaving the hospital the next day at 12 noon, whether my results were through or not.

This created a panic in the hospital. It was the weekend and they did not know whether they could get my results in time. But at 11.30am, the following day, the doctor appeared and said that it had been a stress attack. I was free to leave and we went to Africa as planned.

Our trip to Africa went very well, apart from Gillian's health problems, which she will explain.

We treated a lot of people in Kenya and Paul even did a lecture to a group of English people. I developed a blockage in my bowel as a result of the change in diet. Sylvia McFarlane gave some medicine to ease my constipation but it only made it worse.

We flew to Nairobi from Diani Reef to stay with another Sylvia. By the time we landed in Nairobi, I was in such a state that I could not walk. The pain was terrible. I was trying to push the luggage trolley and collapsed on the floor.

We met Sylvia and she said that she would take us to a friend who we were going to treat. She was married to a doctor who could sort out my problem.

The doctor took one look at my stomach and said: 'Enema for you!'

I thought that he was joking. I got into a panic and thought: 'You are not going to give me an enema' and immediately started saying: 'Paul, Paul, please Ray, get Paul, for God's sake, get Paul.'

The doctor went away to get his equipment. I was panicking, but fortunately Paul arrived and worked on the spasms in the colon. He helped me a lot.

When the doctor came back with all his equipment I said: 'I think I will be alright now.'

Sylvia told him that Paul was there and that he had sorted out the problem. The doctor was amazed. He felt my stomach and realised that it had changed dramatically. But he was very sceptical.

The next big event in our lives was our marriage on May 27, 1995 – over to Ray again:

Getting married to Gillian was very important. It meant that she was showing her commitment, not just to Spirit but to me.

We enjoyed every minute of the day. The marriage was at Bury St Edmunds Registry Office. Paul came through at the reception, held in the Priory Hotel, and gave a speech.

We enjoyed it so much that we would get married again next week if we could!

Chapter 14

Our Healing Centre

Ray and Gillian continued with their busy programme of demonstrations and clinics in 1995. They also ran a very successful week-long course at Knuston Hall in, Northamptonshire. Then, with the help of two of their patients, they realised their dream of opening a healing centre, when they bought Fir Tree Lodge in Lutterworth. Soon after their move, they founded the International Healing Federation, so that Paul could train healers and reach a wider audience. Fir Tree Lodge really took off after Ray, Paul and Gillian were filmed in Spring 1996, for a BBC series, 'Secrets of the Paranormal'. There was an inexhaustible demand for Paul's healing. Ray resigned from the National Federation of Healers after his TV appearance. The National Federation accused Ray of bringing healing into disrepute by going into trance on national TV. Fortunately Ray and Gillian were able to join the Corinthian Church, a spiritual healing organisation that follows the writings of St Paul. National newspapers came hot on the heels of the BBC. Ray, Gillian and Paul had a lot of publicity in the News of the World. Paul even healed the back of Phil Taylor, the News of the World's chief reporter. Phil is now the newspaper's Associate Editor. More successful work on the actor, Sir John Mills was also reported in the News of the World.

Throughout 1995 we did a lot of demonstrations at spiritualist churches and centres and of course we continued with our clinics. I was keen to take it a stage further by organising a residential course. I always thought that we should do a week at Arthur Findlay College in Stansted. Unfortunately they did not want us there. I have no idea why. But possibly it was because Ray was a trance healer. So I thought: 'Right, we will do it ourselves.'

We hired Knuston Hall in Northamptonshire in October 1995 for a week-long course. I arranged all the mediums and lecturers. It was a complete sell-out. One hundred people attended.

Eamon Downey and Janet Parker did clairvoyance. Two doctors worked with Paul - Dr Witold Falkowski from Hemel Hempstead Hospital and Dr Walter Fisher, a Norwegian neuro-surgeon.

Paul lectured about the Spirit world and the mechanics of trance and did demonstrations and group healing training. The event inspired us to think again about developing a healing centre.

We had started a clinic in Northampton, for former Flitwick patients. Two of our patients, said that they would find a place for us. They discovered Fir Tree Lodge and another much larger property, which was Grade One listed. The listing rather frightened us off, so we plumped for Fir Tree Lodge.

I fell in love with Fir Tree Lodge immediately. It had a big barn that we earmarked for conversion into a spiritual hospital. We bought Fir Tree Lodge, sold our house in Bury St Edmunds and moved in on Boxing Day 1995. It went like clockwork.

We decided to centre our clinics on Fir Tree Lodge, and cut out Coventry and Northampton. We carried on with Wimbledon, Bury St Edmunds, Hainault, Ruislip, and Tring, but changed to monthly rather than fortnightly visits.

Paul did in-depth spiritual surgery using oils on the skin. Patients came in the morning and stayed all day. We used our two spare bedrooms as treatment rooms with two beds in each room. Ray's office doubled as a treatment room and if we were really busy we used our own bedroom.

Paul's speciality has always been backs, but he often worked on the stomach, uterus and bladder, healed irritable bowel syndrome, colitis, and cleared blockages. He also did serious heart operations, dealing with valve problems and inserted spiritual probes to stimulate heart muscles.

We had at least three clinics a week. I worked with Paul a lot. He used my hands. I was aware that Dr Barbara Lane was working through me. Paul staged many seminars and workshops. The lounge was 40ft x 40ft, so there was plenty of space for special events.

Fortunately I was able to recruit a wonderful secretary called Carol Esplin who did all our admin work. She is still involved with us to this day. Plans were developed to create the spiritual hospital in the barn. This was the next logical step and would have given us our house back, but the hospital went on the back burner when we launched the International Healing Federation (IHF).

This was Paul's idea. His vision was a world-wide membership of thousands of healers all using his methods.

Dr Cotton, a woman who brought medical students to Fir Tree Lodge, introduced us to Vince Lewis. We really liked Vince. Years before, he had been told in a circle that he would meet Saul of Tarsus. Vince writes about this in his testimony in Part Four.

Vince became our manager and set up and ran the IHF. Anne, who is now his wife, became our second secretary, sharing the workload with Carol. Then in 1996, the BBC came to film. Ray can explain this.

Lance Trendall, a patient at Tring was a ghost hunter. The BBC approached him to be involved in a series called Secrets of the Paranormal.

They asked him if he could recommend a good spiritual healer, so he told them about me. The BBC decided that I had an interesting story. The six-programme series featured Lance Trendall, Mathew Manning, Uri Geller, a clairvoyant and a

UFO investigator. Our story was told in the last programme.

The documentary took two months to film. We were approached in March and the final product was screened on 26 May.

We were deluged with enquiries after the show and had to increase the number of clinics at Fir Tree Lodge. Bookings were being taken nine months ahead.

Can you imagine ringing Ray Brown if you had a back pain and being told you could not see him for nine months! My hands became very sore and I started getting RSI because of the pressure of the work.

Then the National Federation of Spiritual Healers went against my work. They said that I had brought them into disrepute, because I had carried out trance healing on television. So rather than cause a fuss, I resigned from the Federation. I had been a member since the early days in Portsmouth with the Christopher West Healing Group.

I told them that I was going to send my certificate back, as they were on a different wavelength to me. Paul had cured three people on television. Surely this was not bringing spiritual healing into disrepute?

Their real problem was that someone in trance could not be insured. The Confederation of Healing Associations, the National Federation's umbrella organisation was not liable for what happened under trance.

We heard about the Corinthian Church, a healing organisation that followed Paul's writings in the Bible. Gillian telephoned the leader of the Corinthians, the Rev Ron Jones. He said that he had been waiting for us to get in touch.

The Corinthians have groups all over the country. But unlike the National Federation, healers are allowed to use all their spiritual gifts. The Corinthians say it is the Spiritual Way. Paul also spoke of it as the Spiritual Way, saying: 'You must use your gifts of the spirit.'

Unfortunately healing has been changed because of the European Union (EU). Healing organisations have been ordered not to touch the body now, but of course this was the central work of the wonderful healer and founder of the National Federation, Harry Edwards. The EU has weird and wonderful ideas about spiritual healing. The bureaucrats do not accept that it is anything to do with Spirit. It is all about the vibrations and energies from the body of the healer. The EU does not like talk of spirit guides. Fortunately the Corinthians are different and are very open to this.

The EU is denying what we truly are, which is 'spiritual' healers. It is almost going back to the old days when it was a crime to do spiritual healing.

The Reverend Ron Jones arranged for Gillian and I to be ordained as Ministers of the Corinthians. Being ordained means that we can officiate at Christenings, burials and weddings and are just like any other clergy. We now operate as roving Senior Principal Ministers teaching about Spirit and training healers.

Journalists appeared after the BBC programme. We had thousands of letters and the telephone rang every minute of the day. The only way we could get any peace was to leave the phone off the hook! Gillian can explain what happened next.

The number of calls blew up the card in our local exchange. I called BT from a friend's phone, because we went three days without a phone.

The engineer said: 'I am sorry, but your line has blown up the card in the exchange and we have to replace it.'

The *News of the World* came to do a piece in 1997. The paper was bombarded with calls. They even had to take on extra staff to handle the enquiries. It was phenomenal. They received lots of letters, which were forwarded to us.

Phil Taylor, then the *News of the World*'s chief reporter (now Associate Editor) came to see us at Wimbledon Spiritualist Church after the initial story. He had a chronic back problem, which was defying the doctors, but Paul healed him. This led to another feature in the paper.

He phoned me a few weeks after his consultation and said that he was feeling sore again and asked for more healing. Ray was not at home and had gone to Portsmouth to see his children.

So Phil arranged to meet Ray at a Little Chef on the A3.

Over to Ray again:

I had a six-seater VW Sharan at the time. The car had darkened windows to keep prying eyes away from our equipment.

Phil arrived, so I let Paul come through. Phil hopped into the back seat and Paul worked on him. Phil climbed out and bent up and down a couple of times, only to return to the car for more healing. We had quite an audience staring at us from the Little Chef windows when it was all over. Phil said: 'I wonder what would happen if this ended up in the paper tomorrow?'

We also helped Sir John Mills, the famous British actor. His agent had seen the coverage in the *News of the World*. Sir John Mills' son Jonathan phoned and asked if we could heal his Dad. He had fallen over onstage in Los Angeles and injured his back. Sir John was due to take part in an event for the Roy Castle charity, and was in so much pain, that it looked as if he would have to cancel the performance.

I said: 'Can he come to us at Fir Tree Lodge because we are very, very, busy.' Jonathan replied: 'No, I doubt very much that I can get him to you, because he is in so much pain.'

We were just about to go on a trip to Sweden, so agreed to pop in and see him on our way to the airport. Paul worked on Sir John's back and as a result he managed to do the charity performance. The *News of the World* followed this up with another picture story.

We returned to do back-up healing on Sir John after the Sweden trip. Sir John asked Paul: 'Excuse me, is it going to hurt as much this time?' Paul replied 'Well, maybe Sir John, I do not know, but maybe.'

So Sir John said to his nurse: 'Bring in the morphine!' It was a great privilege to meet Sir John and help him.

Chapter 15

On the Road Again

Ray and Gillian reluctantly closed down the International Healing Federation in the winter of 1998 because of a series of personal attacks from the membership. They also decided it would be best for their own health and happiness to sell Fir Tree Lodge and they returned to the road in the year 2000. Fortunately their work is still supported by healing groups around the UK who were all trained during the International Healing Federation era.

The International Healing Federation started to cause us problems. We had hundreds of members who only paid an annual subscription. Ray and I had to work flat out to keep it afloat and pay the salaries of our manager and two secretaries. Ray takes up the story again:

My hands began to suffer, then during winter 1998, we started having problems with the membership. Things came to a head when we found some letters written to Vince about me. The person who wrote them thought that the organisation would be better off if I was not at its head.

I did not take kindly to this. Then we found another letter attacking us. So I decided to close the charity that ran the healing organisation.

When Vince came in the next day, I told him that it was the end of the road and that we were closing down the Federation. Then our accountant contacted the Charity Commissioners to let them know that we were winding up and told them that we were going to donate the charity's assets to the Corinthian Church.

We presented the Rev. Ron Jones with a cheque for £17,600 at a demonstration evening in Hailsham. It was a sad day, but at least we had trained many healers who could continue to work with us.

The clinics continued at Fir Tree Lodge. We had pursued the idea of converting the barn into a spiritual hospital. But some friends went against us when the project was at the planning consultation stage and caused a lot of disruption to our work. So we shelved the idea and because of all the problems and the pressure on my health we decided to sell Fir Tree Lodge and return to Bury St Edmunds.

Paul's dream of a permanent healing centre was at an end – for the time being! We realised that we would be much happier going back to working as freelance travelling healers. By doing that we could pace ourselves. Life would be less frantic and we could steer clear of people who tried to control our lives.

Fir Tree Lodge was only on the market for a couple of months. A man came off the street and told us not to sell it to anyone else. He wanted it. We moved out of Fir Tree Lodge in December 1999, lived locally for the next six months, then returned to Bury St Edmunds.

Carol stayed on as our secretary and still does a lot of our bookings. We also kept up a Lutterworth clinic because so many people had come to Fir Tree Lodge from the north.

As well as Lutterworth, we currently do monthly clinics at Bury St Edmunds, Wimbledon, Hainault, Brighton and Tring, although Tring will be ending soon because Jill Ricketts is leaving the UK. This reduced workload really helps my hands.

Carol keeps a database of all the healing groups. Patients are often sent to the nearest group for back-up healing after their initial consultation with Paul. Also people with life-threatening illnesses like cancer, motor neurone disease, multiple sclerosis and Alzheimer's are sent to a local healing group for regular sessions.

Paul can work with these types of illnesses, but unfortunately as it is such extensive work, we have had to shelve it and seek support from our group healers. Ideally we need a residential place to specialise in life-threatening medical problems.

When we were in Fir Tree Lodge, we also had the facilities to hold seminars with Paul who taught about the Spirit world and trained people in healing.

In January 2004, we worked in Seaton, Devon alongside Keith Charles, a medium with whom we appeared in an ITV documentary featuring his extraordinary clairvoyant gift. Keith is known as the 'Psychic Cop'. He is a former CID officer and has helped the police in difficult cases with great success both here and in America. He demonstrates his gift in this country and abroad and provides private readings for those who contact him.

I still seem to be injury prone! In May 2003 we flew to Cyprus for a holiday. There were lots of golfers on the plane. I was getting our bags off the carousel at Larnaca airport. Gillian was away getting a trolley.

A big Dutch guy spotted his bags once they had gone past me. He pushed in, leaned over me and dragged his bag over the top of the other cases. As it swung out, it hit me on the knee.

At that point I was bending over the carousel trying to get my own case. His case hit me on the side of the knee and took off my kneecap. The kneecap went back into place when I stood up, but I was in agony.

By the time we left the airport I could not walk. I had an emergency operation in Paphos and spent the rest of the holiday on my back. The problem did not clear up, so I went to see another surgeon in the autumn. He decided that it needed cleaning out and did another operation.

The operation went really well. But I now have pain in the front of the knee and inside the joint. It is very painful if I have to walk any distance.

Gillian gave Paul a lot of stick: 'Why can't you do Ray's knee? Everyone is asking why can't Paul help?' Paul kept saying to her: 'I will do it when the time is right. I have to wait until the inflammation has gone down.'

He must have been fed up with having his ears bent. I was in bed with flu, watching TV and dozing, then woke up with a start. My hand was on my knee and was fumbling around. I had no control over it and thought: 'What is going on here?'

I immediately sent up a message to His Nibs: 'Make sure you do not come any higher!' He did the operation and it is feeling a lot better. Now back to Gillian to close the chapter:

As we get older, Paul will want to focus on teaching and doing less healing. I suppose he is waiting for us to slow down and decide what we want to do.

Ray and I are sure that we have much useful work to do. We have many more years of active healing ahead of us – so long as Ray's hands hold out!

Chapter 16

Ray's Eyesight

Paul can see perfectly without glasses. Ray has always had poor eyesight and has always worn glasses. Here Ray explains what he has done to improve his vision.

Up until I met Gillian, I wore glasses that corrected my eyes. My right eye had 13.6 vision and my left eye was 9.8, a long, long way from perfect vision! I could not find my way round a darkened room without my glasses.

In Chapter Six, I told the story of the time when Ted Brown, or the Spirit that was talking through him, asked me what time it was. It was a dark room and I could not see the clock. I told him: 'Well you are a spirit, you should be able to see the clock because I cannot see it without my glasses.' I was just being straightforward but the spirit or the medium took it the wrong way.

The funny thing is that Paul has always been able to see everything. He could even read the paperwork at the back of the churches or halls during demonstrations. He did not need to wear glasses. People became used to seeing me wear glasses and him without them.

I wore contact lenses for a while after I met Gillian. Then I started having terrible problems driving in the dark. It did not matter whether I was wearing contact lenses or glasses, but car headlights coming from the opposite direction seemed to be heading for me. It was both dangerous and frightening.

We heard about corrective laser treatment and ended up seeing a specialist, Dr Chaudry in Leicester. He is one of the top eye surgeons in Britain. I know that he was one of the pioneers for retina detachment laser treatment.

He took one look and said that there was no way he could laser my eyes, they were too bad. If he carried out the standard treatment, I would have no eyes left! He explained that the only way to get round it was to do a clear lens extraction on my right eye. My lens was perfectly healthy, just shortsighted.

It would be the same as a cataract operation. He would remove the lens and put in a new lens. Dr Chaudry said that he did not normally do this operation on a person who could see well with glasses, but said that if I was willing to take the risk he would do the necessary.

I signed all the paperwork and he successfully operated on my right eye. My vision improved from 13.6 to 6.1, a massive change. Then he lasered the right eye and brought it to 0.6. The job was completed when he lasered my left eye, which now has 0.2 vision. It changed my life completely!

Paul was completely confused after the operation. But because he did not want me to damage my eyes, which have been very sensitive since the treatment, he began wearing my reading glasses. This wrong-foots people because they expect me to wear glasses. To be honest, I think that Paul enjoys it, because nobody, except for Gillian, knows when he is there.

Sometimes he will sit in the clinic during the lunchtime break and listen to friends or healers who think they are talking to me. It is not until Gillian tells them that Paul is with them, or he speaks in his posh voice, that they realise he is present!

Ray and I have now told our separate and joint stories up to the present time. In the third part of the book it's Paul's turn to have his say and explain in his own words, his own life, going back 2000 years, his teachings then and his teachings now – and how they have changed. He also spells out in detail what the world of Spirit is like and why and how he has chosen to bridge these two very different worlds.

Part Three

Paul of Tarsus

I come into your world to heal the sick.
For I am no greater than you and you are no lesser than I.

I am just Paul, a servant of God, a mere grain of sand
in a vast desert, so being one grain of sand I am part of the whole.

Love is all you need. Love is all you have.

God is like the sun, always somewhere.

Always know that there is a place for you in God.

Do not seek power, you already have it given to you by God.

Without God nobody would be.

Healing is love. Let all you do be done in love.

Birth is the opportunity. Death is the reward.

There is not evil, only ignorance.

I am with you always.

Chapter 17

Saul and Paul

In this chapter Paul outlines in his own words the story of his life on Earth 2000 years ago, his experience on the road to Damascus and his continuing belief in Jesus' teachings and the love of God. Later he explains that he no longer defines his own mission as Christianity and says he wishes there was only one spiritual philosophy on this troubled Earth. Paul maintains that his new teachings are the easiest to understand and follow.

I was born Saul of Tarsus. Paul was my Roman name. My full name was Gaius Julius Paulus. My surname was taken from my father's citizenship. I was brought up in the Jewish faith as a Roman citizen at Tarsus, now named Cilicia, during the reign of Caesar Augustus.

My father was not of Roman lineage, but as he was a very wealthy privileged man of some prominence, he inherited the citizenship. My mother was Judean and I had a brother and a sister.

To be anyone in my time you had to be Roman, but even then there was no guarantee that you would survive until old age, as they were very violent times. During the time of Christ, Galilee was a dangerous place because of rebellious partisans who attempted to fight the Romans, the invaders of our land.

As a young boy I was often sent away, so I did not have the opportunity to see a lot of my father, but he was a good father and as the head of the family he was very strict. Contrary to what is believed in today's modern world, fathers were only strict on their sons, not their daughters.

Many people believe that I did not like women, that I hated women.

That is not true. It was the faith I was brought up in that was hard on women. Some people joke that I loved camels more than women. Well I suppose that I was with camels more than women!

Tarsus was a very beautiful part of the world, situated about ten miles from the coast. The land was immensely rich and fertile, and if you looked to the north, you could see the snow capped Taurus Mountains in the distance.

I spent many hours as a young boy down at the busy harbour, happily watching the ships as they sailed to and from Cyprus, Greece, Syria, Crete, and Egypt carrying their cargoes of herbs, spices and fabrics.

When I was a young man I went to Jerusalem to study theology under Rabbi Gamaliel. At the same time, I followed my own way and seriously studied the scriptures from the Greek Bible, the Septuagint.

As Saul, I spent some of my early days in Galilee and, although I had heard of Jesus Christ and John the Baptist, I did not meet with them. I worked in my father's business and preached whenever and wherever I could. I became very absorbed in the religion of the Jewish people and eventually took up teaching in the temples and tabernacles of Jerusalem.

I was very happy in Jerusalem and was able to move around the Hellenic city with freedom to labour, study, and seek out many learned teachers and priests. I decided not to become a Pharisee as my father had intended. As a young man my father had greatly influenced my life and I had a profound respect for him, but I was excited, enthusiastic, and thirsty for knowledge. I was not ready to respect his wishes and become a Pharisee. So much was happening and I was not ready to make a decision on what I wanted to do.

I became acquainted with the Sadducees, then became interested in a sect known as the Essenes. I visited their community on the shores of the Dead Sea. It was there that I learned from an old man, that the

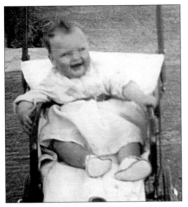

Right: Gertie, Native American Indian woman on the camp at Atherstone-on-Stour pushing Ray in a pram

Above: Ray as a baby

Above: Marcia, Ray's Mum

Right: Ray as a toddler

Left: Ivor and Marcia Brown's wedding

Right: Peter Brown, step-sister and Ray

Left: Marcia Brown
with Bob Black

Right: Ray at seventeen

Left: Ray healing with members of the Christopher West Healing Group

Above: Christopher West Healing Group. Ray third from right

Above: Ray's first wedding. Back row: Aunt Jean and brother Peter.
Front row: Ray with Helen, Arthur Thorn (Helen's father) and Marcia Brown

Right: Ray's second
marriage to Sally

Above: Gillian's Dad, Roy

Above right: Roy and Connie's wedding

Right: Gillian with Mum, Connie

Above: Gillian's grandmother, Jessie

Right: Gillian with
Stepdad, Arthur Yates

Above: Ray and Gillian's wedding

Right: Psychic painting of
Paul by Diane Webbe

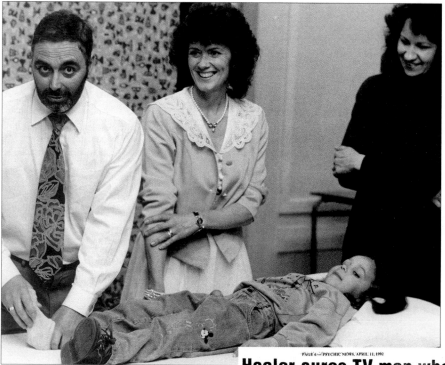

Above: Paul and Gillian at a demonstration in Essex

Below and right: Ray's UK work begins to make headlines in the journal, *Pyschic News...*

Healer cures TV man who was sent along to film him

PAUL — the 2,000-year-old spirit doctor who heals through medium Ray Brown — scored an instant success when he cured a member of the TV team sent to film him.

Last month, Ray was invited by Free For All, a Channel Four film production team, to take part in a programme featuring the Bristol Cancer Help Centre. Paul is currently treating one of the patients taking part in the survey.

"Whilst working," his assistant Gillian Sitton explained, "one of their production team — his name was Phil — walked in with an injured back."

Luckily for Phil, Ray, who was entranced by the "dead" Judaean surgeon at the time, offered to help. To Phil's surprise, he was able to put the trouble right at once.

"The team were amazed," Gillian commented. "They said Phil had been moaning for weeks and driving them all up the wall."

The spirit surgeon also gives lectures on all aspects of Spiritualism and healing, as well as training healers to become proficient in their work.

Last month, the Rainbow Enlightenment Foundation — a new organisation which seeks to raise people's awareness — opened a clinic at Histon House, Steppingley, Bedfordshire.

Ray was invited to take part in the opening programme organised by the foundation.

TRANCE healer Ray Brown "amazed" a camera crew after he gave one of them successful treatment.

Paul entranced Ray and "gave a splendid demonstration of healing to the 300 people who packed the school hall," said Gillian.

One patient who went to the spirit doctor for treatment was Janet Petigrew.

"At first, she was very reticent about letting Paul work on her dislocated toe," Gillian

spirit doctor how she had suffered with pain in her neck, shoulders, hips and legs since she had a bad fall three years ago.

As she left the platform free from pain after a successful healing, Mrs Farrell was overjoyed she "forced back tears of relief."

Arthritis patient, Elizabeth Gander — the "only patient managed to get on to the platform with the aid of a walking stick" — was another happy woman after the spirit doctor treated her knees and legs.

"To her amazement she was soon walking up and down the platform with Paul," said Gillian. "She was able to bend her knees without the aid of her stick."

Ray's healing demonstration was followed by some "brilliant evidence of life after death by clairvoyant R. Moulding," Gillian comments.

"The whole evening was a great success for Spiritualism and the foundation."

Despite protests received from residents "worried at the work of the devil" was performed at the meeting local reporters who witnessed Ray at work "found the complete reverse.

"After watching him being patients and talking with him afterwards," said Gillian, "they were spellbound.

"The article they wrote in their paper afterwards has brought hundreds more for healing."

commented. "It was so painful she could hardly walk."

Though specialists had unsuccessfully tried to put it right before, "Paul soon had it back in its joint," she added.

"Mrs Petigrew was happily walking around the platform afterwards, very pleased to be out of pain."

Josephine Farrell told the

A FORTHRIGHT reply to criticism levelled at him by healer and lecturer Tom Johanson (PN August 22) has been received from Paul, the 2,000-year-old spirit guide of healer Ray Brown.

During a trance sitting, Paul made it clear how he wished to reply to some of the points raised by Mr Johanson.

His comments, which he prefaces with the words, "All is not karma," are given below:

It is man on the earthplane who has learned nothing in the last 2,000 years. It is still the same today as it was 4,000 years ago.

In fact, man has not learned anything since time began. The greed and destruction are still the same as in Moses' time.

People come to me, very distressed and full of guilt, because they have been told their illnesses are karmic.

Teachers who state that you are put here to pay karmic debts through illness are wrong.

Can it be through the laws of karma that you start smoking, which causes cancer? Can it be karmic that you work so hard and get so stressed that you build up illnesses?

You cannot say "All is karma." There are thousands of people dying from starvation because others will not give them food. They would rather sell it for gain or make a profit out of it.

There is more than enough food put upon this earth to feed every mouth. It is the powers governing the world who decide whether people eat or not, not God.

These things are done by physical people, not by the spirit world, not God. This is not karma.

For one to say that you have to suffer to learn is wrong. Karma, as you call it, is changed every day.

If karma were true on earth, should you not then go along with the views of the Jehovah's Witnesses and not accept a blood transfusion? Should no transplants be carried out because it is your karma to die?

If you step out into the road and a car knocks you down, that is of this earth, it is not karma.

As I See It

Doubting karma

When you pass into the spirit world, the first thing you have to come to terms with is the trauma of your passing.

You then have to settle into the spirit realms by being cleared of all your earthly feelings.

You are given time to adjust; the first level is a zone of resettlement, your dependency area.

Then you move on to level two, where you come to terms with your previous existence,

accepting responsibility for all that you have done and working out every thought and deed against another soul.

When you are truly repentent, then, and only then, do you have the right of choice to return for another earthly existence or to progress on through the spirit realms.

You work out your karmic debts in the spirit world, not on the earthplane. YOU are your own judge.

If everything is karma, then

cause of the ways of your world.

It seems that however many times man comes back, he still makes the same mistakes over and over again.

Your world has not changed. love is not jealous or boastful; it is not arrogant or rude. Love does not insist on its own way; but rejoices in the right. Love bears all things, believes all things, hopes all things, endures all things. Love never ends."

When you come back, and you reach the age to think for yourselves, you will be doing the same as everyone else, making the same mistakes.

Why not, then, stay in the spirit world and move on, be-

May I, in love, quote you the Letters of Paul, Corinthians I, Chapter 13, Verse 4:

"Love is patient and kind;

Healer performs 'miracle' in Spain when giving treatment

A MAN with severe back pain who had difficulty in walking unaided was able to "skip and bend" for the first time in 10 years after healing by Ray Brown's spirit guide, Paul, during a demonstration in Alicante, Spain, last month.

The delighted patient — he had undergone several unsuccessful operations — told the healer he had changed his life. "It's a miracle," he said. "I can't believe this has happened to me."

Ray and his assistant Gillian demonstrated in a social club on a sports complex in Alicante before a mixed audience of holidaymakers and residents of many nationalities.

"They were mainly retired people who have moved to Spain because of the salt lakes and the warm climate," Gillian explained.

The spirit guide was later challenged by a German patient, Max Sharp, to heal his stiff knees and get him walking again.

Mr Sharp commented that spiritual healing was against the law in Germany unless medical qualifications were held.

"We were amazed at the number of English, German and Swiss people living there," said Gillian.

Most, she thought, had been attracted by the warm Spanish climate.

Keep-fit instructor Jean White sought healing from Ray for a painful foot and neck which made it difficult for her to work.

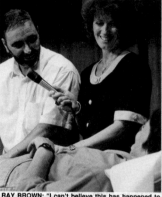

RAY BROWN: "I can't believe this has happened to me," says patient.

"The arch in her foot had dropped," Gillian explain[ed]. "The bones had moved and [she] had a nasty arthritic big t[oe]. She was also suffering from [a] disc problem in her neck."

Paul "released the arthr[itic] crystals from the bones [and] joints and soon had her wa[lking] ing properly again," Gill[ian] stated.

So successful was the de[m]onstration that Ray was ask[ed] if he would consider movin[g to] Spain permanently.

"Those present had ne[ver]...

her.

"She was with us for three days," said Gillian. "In that time she was able to eat properly."

After a spirit operation performed by Paul, Lois returned to America. Now she is making arrangements for Ray to visit her Spiritualist church in the New Year.

Since their return, Ray and Gillian also gave a successful demonstration of spiritual healing before an audience of 50 people at Flitwick, Bedfordshire.

Among the many patients treated was Teresa Bowen, of Barton Le Cley, Beds.

Twelve years ago, Miss Bowen underwent an operation for the removal of a cyst in her right eye. She has suffered pain on "the right side of her face and over the back of her head" ever since.

Gillian told how the patient was "amazed" later when the healer was able to touch the injured area without her feeling any pain whatsoever.

Another happy patient was

Suffolk trance healer gives terminally ill patient new hope

Healer in mercy dash to Germany

...and his work in Europe attracts further *Psychic News* coverage

JUST days after a mercy trip to Germany by Suffolk healer Ray Brown, a terminally ill patient was able to "go out walking with his dog," his daughter, Ruth, told PN last week.

Helmut Kompel, 63, was told by doctors he had one year to live last April. He suffered from cancer of the gullet, which had spread to his chest and stomach.

"He had an operation last March," his daughter Ruth Mahlert explained. "Doctors performed an operation in which they removed his gullet and replaced it with a tube so that he could eat and drink.

"The tumour was too large for them to take away and he suffered much pain. He was very feeble and had lost a lot of weight, but his will to live was very strong."

No chemotherapy or treatment of any kind was considered advisable and the patient was sent back home.

Desperate to obtain help for her ailing father, Ruth recalled seeing Ray demonstrating healing on a German television programme.

"I thought 'this is our last hope'," she explained. "I wrote to the TV station and they sent me Ray's address.

"My brother, Harald, who speaks English very well, telephoned him. I also wrote to

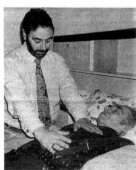

ABOVE: Ray Brown, entranced by his guide Paul, gives healing to cancer-ridden Helmut Kompel.

Ray, saying we all loved father very much and could he please help us."

The desperate brother and sister suggested they should attempt to bring their sick father to Britain for healing.

Ray was shocked. He was convinced such an arduous trip would seriously jeopardise Mr

Kompel's condition.

After some discussion, it was agreed Ray and his assistant Gillian Sitton would fly out to Frankfurt, where Ruth and Harald would meet them and drive them 150 miles to the small village of Kothen, near Fulda.

"The village was way up in

the mountains and knee deep in snow," said Gillian. "When we arrived Helmut was a very sorry sight and in a tremendous amount of pain."

Over the weekend they stayed with the Kompel family, Ray gave healing and went into trance so that his spirit guide, Paul, could perform psychic surgery.

"Three psychic operations were performed," said Gillian, "to arrest the growth that was constricting his lungs, liver and kidneys."

Paul uses only spirit instruments to perform his operations, never physical knives or blades.

"He worked on the spasms in the gut, untrapped and repaired many nerves in the throat and chest area," she explained. "He used very strong healing rays to penetrate the tumour."

At the end of the final healing, Helmut's breathing had "become stronger, he was eating, drinking and walking about.

"He felt so much better after all the pain had gone," Gillian explained.

"We were so happy," Ruth, added "It was a great weekend for all of us.

"Although my family is religious and we believe in life after death, I had never met a spiritual healer before. They are not known in Germany."

As no healers could be

■ Turn to page 4, column 1

Mediumship and trance healing go public in Japan

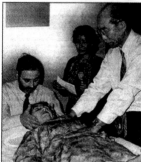

JAPAN'S first ever public demonstration of clairvoyance and spiritual healing took place last month.

Promoted by LAD Promotions, its chairman Derek Robinson described the trip as "the experience of a lifetime."

Mediums Jill Hay and Alan Law demonstrated alongside trance healer Ray Brown and his assistant Gillian Sitton in the towns of Sendai, Nagoya and Kyoto.

The group visited the country at the invitation of the Rev Michael Yamamoto of the Japanese Spiritual Institute.

When in Britain, Mr Yamamoto had attended Wimbledon Spiritualist Church, South West London, of which Derek is president.

The trip to Japan served to strengthen the link between Spiritualists in both countries.

"The medi[...] with delight [...] said Derek. "[...]

equally fascinated by the demonstration of trance healing given by Ray Brown."

Translators, including Mr Yamamoto's daughter, Ria, were on hand to give assistance and the language barrier presented no problem.

In Sendai, demonstrating before an audience of 300 people, Jill and Alan described communicators, their relationship to the recipients, dates of passing, birthdays and anniversaries.

"They gave a host of evidential facts," Gillian told PN last week. "Every message was accepted with applause."

his spirit doctor, Paul.

In Nagoya, Gillian witnessed 400 astonished Japanese listening to a spirit mother "teasing her daughters about shoes and trousers recently bought which were too tight."

Another spirit communicator provided Survival evidence when speaking to his family about a new car they intended to purchase.

"Jill gave evidence of a man who had drowned in a boating accident and wished to contact his brother," Gillian added.

"Another woman was in tears when she received a message from her dead husband. He had no time to say goodbye when dying suddenly from a heart attack."

One outstanding demonstration of Survival came when Jill and Alan, working together, made contact with a 15th century Bud-

healing," Gillian explained.

"The mediums gave his name and described his dress. This was confirmed by the recipient as he had been given this in a picture two years ago."

Healing by Ray's spirit guide, Paul, enabled Katsu Fukuda to walk again, after being confined to a wheelchair since an injury to her spine in 1988.

"The audience applauded with amazement and happiness," said Gillian.

Another patient, Hisako Chiba, also underwent a spirit operation which left her free of pain.

"The Japanese were overwhelmed with the power of spiritual healing," Gillian commented.

Spiritualism in Japan, Derek explained, focused mainly on healing and teaching.

"Members of the Institute were very eager to learn about

for a development circle and expressed his willingness to return to Japan before too long in [...] to give the group further [...]ction."

[...]fter the group's return to

England, Alan Law commented: "The Japanese are wonderful people.

"I wish Spiritualists in this country had even a small part of their enthusiasm and dedication."

MICHAEL Yamamoto (right) assisting an entranced Ray Brown in Nagoya last month.

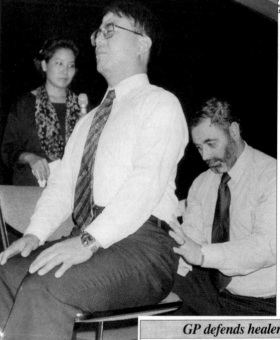

Left: Paul gets to work in Japan...

Above and below: ...and *Psychic News* continues its coverage of his work there, and in the UK

Opposite: ...and in Africa

GP defends healer after press attack

A MEDICAL practitioner has made a stand against the public denigration of trance healer Ray Brown and his guide Paul, after comments made in a national newspaper implied that Ray is suffering "delusions".

Liverpool practitioner, Dr Marjorie Cotton felt impelled to hit back at recent comments made by Professor Richard Dawkins which were published in the Sunday Times. The paper devoted a half-page article to Dawkin's attack on the "current epidemic of 'paranormal' programmes on television", in which he complained that television companies are feeding the public on paranormal "drivel" which he likened to little more than "conjuring tricks".

Referring to the BBC2 *Secrets of the Paranormal* series which featured Ray and Paul's work, Dawkins wrote: "...a builder turned 'healer' is given the prestige of the channel to tell us that his body is inhabited by a doctor

called Paul of Judaea, dead 2,000 years.

He went on: "Some sad people think they are Napoleon reincarnated, but we do not expect them to be granted a prime-time 'factual' television slot to air their delusions."

Dr Cotton, who is able to testify to Ray's abilities, having observed him at work at a number of healing clinics, appealed to both the Sunday Times and Professor Dawkins for a more "open minded" appraisal of Ray and Paul's work.

In a letter to Professor Dawkins, she stated: "There is no doubt in my mind that Ray Brown is not suffering from any delusional psychosis..."

In another letter, addressed to the editor of the Sunday Times, Dr Cotton suggested the newspaper might be "a suitable vehicle" to research and publish a feature on Ray's work with Paul.

When PN contacted Dr Cotton last week, she admitted that neither letter had so far provided a response.

She added, "Having seen for myself the way in which Ray and Paul are able to help people, I couldn't just sit back and not do anything. Anything that supports their work

Trance healer Ray Brown

and helps to bring it to a wider audience can only be for the good.

"The BBC produced a factual and unbiased presentation of Ray's work which allowed people to judge for themselves. It brought healing to the public's attention and resulted in Ray being able to help many more needy people."

Dr Cotton's own interest in healing was sparked off when a patient

lent her a book by Harry Edwards. Fascinated by the healer's work, she says she contacted the Harry Edwards Healing Sanctuary and started to request absent healing for her patients.

Her interest grew and then in May this year she attended her first healing clinic with Ray Brown and Paul, which she now attends on a monthly basis.

Psychic **PN** *News*

SATURDAY JANUARY 11 1992

THE WORLD'S ONLY INDEPENDENT
SPIRITUALIST WEEKLY NEWSPAPER

Spiritual healer goes to Africa

WORKING for eight hours a day in temperatures in the 100s, trance healer Ray Brown and his assistant Gillian "treated 106 patients with excellent results" during their two-week visit to Africa, last month.

Ray and Gillian were invited to Mombasa by trance medium Sylvia Macfarland. They treated patients in her healing sanctuary at Diani Reef.

"We worked in such incredible conditions," said Gillian. "It proved very successful indeed.

"We had people of many nationalities flying in from all over Africa to receive treatment. The interest was tremendous. We were so pleased with the results."

Many of the patients, she added, had visited doctors in Europe, who had "been unable to diagnose or help."

Working through his entranced medium, Ray's spirit doctor, Paul, "treated everything from stomach and bowel problems, sinus, sciatica, migraine, heart and lung conditions to growths."

A 10-year-old girl, Rakhe Jetha, who suffered brain damage at birth, "walked assisted by one hand only" after treatment by Paul.

Before visiting the healer, the child "had to be carried everywhere by her handservant.

"Paul worked on the brain cells of the child. He will complete his work on his return to Africa later this year."

Another satisfied patient, Felicity Holden, flew from Nairobi to see Ray.

Felicity was suffering continual pain in her back and legs as a result of her spine being fused in two places.

"During her stay of two days," Gillian commented, "Paul cleared her of pain. She could straighten her back and feel tall once again."

The delighted patient later told Ray: "Words are not adequate to convey my thanks and gratitude. Thank you both for coming into my life."

A mother of 20 children, Turene Lucas, from the Seychelles flew home "very happy" after the spirit doctor "untrapped the nerves around her ribs." Turene had fractured them a year earlier.

Two women — Lillian Kritzner and Wendy Chiara — with gynecological problems were also successfully treated.

Wendy, who was in Mombasa on business from England, had suffered pain every morning for eight years. Doctors and specialists were unable to help her.

After treatment from Paul, the spasms eased and she was "at last relieved of the pain."

Lillian had undergone three abortions after contracting malaria and was "in agony" as a result of internal spasms. After seeing Paul, "she was cured in one visit," said Gillian.

Lorraine Brummer, who had a sinus problem, "found that every time she drank alcohol her face became very painful.

"Paul untrapped the nerve causing this," Gillian explained. "The next day she was drinking wine with her meals!"

A professional singer called Shakoor also visited the spirit doctor for treatment.

"He was losing his voice through the thickening of the vocal cords, which had become knotted in scar tissue after undergoing two operations," said Gillian.

After healing from Paul, Shakoor is now "practising his singing again."

The healing mission to Mombasa was so successful, said Gillian, "we have been asked to go out again for three weeks at a time in July and December this year."

After working with Sylvia and her team of helpers, spirit clinic in Mombasa" and has instructed another spirit doctor "who specialises in tropical diseases" to carry on his work.

On their visits later this year, Ray and Gillian have also been invited to travel to Nairobi "to do healing and to initiate a clinic there."

Before visiting Africa, Ray worked with a team of cameramen sent to Britain by Bavarian State Television in order to film him giving healing.

Above: John Bundock being ordained into the Corinthian Church by Ray

Danger follows healer in Africa

SUFFOLK healer Ray Brown survived death by drowning, a charging buffalo, an encounter with two lions and a malaria attack, during an action-packed East African healing tour, his assistant Gillian Sitton told PN last week.

And Gillian herself received a dramatic healing from Ray's spirit guide, Paul, when she collapsed in intense pain at Nairobi Airport, while waiting for their connecting flight home to Britain.

"I was suffering from a parasitic infection, caused by drinking some impure water while in Mombasa," she said.

"I had been feeling ill during that week, but when I arrived at the airport the cramps became so severe that I was doubled up with pain."

Rushed to a local doctor, Gillian told PN she begged Ray to go into trance so that Paul might come through and help her.

"While the doctor was looking for the necessary equipment to deal with the situation, Paul entranced Ray and performed a spirit operation on Gillian.

"Within 10 minutes, the bowel blockage causing the pain began to disperse," said Gillian. "The doctor had no need to give me any treatment."

Gillian was able to board the plane for the flight home, but she was so exhausted from the after effects of the infection that special arrangements were made for her to lie down during the entire trip.

"But," she said, "for the rest of my journey I was free from the excruciating colon pains that had stopped me dead in my tracks, thanks to my entire flight doctor!

"It took weeks for the parasitic bug to leave my body entirely. Without Paul's healing, I don't know what I would have done."

Ray and Gillian commenced their tour late in June, first flying out to Nairobi to work at a healing clinic in Limuru run by Angela Lakin.

Angela had first contacted the Nairobi clinic as "very successful. People came from far and wide to see spirit surgeon Paul."

Indeed a 35-year-old woman, Melony Sarlinson, travelled from Bahrain, an island in the Persian Gulf, especially to receive treatment from their spirit doctor.

Melony was in considerable pain as a result of three vertebrae being fused in her spine. After treatment from the spirit healer, she was able to walk properly again.

Another patient, a nurse working for the poor in a local free hospital, was also able to throw away her walking stick after treatment for injuries sustained from a fall.

An English resident living in Nairobi who had been unable to eat solid food because of throat spasms was "able to eat normally for the first time in years" after visiting the clinic.

"We had a lot of people coming to us with hiatus hernia problems," said Gillian.

"We have stacks of testimonials from people who have been cured of the miseries that this illness causes."

Another patient who sought help from the spirit surgeon was Sister Verdanti from the Brahma Kumaris Ashram in Nairobi.

The Brahma Kumaris are a group of women who live together in a community, support themselves and work with the poor on a world-wide basis.

"They travel all over Africa helping people," Gillian explained, "giving aid both to the poor and to those wishing to develop their spirituality.

"Sister Verdanti had been in continual pain with her neck," Gillian commented. "She was unable to meditate or sit in the lotus position. But after just one treatment from Paul she was cured."

On leaving Nairobi, Ray and Gillian flew to Mombasa,

cially to receive treatment from the spirit doctor.

Kenya, to give healing at their clinic, run by Sylvia Macfarland.

"Last time we were in Mombasa, Paul came through to teach local healers," said Gillian. "Sylvia was a trance medium when we met her, so it was easy to pass a spirit doctor — they are also trained by Paul — to her to work with."

It was in Mombasa that Ray was offered a short safari trip as a means of some quiet relaxation during his arduous tour.

"We went on the Masai Mara Safari Trip," Gillian explained. "The people we were staying with ran that safari. It was similar to the one on which Suffolk girl Julie Ward — who also came from Bury St Edmunds — was killed."

The Brahma Kumaris invited both Ray and Gillian to work at their ashram for a meal in appreciation of the healing received.

ABOVE: Spiritual healer Ray Brown is seen treating a 10-year-old girl suffering from brain damage.

On recovering from that ordeal, a second shock awaited the healer. The jeep stalled — right in sight of two fully grown lions!

"They were male lions, too," said Ray. "Nevertheless, we had to get out of the jeep in order to push it so that it would start again."

Watched in silence by the two lions, Ray, the driver and an American passenger, warily descended and attempted to get the engine to start.

As soon as the engine purred into action, the trio hastily got in and drove away as fast as they could to safety.

But Ray's troubles were not over. Again seeking a moment's relaxation, the healer went scuba diving.

"Ray's day of nearly killed him." Gillian commented. "I wouldn't go out to sea because it was too rough."

Going under, Ray "began to feel pressure on his ears."

The healer was 30ft under by an irate buffalo, who charged it.

■ **Turn to page 4, column 1**

Above: Quintin Smith, Gillian and Ray at Quintin's ordination into the Corinthian Church

Spirit surgeon in first British TV demonstration

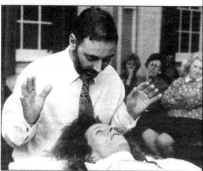

RAY BROWN, entranced by Paul, at a public demonstration of healing.

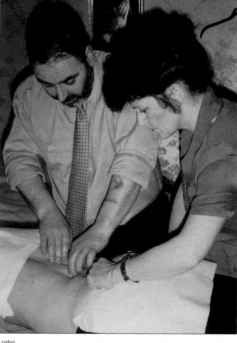

Above: Operation at Fir Tree Lodge

FOR the first time in the UK, 2,000-year-old Judean spirit surgeon Paul — guide of Suffolk healer Ray Brown — has been interviewed on television.

Appearing on Anglia TV's "Magic and Mystery Show," his overshadowment of Ray, from Bury St Edmunds, was filmed — as were two successful spirit operations — and shown to a studio audience.

Questioned by a TV interviewer while under close scrutiny, Paul described his fascinating past life as a physician in Judea around the time of Christ.

Although he admitted he never knew the spiritual master, "it was he who really brought me to my end," explained the guide, "his beliefs and my following of them."

After accepting Christ's teachings, the spirit doctor turned against the Roman Senate and was beheaded.

"As a Roman Citizen I could not be crucified or stoned as Jewish people would have been," he said.

"Yet I was a Christian at my passing."

When asked about his relationship with the spirit surgeon, former builder Ray, 47, explained that he is able to communicate with him only at the beginning of a sitting, just before being taken over.

"Once he is in and I am out, there is no further communication whatsoever," added the healer.

How did he reply to the watching sceptics? "The proof of the pudding is in the eating," said Ray. "I would be back on the building sites if this wasn't working."

After the programme had been transmitted, the healer told PN a large amount of material had been cut.

Although an old woman who entered his room in a wheelchair was pictured walking out, he felt some of the most impressive scenes were not included in the final film.

"The woman could not use her head, yet soon raised it above her head after Paul's treatment," said Ray. "She also remarked to having not done that in 20 years."

With the other patient, a young woman, the healer regretted her severe back problems and subsequent loss of pain were omitted. The cameras simply focussed on her knee trouble, "which was nothing."

Interestingly, Paul found no extra difficulty in overshadowing Ray with TV cameras present and, according to the healer, a "quiet, calm man who didn't mind them filming, so long as there was no interference during spirit operations."

Unfortunately, the actual process of overshadowment was shortened in the final edited version of the film. What seemed to be almost an instant change left some in the studio audience

sceptical.

"I don't know how talk as Ray, take his g off, and suddenly spe Paul," said one woma healer was not given chance to reply.

"I was 21 when th first came through me said to PN.

"And he has work my body every day fo last four years. Like on a tight suit again again, it gets easier a quicker."

What about anothe comment raised, that seemed to have maste modern English very quickly?

"I thought this was rather silly," said Ray. "He learnt the language in the spirit world. He is not going to speak ancient Judean when nobody would understand him!"

Sceptic Dr Susan Blackmore, who argued on the film that people were being healed because of extra care and attention, not due to the intervention of a spirit guide, has since expressed interest in seeing Paul work.

Above and right: Ray's work attracts the attention of television – and controversy follows

OVER 60 YEARS' WEEKLY REPORTING ON SPIRITUALISM AND THE PARANORMAL

Psychic News

No 3341   Saturday, June 22, 1996   35p

The Art of Dreaming

AN exhibition of the dream drawings of Dutch artist Paul Klemann opened this week at a West London art gallery.

The exhibition which runs until July 15 will be the first time the artist has exhibited in England.

Paul whose work is held in many Dutch collections sets his alarm clock and wakes himself up several times a night to scribble down notes. Later, when he arises from his slumbers he elaborates on the notes and makes them into sequences of sketches on A4 sheets of paper.

The artist says he does not aim for a high artistic level with his drawings. Neither is he interested in the analysis. Rather he is interested in the story "from a world in which we humans escape from our organised daily existence."

To coincide with the exhibition a 104-page book, published jointly by the artist and the gallery, will be launched at the exhibition. The book features an interview with the artist, dream texts, preliminary sketches and 43 illustrations of which 15 are in colour.

Ray Brown Quits NFSH Over TV Documentary

RAY Brown, a member of the National Federation of Spiritual Healers for over a quarter of a century has relinquished his membership after complaints from other members about the way he carried out his work during a recent television documentary.

Ray, whose life and work with his guide Paul was featured on the BBC2 series 'Secrets of the Paranormal' is alleged to have "blatantly broken" the NFSH Code of Conduct on several occasions during the documentary.

In a letter to the healer, National Chairwoman, Shirley Brooker said that a number of complaints had been received from members who were "distressed" by the programme in which Ray's

of Conduct were blatantly broken. For example, clothing was removed, you were working in a public demonstration in trance, a form of medical diagnosis was given and also vigorous massage.

"Whilst you are entitled as a private individual to heal in the manner of your choice, as a member of the NFSH you are not allowed to do so. The complaints mentary.

"We have voiced the opinion that you have brought the NFSH into disrepute."

The letter ended by saying the disciplinary committee was discussing the matter of his continued membership and another letter would be forthcoming in due course.

Resigning with immediate effect, he wrote to the NFSH telling them "I am completely disgusted by the way you have treated me, and feel sad as I was one of the youngest members you ever had and have supported you in every

Ray Brown - claims hundreds of healers work in trance, many of them NFSH members

He added "Members say that the documentary about my life has brought the NFSH into disrepute.

yet my guide Paul cured on national television four people in dire pain, which has brought to my door thousands of requests for help and convinced some of the strongest sceptics that spiritual healing works."

He received over a 1,000 phone calls and letters in the weeks following the programme with many congratulations and requests for help. Two GPs had shown an interest in Paul's work and wanted to send patients to him for treatment.

He asks "Is this bringing spiritual healing into disrepute? I was under the impression that this is what the Federation wanted, and yet when I mentioned to them that I was working with doctors, no recognition was given by anyone, probably because it might be heard by Federation healers

Some of the healers who feature in Part Four.

Left: Ray and Pat Cowen

Above: Group Healing: Paul with Vince & Anne Lewis

Left: Jo and Peggy Aschwanden

Above: Charlie Hammond, Ken Parr (back row) with Ray, Georgie Hammond (left) and Jeanne Lambourne (right)

Working with the medical profession:

Above: Ray photographed at Knuston Hall in 1995 with Norwegian neuro-surgeon Walter Fisher *(right)* and Dr. Witold Falkowski *(left)* from Hemel Hempstead Hospital in the UK

Below: Psychic News reports on further collaborations

Healer Ray Brown in new Initiative with GP and Medical Students

On Thursday February 27 history will be made when a group of medical students accompanied by General Practitioner and advocate of Spiritual Healing Marjorie Cotton spend two to three days at Ray Brown's Healing Centre.

Ray Brown works mediumistically with his guide who is known as Paul. The students are looking forward to the opportunity to ask Paul questions about his work. As Doctor Cotton says, "Medical students are now realising that not everything can be explained in terms of anatomy and physiology - what they now refer to as 'form and function'.

They have been introduced to the concept of energies in the healing process.

In therapeutic touch this was explained to them as being explainable in terms of quantum physics and was purely a balancing of the body's own energy field. This process necessitates that the therapist be 'centred'. This is the development of a calm, focussed state of mind. Focussing on the here and now. It involves having a clear sense of oneself as a unitary whole and differs from concentration or paying attention in that it is not associated with mental effort."

On a previous healing study day with a spiritual healer working in a GP's practice they took part in experiments where they were able to sense energies for themselves.

"As I have been interested in and studied the work of Harry Edwards", states Dr Cotton, "I realised that a consideration of the power of spirit was essential to an understanding of spiritual healing. Truth is not subjective but is absolute. Fear and ignorance should not prevent us from grasping a truth however uncomfortably this may sit with the cultural and religious norms."

Ray Brown's work was the subject of a BBC2 documentary and the overshadowing of his physical body during the time when Paul was working with him was quite marked.

Paul's hope is to be able to work alongside conventional doctors. As for Dr Marjorie Cotton, she states , "I am hoping that the students will now become more compassionate doctors who may be more open to working with healers and other complementary therapists. Some of them may wish to explore their own healing potential, although they are beginning to realise that this potential can be expressed in the role of the truly caring doctor."

Any readers who may wish to consult Paul may make an appointment to do so by telelphoning ; 01455 559880.

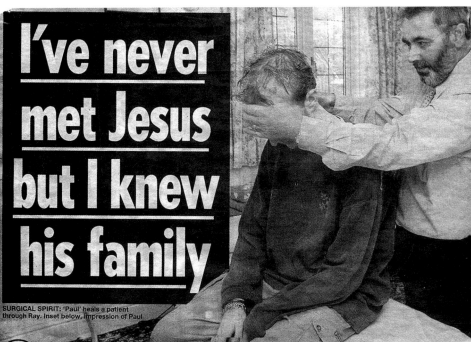

I've never met Jesus but I knew his family

SURGICAL SPIRIT: 'Paul' heals a patient through Ray. Inset below, impression of Paul

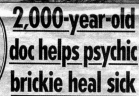

2,000-year-old doc helps psychic brickie heal sick

CURE 1

CURE 2

CURE 3

RICKIE Ray Brown has turned into a miraculous faith healer after claiming his body was invaded by the spirit of a 2,000-year-old surgeon nicknamed The Skirt.

So far he has helped people suffering from crippling back conditions, stomach disorders, arthritis, cerebral palsy, multiple sclerosis, even cancer.

Ray, of Bitteswell, Leics, says the real name of spirit who takes him over is Paul—a rabbi who practised in Judea at the time of Christ, came to follow Jesus, and was finally executed by the Romans.

We asked Ray if he would summon up Paul, nicknamed The Skirt for his historic pleated dress. Ray sat quietly on the sofa and screwed up his eyes as the transition took place. Instead of Ray's gravelly voice came smooth, polished tones.

This is the year's most incredible interview—between a doctor apparently lived at the time of Christ and a reporter approaching the dawn of a new millennium:

What can you tell us about your time on Earth?

I was a Jewish boy who was brought up around Judea and Jerusalem in the time of Jesus the Christ. I never met him but I knew of the family, his uncles. I knew the Baptists very well. It was a very close community.

What about Mary?

I knew Mary, but not very well.

What was it like working with Romans as slaves?

My work wasn't really to keep them all but to see if they were still fit to be slaves. If they weren't, they were dis-

By ROSIE DUNN

down they went with it. I was in transportation to Rome but I was a rabbi and had medical knowledge so I was not chained.

Q: What did people do for entertainment?

A: There was bear baiting, throwing people to the lions if the Romans got bored. I was run around an arena a couple of times being chased by chariots. That was sport to them. They knocked us because we were Jewish—I was a Christian by the end.

I saw lots of people die, it was very common. If someone injured a soldier

LITTLE Charlie Gallegos nearly died after his brain was starved of oxygen in a ski accident two years ago.

The Dutch tot's parents Paul and Natalie turned to Ray when doctors said Charlie would never revive.

Today Charlie, aged seven, can chew, swallow and kick. He can even laugh again.

Natalie, 39, said: "The improvements are enormous. Ray's intensive healing has given a life back to our boy."

LEN MACKENZIE was a virtual cripple when he met Ray Brown in 1995.

The Leicestershire site worker was in agony after damaging three vertebrae in his back. His only hope was a major op to fuse his spine.

Len, 55, said: "I went to see Ray. He said he would move nerves to stop the pain.

"Seconds later I had total relief. The pain came back so he did a spiritual operation. My back has been fine since."

LEE THURSTON can enjoy l with son Harry since R Brown got his hands on him Eltham, south London, s The 31-year-old, fro fered from a ruptured disc his lower spine.

Lee said: "Ray told me could see the problem. I w fully clothed at the time. pinched my leg and I jumpe He pushed at my spine a that was it.

"Two weeks later the pa disappeared for good."

Ray, 51, explained: "When he carries out his spiritual surgery through me he uses spiritual instruments that are not visible to the human eye.

"He doesn't need to remove a patient's clothing to diagnose what is the matter but can cure internal conditions without breaking the skin.

"He literally carries out a spiritual operation and uses spiritual clamps or stitches to heal internal wounds.

"By laying his hands on the affected area Paul is able to establish what the problem is and treat it."

Recalling his first visitation by the spirit surgeon, he added: "It was like a sledgehammer hitting me. I saw blazing

to two different men. We just treat F as part of the family. They're b lovely men."

Ray has a portrait of Paul painted him by a psychic artist. Paul himsel said to have confirmed the likenes

"If I was a fake I'd be back on building sites by now," added Ray

Consultant psychiatrist Dr And Powell told the News of the Wo spent with Ray, I saw patients wit history of severe medical problems w responded immediately."

Gillean Cray, a columnist from Church of England's newspaper,

---

Above: The British mass circulation Sunday newspaper the *News of the World* reports positively on Ray and Gillian's work (*News of the World* 15 February 1998)...

I'LL CURE YOU ALL!

NEWS OF THE WORLD BRINGS YOU THE OLDEST EXCLUSIVE EVER

I've never met Jesus but I knew his family

2,000-year-old doc helps psychic brickie heal sick

HEALER: Ray gets to work in our exclusive last week

Ex-brickie proves his miracles work

By AYLIA FOX

PSYCHIC healer Ray Brown performed miracle cures on astonished News of the World readers this week as thousands queued up to receive his unique 'spirit surgery'.

Last Sunday we told how the former brickie, who once built walls for a living, is possessed by the ghost of a 2,000-year-old surgeon called Paul.

Paul is said to perform his medical procedures through Ray using no visible instruments, though his power has the effect of surgical equipment.

We published Ray's phone number for readers in need of treatment–and his line almost melted down. Last Sunday alone, between 8am and 4.30pm, Ray received 480 calls before his phone conked out!

Now, a week on, they're still coming in at a rate of over 50 an hour. That's on top of the hundreds received at the News of the World's London offices.

We spoke to readers who visited the Browns for treatment that changed their lives

Shoe Guinness-Taylor was told by doctors five months ago she needed an operation to remove nine benign breast cysts.

The partner of brewing family heir Lord Moyne said: "I wanted to avoid being cut open if I could.

Injury

"I knew a bit about psychic surgery. Once I saw Ray's number I knew I had to meet him."

Shoe, 53, flew from her home in Dublin to see Ray on Monday. She said: "I felt the cysts drain away."

As with all his patients, Ray advised Shoe to re consult her doctor, but she insisted: "There's no need. I'm cured."

Kevin Reynolds, 38, visited Ray after months of physiotherapy and osteopathy had failed to rid him of a neck injury.

Spirit surgeon Paul manipulated the Leicester sales rep's spine. The pain simply went. "It was like magic," said Kevin. "A

THUMBS UP: Shoe's

swelling on my neck had disappeared. I'd recommend him to anyone."

Ray, 51, of Bitteswell, Leics, sees up to 35 patients a day, who pay £25 per session.

He is now booked solid for the next three months.

Fees are put back into his charity the Healing Rays Fellowship. It funds 12 clinics per month he

Picture: BRIAN ROBERTS

so happy after healing

runs nationwide. Ray and wife Gillian also go on healing missions abroad.

THE News of the...
put Ray to the ul...
test—to cure Chi...
ture Writer Phil T...
bad back. Phil sa...
"I suffered a ...
disc in my lower ...
which for two da...
me unable to mo...
"After physiot...
costing over £50...
turned to work...
weeks later, still...
nagging pain.
"I met Ray at ...
his clinics—a ...
ualist church in ...
bledon, south-we...
don. He 'summon...

He eve... fixes... man Ph... bad ba...

BETTER: Write...
Paul' and his ...
voice change...
smooth tones.
"Then he fe...
lower back and v...
the EXACT point...
I was suffering...
"He said, 'You...
seems to be OK...
have a trapped n...
"He pushed ...
spine and said ...
should do the thi...
"He told me h...
and touch my ...
something I ...
dared do for a m...
"But suddenly ...
do it without an...
Two weeks on, i...
a little sore. Ray...
the nerve is tend...
wants to see me...
I have booked ...
pointment."

FR GILLEAN ...
IN our report ...
faith healing ...
week, the News ...
World suggeste...
the Rev Gillean...
endorses the w...
healer Ray Brown...
is not the Can...
Father Craig ha...
met Mr Brown.
In fact Father...
Rector of St Ge...
The East, in eas...
don, has askest...
point out that, ...
in The Church ...
about a TV pro...
featuring Mr Br...
commented he...
hardly have bee...
sceptical, but t...
visual evidenc...
compelling to ...
least.

Psychic saves sick Sir John's one-man show

VETERAN star Sir John Mills has told how he turned to a psychic healer to overcome crippling back pain . . . and was CURED.

The 91-year-old Oscar winner crushed his vertebrae after falling off stage.

Sir John, one of Britain's best-loved actors and a close friend of the Queen Mum, was in so much pain he could not walk or stand up straight and even had difficulty lying down.

Fearing he would have to cancel a charity performance of his one-man show, An Evening With Sir John, he tried physios, osteopaths, acupuncturists and even faith healers. But none worked.

Then his writer-director son Jonathan heard about the amazing healing powers of Ray Brown following an article published in the News of the World.

We told how the former brickie claims to be possessed by the ghost of a 2,000-year-old surgeon called Paul. Hoping against hope for a cure, Sir John asked Ray to visit his Buckinghamshire home –and the results were stunning.

The actor, who was performing in aid of the Roy Castle Cancer Fund, said: "It's fantastic what Ray has done.

Picture: NICK BOWMAN

CURED: Sir John had tried everything

BY PHIL TAYLOR
CHIEF REPORTER

Amazing

"He has worked wonders. I was in such pain I was on the verge of cancelling my one-man show.

"With just a week to go my back was chronic. But then Ray came to my aid and told me: 'Don't worry, you will make the show.'

"Ray examined me and said 'You have got trapped nerves and they need to be

put back in place." Over the next week, Ray says he used spirit Paul's powers to perform psychic surgery on Sir John.

Sir John added: "I made such an amazing recovery that I was able to go on stage and perform my full two-hour show."

Ray, 53, of Lutterworth, Leics, said: "Sir John had taken all the conventional treatment and nothing had worked at all.

"We were his last resort and we helped him."

HELPER: Sir John and Ray

…which leads to a new wave of nationwide acclaim (*above: News of the World* 22 February 1998) and the healing of the chief reporter Phil Taylor's back …

…and (*left*) to a further dramatic intervention to save a great British actor's solo charity performance (*News of the World* spring 1998)

NEWS OF THE WORLD

SUNDAY

prophet Jesus of Nazareth was in Galilee preaching new doctrines, healing the sick, attracting huge crowds and upsetting the Romans.

Then I decided to meet the holy man Bannus, who took up the quest of John the Baptist after he was executed. I felt strangely drawn to this man who was to have a great influence on my life. Bannus invited me to stay at the monastery, which I did for some time, but I became restless and was keen to move on.

In about 30 AD, during a visit to Jerusalem, Jesus was arrested and accused of blasphemy by the hierarchy of the church, who felt threatened by his teachings. He was crucified on the orders of Pontius Pilate. Many followers of Jesus saw him as first and foremost a Jewish nationalist. Although the Romans crucified him, they were urged to do so by the Jewish hierarchy who believed that his teachings undermined their authority and challenged traditional Judaism.

They also resented his claim during the Sermon on the Mount, that inner virtue is more important than conformity to rules of behaviour. Jewish priests regarded as blasphemous, Jesus' followers claims, that he was the Messiah and Son of God. Many of Jesus' disciples, who had fled at the time of his arrest, eventually returned to Jerusalem where they established a synagogue and formed the Nazarene movement. The Nazarenes were native inhabitants of Nazareth of Jewish origins, who became members of a movement of early Christians, and chose to retain several of the prescribed Jewish observations.

I have been asked if Jesus really did die on the cross. Was he revived in the tomb to live another 40 years? There are suggestions that Jesus was part of a political conspiracy against the Roman Empire. If this is so, then the Evangelists deceived the people and the Gospels can be of little comfort to Christians. I am certainly not here to create a storm. However to satisfy any curiosity, I can say with certainty that death on the cross is a slow and horrific way to die. I never saw anyone come out of it alive.

Jesus died physically and his spirit manifested itself and materialised to his disciples. The purpose of the resurrection was to prove that there was life after death. The Gospels bring this good news to Christians. I know that he came back from Spirit because I have also come back from Spirit. The only difference is that I use another person's body.

The belief in the resurrection was so strong amongst the disciples, that it enabled them and their successors in the early Christian church, to endure persecution and death in the certainty that Jesus was the Messiah.

About the time of the crucifixion, I had left the Essenes to return to Jerusalem. I had made up my mind to become a Pharisee. The Nazarene sect was becoming a threat to Hellenic Jewry. Because I was a Greek-speaking Jew and Roman citizen, I was chosen by the high priest to lead the revolt against the Nazarenes, and seek out the leader of their group, a man named Stephen.

We eventually found Stephen preaching and stoned him to death. We then continued to terrorise and beat the Hellenic Nazarenes of Jerusalem. As a result many fled the city.

I believed that what I was doing was right. However I did become increasingly troubled, and started to regret the terrible suffering that I had inflicted upon others. In fact, the guilt weighed so heavily upon me that it badly affected my health.

It did not help when I heard how much my actions had distressed my family, who begged me to give it all up. As a result I became very confused and uncertain about my thoughts and actions. Little did I realise at that time, that I had reached a crucial point in my life, or realise I was destined to pass through it and help shape a new Christian world.

It was on the desert road to Damascus, in pursuit of the apostle Peter, that my life dramatically changed and led to my eventual conversion to Christianity. I had hired some muleteers who knew the road and some handlers to carry my equipment and lead the camel train. It was a long arduous five-day journey and I was feeling tired and wretched. I was very sick from the fever, which was quite a common illness in those days. Nevertheless I pushed on.

One day there was a sudden formidable change in the weather, which agitated my horse. Dark black clouds began to drift down over the mountains and the air became very cold, chilling me to the bone. I was only wearing a thin robe and desperately needed my thick cloak, but I could not see any of the handlers or muleteers.

Some hours later a tempestuous icy wind descended and frightened my horse, which suddenly bolted throwing me to the ground. Shocked and weak, I froze on the spot, unable to move. As the wind mellowed a vision appeared to me, but I did not take much notice of it. I thought that it was the fever playing tricks on me.

Three days later the vision appeared again and I heard a voice saying: 'Why do you persecute me Saul.'

I was so weak and ill that I do not know how I found the courage or energy to ask who it was, but somehow I did, and he replied: 'I am Jesus of Nazareth who you are persecuting. It is vain for you to kick against the goads.' I asked him: 'What should I do?' He replied: 'You must go into Damascus where you will be told what to do.'

My whole body was shaking uncontrollably due to a combination of the fever and shock at seeing this vision; a vision that I was convinced had actually spoken to me. I struggled onto my feet and realised that I could not see. I was numb with fear. According to my muleteers, I collapsed into unconsciousness in the doorway of a shelter. They wrapped me in a cloak, massaged my limbs to help improve my circulation, and eventually brought me round.

It was not a bright flashing light that blinded me as written in the Bible.

Sceptics find it very difficult to accept this happening and seek to question my integrity. But how many of you have been influenced by an experience, or by the spoken word? Just one fleeting moment in your life that has caused you to reflect and help change your ways for better or for worse?

I believe in myself and that is what is important. There have always been prophets, and many people have seen visions. I saw a vision, and as a result converted to what is now known as Christianity and taught the preachings of the prophet Jesus Christ. I am no different.

The following morning the fever had abated. I was led to Damascus and went to a house where I met the high priest Ananias, an Orthodox Jew, who had become a follower of Christ. This stranger told me that he knew I was on the way and was told by the Lord to restore my sight, and fill me with the Holy Spirit. As instructed by the Lord he bathed and treated my eyes until my sight was restored. Because I was still very weak and exhausted from a combination of difficult and tiring journeys, the fever, loss of appetite and the spiritual experience on the road to Damascus, I was invited by Ananias to stay in his quarters until I regained my strength and was ready to move on.

One day Ananias invited me to be baptised. He led me to a stream by his house, where I was immersed in the water. From that moment I understood my errors, found the courage to repent, and asked the Lord for forgiveness. My prayers were answered and I was filled with the Holy Spirit. The Holy Spirit had come upon me. I felt uplifted. I felt renewed. I had become a follower of the Lord Jesus Christ.

I began to spread the teachings of Jesus and Christianity. Instead of persecuting the Nazarenes for their beliefs, I became one of them. I am nothing. I wish to be nothing. That is the way that it has been throughout my life, until given life again by God. I talk of Jesus so much because he was my master. I will listen to anyone if they are being truthful. You must be true to yourself and be yourself. Love yourself first and humble yourself before others.

Jesus was a prophet, a man with a vision, who broke away from the religion of the Orthodox Jews and the strict inextricable laws of Moses, to teach us about God and the spirit world that we all return to. He showed us the way to reach God and become fulfilled, to be true to ourselves and accountable for our actions. The very people he forgave allowed him to die for those beliefs.

I lost my head for him, because he spoke to me about love and truth. He was persecuted and died for his beliefs and it opened my heart. In my time it was known as blind faith, which meant believing in someone you could not see. God is the force of all life and he is there in every one of you. It is believing that is difficult.

I met many of Jesus' disciples, who were mostly fishermen, and came to know them quite well. Because of my privileged upbringing and education I was looked upon as being the most literate and persuasive with words.

Greek, the common language of the Roman Empire, was my main tongue. But I could also speak several other languages, including Hebrew and Aramaic, which is the southern Semitic language that Jesus spoke. This impressed the disciples greatly, so they asked me to be their spokesman.

As Christ's ambassador I set out on my pilgrimage across land and sea to spread his teachings. I endured many reprisals and hostilities for my beliefs, but I kept my faith. I travelled with the Roman armies on galleys across the Mediterranean when I was in transit to Rome from Caesarea under close arrest. They could not put me in chains, because I was a Roman citizen, and had not been condemned by the Emperor. I was only put in chains once, at Caesarea, but that was soon rectified.

Every night I was locked in a cell but was allowed to walk freely during the day. I carried on preaching, then went to bed at night, just waiting for Caesar to decide when it was time for me to leave my cell. I did not take the opportunity to escape when an earthquake damaged my cell at

Philippi. There was not much sense in running away. My guard would have been killed for letting me escape. I did not want him to die for my sake.

My cells were small, dank, dark and very smelly. It was almost impossible to stand upright in some of them and as a result I developed a stoop. Illness constantly plagued me due to lack of nourishment and the terrible conditions in which I was confined. I suffered from malaria and my joints became arthritic and painful. My eyesight was poor and became especially bad towards the end of my life. My head was scarred from being stoned and I had scourges on my body from being whipped. I was whipped almost everywhere I went.

Nothing deterred me from preaching, which made the Emperor very nervous. He could not understand why the people listened to my preaching about Jesus and God. This confused him. He also wavered over my death sentence because of my Roman citizenship.

The Romans had no respect for life. They were cruel barbarians who were terrifying to watch in battle and treated galley slaves with contempt. Sadly, many of them were beyond caring, as they knew they would not live very long, at the most two or three years. Many of them died through drinking seawater, or malnutrition. I could not ignore their suffering. Because I was not shackled I tried to help them as much as I could and comforted them as they lay dying.

Roman galleys were not very seaworthy. They were bulky and top heavy, and as a consequence often sank. On at least three occasions I was shipwrecked, and was also adrift at sea for a day and a night. The Malta shipwreck stands out in my mind. Only the fittest managed to reach the shore. It did not matter to the Romans how many slaves they lost at sea. Life was cheap and slaves were easily replaced when the ships reached port.

When I upset the Jewish people of Paphos they turned against me and became my accusers, for they believed I had betrayed them. Three judges, who were members of the San Hedren, ordered me to be whipped.

I was lashed on five occasions. When it happened, I was either bound by my hands to a pillar, or thrown to the ground by my persecutors, who then brutally stamped upon my head, grinding my face into the hot gritty dust.

When I was about 65, I was delivered as a prisoner to the Romans by Governor Festus of Caesarea and suffered unmercifully at their hands. I was flogged, tried, then sentenced to death by Nero, who had me beheaded for preaching Christianity and spreading the word of God. I died for Jesus. However it was not a public execution, as many believe.

I was taken to the Imperial court to stand before Nero. There were many people present in the hall including officials of the city. They had come to laugh at me and scorn me, as they believed I was stirring up trouble and was some kind of magician.

They also accused me of setting all people against the Emperor and the law, and leading people into the most evil things. I denied all accusations but the lawyers were extremely deceitful and developed further accusations.

I became very angry and fought back with all my mental resources and the love of my Lord Jesus. I spoke of the one true God, of life after death and the salvation of all people, and I spoke of my blinding and encounter with my Master in the vision outside Damascus.

Many listened intently and I could see that Nero was afraid. At last I was in Rome to pronounce to the entire world the truth of the Master's coming. My accusers urged Nero to sentence me quickly, so that I could speak no more. He stood up, waived his hand at me, and said I was a threat and a danger to his authority and that I should be crucified. But because I was a Roman citizen I would have to die by the sword.

They took me away and put me in a dreadful underground prison, known as the Sepulchre. I was among thieves, robbers and murderers who fought most of the time. Rats infested the prison and many of the prisoners were eaten alive. Most of the prisoners were in a terrible state and I helped those who wished to be helped whenever I could. Those who listened to my words gained comfort. In return they helped me to sleep by taking watch, so that the rats would not get me.

My health deteriorated rapidly and I could barely walk. Meanwhile Timothy had asked the centurion's permission to help me during my execution outside the gates of Rome. The centurion was very kind to me and allowed me to kneel and pray before my execution. After my prayers to my saviour Jesus, I told the centurion that I was ready to be taken. My eyes met with Timothy as we nodded our goodbyes in silence. Then the guards took me to the block on which I laid my head. I prayed for the moment to come.

They took my head. It was over. My body was thrown into a pit where it lay with many other festering bodies. On the following day, my faithful friends Mark, Luke, Onesimus and Timothy lifted my body from the pit, wrapped it in my purple cloak and took it to a grave they had prepared for me. It was over. My work was done. My journey had ended. I had kept the faith.

As one of the forerunners of the Christian church I failed in some aspects of my mission. If I had done a truly good job, there would be no greed or poverty and there would be no war. Instead of fighting against each other, all people would love and care for one another, as Jesus taught, and not say my God is better than your God.

There is only one God. There are many religions and many faiths that believe they have the right God. God has no preference to any religion. All God wants is for people to live in harmony and love one another. The Church of Rome was started in a simple way and was built by me and the disciples; the people who believed the words of Jesus. But it has been changed out of all recognition. Today people are no more different than they were in my time. Sadly nothing has changed, as there is still greed and poverty. Terrible acts of cruelty are inflicted because of people's creed or race.

People use God and Jesus as though they are allies to assist them in anything they want to do in the name of religion. Jesus taught love not war. The world is in a very sad state of affairs, which makes me sad too. The reason that congregational places, churches, were built in my time was to enable all people to meet in one place. A beautiful thought, but out of this came greed. If I were a man on Earth today, I would be a free spirit. Free to communicate with the world of Spirit and develop spiritually in my own way and pursue my own pathway.

You can feel universal power wherever you are if you choose to. For love is the spirit of life. There is no beginning and there is no end. The universal power is amongst you. It is all around you and lives within you. It is a power that you are a part of and will always be a part of, till the end of time.

All peoples and races, as different as they are, should sit together and become one. That is why we are here; for the unity of souls, people, and the universe. Love is the greatest gift given, because without it you do not really exist, you are empty.

I love myself. The reason that I love myself is because I know that my creator loves me. He is my existence. He is the reason I am here. He is the reason that I am walking among you 2000 years on. He is the reason that I passed on in the first place.

Chapter Eighteen

Paul's Spiritual Teachings

In this chapter Paul describes what happens to us after we die. He charts our progress in Spirit and our eventual return to the source, God, the great universal power. Paul explains that we can reincarnate, but he does not recommend this course of action. He teaches how we and we alone judge ourselves and clear our own karmic debts in Spirit. Some religions teach that we reincarnate on Earth to clear our karmic debts – but Paul explains that this is not so. Paul also gives us new guidance for our lives on Earth, and encourages us to love and cherish all people, animals and the natural beauty of our planet.

When you leave the Earth plane and pass into Spirit, you go into your own time. It would be very unfair to place you back two thousand years in time because you would be so confused. We would not understand you, and you would not understand us. As people pass over they need to pick up with their relatives and be with those they know. So every one goes into their own time and dimension with their own people.

Before I go any further I will explain the diagrams on pages 122 and 123 that represent a symbolic cross section of Earth and the successive spheres of the spiritual realm.

As you can see at the foot of each page there are concentric circles numbered from one to ten. In the middle is the Earth plane. Around the Earth plane is an area called No-mans land.

Each circle represents a level, or sphere if you prefer to call it that. From the Earth plane we move outwards from one level to another, until we get to the outer circle, which is Level Ten. When you reach Level Ten, you move on into infinity, to God the source of all light and power. This is where you came from in the first place. But I will cover that later.

What you have to realise is, that there are also levels within the different levels. Imagine you are looking at an opaque three-dimensional object, preferably a pyramid shape. You can see what is in front and you can also see most of the sides, but you cannot see what is behind it. As you can see from the diagrams on the following pages there are nine levels shown, each in a pyramid or triangle shape and each triangle is divided into four inner levels.

These are the four levels within each level and there are clearance and preparation levels for transportation from one level to another in each level. I appreciate that this might be a difficult concept to understand. The arrows show the path of progress through Levels One to Four.

Spirits do not come down from on high. We pass from our own dimension which is Spirit into your dimension, the Earth plane. The only reason that you cannot move between dimensions is that you are attached to your body. If you tried, you would hurt yourself. I could walk Raymond to a wall and he would hurt his nose, but I could pass through to the other side as I am in a different dimension.

Long ago people were able to communicate by thought waves. But this ability has become lost through the evolution of man. There are some people that you call clairvoyants, who have this ability. Spirit uses these people to pass messages from our world to yours to help those in need. Everything in Spirit is done from within. At times I change my thought waves into power, because that is all I need to do.

There are exit points around the world that we call vortexes. They sit between your world and the spirit world. You are gathered together at these exit points, to be taken away and pass straight to Level One. Everyone goes into Spirit from where they pass on, i.e. if you die in Sweden, you have to be transported from one of the exit points in Sweden.

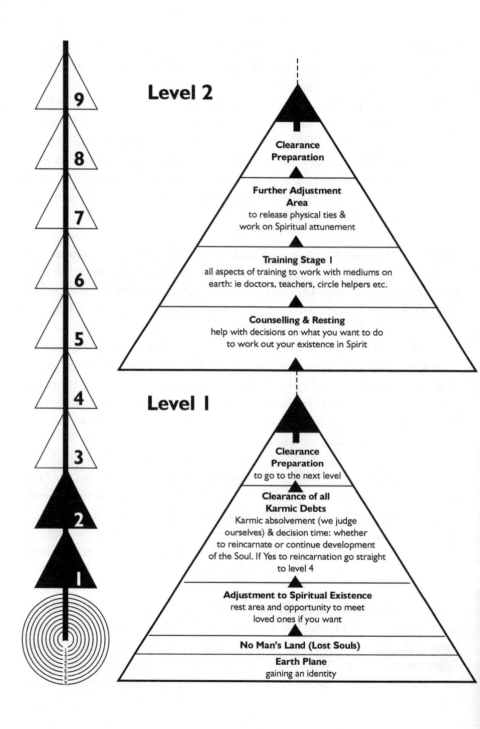

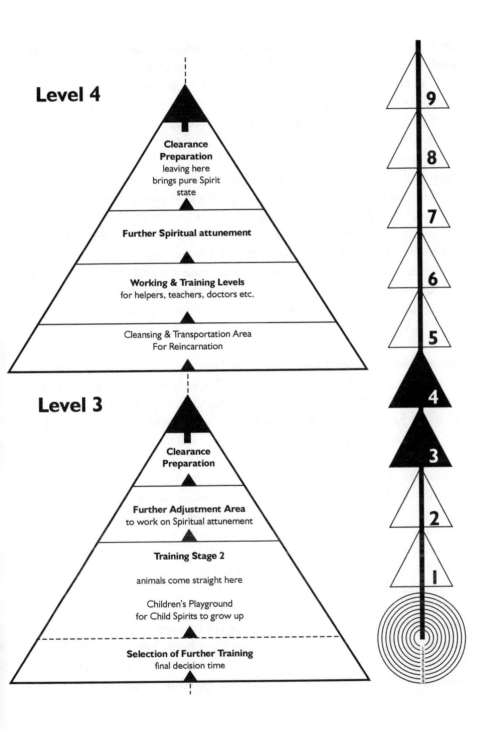

Level 4

Clearance Preparation
leaving here
brings pure Spirit
state

Further Spiritual attunement

Working & Training Levels
for helpers, teachers, doctors etc.

Cleansing & Transportation Area
For Reincarnation

Level 3

Clearance Preparation

Further Adjustment Area
to work on Spiritual attunement

Training Stage 2

animals come straight here

Children's Playground
for Child Spirits to grow up

Selection of Further Training
final decision time

9

8

7

6

5

4

3

2

1

Some people who leave the Earth plane very suddenly through a fatal accident go into No-mans land. Raymond's mother was lost for some time because of the way she passed over. She passed into Spirit so quickly because of her sudden traumatic death that she wandered off, and became lost before anyone could collect her.

If you pass into the spirit world very quickly after sudden death, you might still think that you are alive and will try to communicate with the people around you. In this area of darkness between the Earth plane and Spirit it is possible to get lost. This is what we call No-man's land. The reason why it is called No-man's land is because it is literally that. A person can be lost in No-man's land for any amount of time. Sometimes Spirit cannot rescue them because they keep hanging on to thoughts of the Earth plane and do not believe that they have passed on. It is not unusual to pick up somebody even from my time that wandered into this vortex, this dark empty space.

Thousands and thousands of spiritual beings are trained to collect and help other spiritual beings that get lost. These spirits have to go into the vortex to entice them into the light. Many spiritual beings want to help others in Spirit. Not everyone wants to be a doctor or a teacher; they just want to do something to help

The teams of spirit people who help find spirits in No-man's land are linked to home circles in your world. People sit to help these lost souls, by allowing them to take over someone in the group, a specially trained medium. They talk to the lost spirit and try to convince them that they have passed on to the next life, and to look to the light to get help. Most times they are successful but if they are not, then Spirit tries again and again until they succeed.

These groups are much admired by us because rescue work is not very pleasant and Spirit is very grateful for their help. The greatest gift that can be given is to help another out of this darkness into the light. Whether you are collected from No-mans land or whether you pass straight through this vortex, you always go to Level One, the clearance and dependency level. This is where your earthly life ends and your spiritual life begins. It is the level where clearing the physical and becoming spiritual once again happens. Medical operations take place to help you through this process.

The clearance operations get rid of physical attachments and make you whole again. Many people come back to us in great distress after a bad passing. They are traumatised and we need to help clear this bad memory. Their earthly life has passed, it has gone, but they still find it difficult to let go. If you have had your leg amputated on Earth, it will return when you come into spirit. We help you to accept this change. Once you have had clearance you are then free of the body and also any pain and suffering that you had on Earth.

A vast team of helpers, doctors and nurses work to make clearance possible. They are specially trained to take care of those coming into Spirit. When you die and pass over into our world, you will meet up with your loved ones and friends. It is very important in the first stages of Spirit that you see them as they were when on Earth. You would not wish to see them as lights buzzing about. You would not recognise them, and the spirit world would appear very strange indeed.

When you pass on, you might not want to meet any of your relatives. I did not want to meet mine at first, but then that was my choice. For the first few years in spirit I chose not to meet anyone. I just wanted to rest and bring myself together.

As you go further and further away from the magnetism of Earth, and develop through the higher levels, you become what I can only describe as pure light. You do not really need identity. You have it. You feel it. You are it. I know who I am. People know who I am. It is only when I go back down to the lower levels that I need to take on my identity to be recognised.

As I explained, everyone passing into Spirit has to go through Level One. Even I have to do this every time I come from your world back into mine. When I sit in Raymond's body, I pick up earthly vibrations. I have to go through Level One to be cleared of these vibrations before I can go on. It does not take me long, because I am already Spirit.

The levels in Level One are cleansing and preparation levels for your life in Spirit. You can be on this level for many years. I am giving you this in Earthly time, because time is important to you here. Once you have passed on, time is irrelevant. You are Spirit and spiritual existence is eternal.

You will depend upon others a great deal when you reach the spirit world, as much as you depended on your mother, father, doctors and other people in your life. On the Earth plane you have a dependency level and in Spirit it is no different. You need care, attention and love and everyone in Spirit is there to make sure that you get it.

Your loved ones are very eager to help you in Spirit and encourage you. The traumatic experience of being born is no different to your passing. It is a birth, but this time you are being born into Spirit. Your loved ones congregate to receive you and help you to leave that body which you do not need anymore and go to them.

Many people find it a struggle to let go of their Earthly existence. If you have loved your world, you will find it very difficult to depart. Even if your body says I have had enough of this existence, the ties between the Earth plane and yourself will be very, very strong.

When it comes to departing from this world many of you will face this conflict. I have been through it myself. When I was in the dungeon waiting for my execution I desperately wanted to get out of there. I had had enough and wanted the execution to take place. But when the final moment came, even after all the torture, stoning and flogging I had suffered, I was afraid.

Think of Jesus Christ, a man amongst men who came from God, as you and I did. Some say he was a prophet. Some say he was a healer. Others believe that he was a medium or that he had magical powers. But with all his knowledge and belief, the night before he knew he was going to be killed, he was afraid. Dying on the Cross was not easy. I know it is just another form of dying, but it was the way that it was done that made it so terrifying.

I have seen fear in very sick slaves on the Roman galleys who said: 'Please take me, I want to die.' But as soon as the ship's captain said: 'This slave is no good, throw him over the side,' they called out, saying: 'No I do not want to die.' That is fear. Most of you, right up until the last moment, will grip on to life until it is taken away from you. Then suddenly peace and love will surround you and you will lift out from your body.

It is a wonderful feeling. The fear has gone. The pain has gone and peace has arrived. We will be there to collect you. You will have become Spirit again. Once you have settled down and rested your spiritual being and enjoyed plenty of time with your loved ones, you will feel the need to move to the area where you will clear your karmic debts.

This is an area vital to your spiritual existence. You cannot move on without going through this. It could take you hundreds or even thousands of years to clear. The most important thing you must realise is that you are responsible for your every word, deed and action on the Earth plane.

You cannot avoid the Laws of Karma. There are those on Earth who are of the opinion that karmic debts are cleared down here. Forget that idea, all karmic debts are cleared in Spirit.

Think about this. A young child is on his way home from school, and is kidnapped by a man. The child is beaten, sexually assaulted and left for dead at the side of the road. He survives, but this experience has left him with terrible physical disabilities and a fear of going out alone.

Are you asking the child and his parents to accept that he had to go through this experience because he did a similar thing to someone else in a previous life and this is his karmic lesson?

If you are, then what about the man who committed this terrible act? Would he not have to go back into Spirit, reincarnate and start all over again on Earth to clear his karmic debt? If that is the case then everyone in Spirit would be on a perpetual cycle of being reborn and returning to Earth to clear their karmic debts.

No, everything that happens on Earth is a result of 'Cause and Effect'. The 'Cause' in the child's case was that the man, sick in mind, committed a terrible act for which he will have accumulated karma. The 'Effect' is the harm that the experience has caused the child, which may affect his whole Earthly life.

If you step out in front of a bus and end up brain damaged in a wheel-chair for the rest of your life, are you to believe this is your karma. No, once again the 'Cause' was that you did not look where you were going, and the 'Effect' was the wheelchair existence. It is very unkind to tell people who have disabilities or suffered accidents that the blame is theirs for something that they did in a past life.

A final example. What karmic debt did Jesus have to clear when he died so unmercifully on the Cross? No, you do not clear karmic debts on Earth, you clear them in Spirit.

You will be reminded of all your good and bad deeds, no matter how small. You will feel all the pain and suffering caused by your actions on Earth. There is no one waiting to deal out punishment to you. You judge yourself. The need to repent and put right all those sins, which will engulf your very being. Once you have cleared all your karmic debts, you can go forward in Spirit or reincarnate onto the Earth plane.

Before we go any further let me tell you why you are here in the first place. Have you ever thought what holds this planet together and the life force around it? Your world is spinning in a vast universe of space. The power around you is called universal power. But have you ever given a thought to what has created this world? If God or the source were not there, the Earth would not exist and neither would you.

You are here because the Infinite Spirit, the source of all life, God, has allowed you to experience life. You are born into this world for the same purpose, to gain an identity and to have an Earth experience that will allow you as a perfect soul, to bring your pure light and love to the Earth plane and help change it for the better. But unfortunately this is rarely achieved due to life on Earth.

I have dealt with people who have been down more than once. I say fine that was another existence on Earth, are you ready to stay in Spirit? So many of them say to me: 'I do not really know. I will have to think about it.' What it all boils down to is that they have lived another existence, and that they have trodden the same path as before.

There are many people on your Earth who teach that you reincarnate repeatedly until you reach the higher spiritual realms. They also teach that you have a choice of male or female, where you go, who your parents are to be, and your subsequent lifestyle.

I know that there are many teachings of this kind on karmic debt and reincarnation. They are deep subjects and I am not here to upset anyone's beliefs. But I am here to tell you what I know to be the truth.

I have gone through all the levels of progression to Level Nine, and have helped many people overcome these beliefs that come from your Eastern religions. The only choice you have is: 'Yes, I wish to reincarnate or no I wish to progress in Spirit.' There is a greater power than you or I that decides when and where you will be placed.

Think about this example. A person in India is going to give birth to a child who is severely disabled, unable to communicate, and blind. A person in England is going to give birth to a child into a privileged family.

Here is your choice: years of being trapped in a body unable to do very much or a wealthy and healthy life. Which one would you choose? I am sure you would choose the better life. But what of the disabled child, a spirit has to be placed for that child to be born, if not most of the children on earth would be stillborn. No, we cannot leave the choice to you.

Of course because of the teachings on Earth we might get the answer: 'Oh I would choose the child who is disabled because I feel I need to go through that experience and learn something from it, and clear karma from this life.' But what are you going to learn in a body that is trapped and disabled that you did not learn in your previous life?

When you come back into Spirit we try and make you understand the ways of progression. But we are not always successful and the choice is made to reincarnate. Back you go to start all over again, making the same mistakes and end up in Level One when you return. And so it goes on. Level One, back to Earth, then Level One again. You never get past Level One.

Some people are taught that by coming back through all these different lives they are raising themselves through the levels in spirit, that this is the way of progression - and are referred to as 'Old Souls'.

No, you are all equal on Earth. Just because you have been here many times, it does not put you higher up the ladder than anyone else. Everyone goes back to Level One until they decide to stay in Spirit and move on.

Let us suppose that you have cleared all your karma and your decision is to reincarnate. You bypass Levels Two and Three and are taken directly to Level Four where you are prepared and purified ready for transportation.

During the reincarnation process your life force is suspended. You are put in what you might call a holding bay. Although your life force is suspended, it cannot be shut down. You are cleared of your previous earthly existence, because you cannot have the same identity. You are cleansed and prepared to re-enter this world.

When you go into the holding area, our contact with you in Spirit is finished. We have done our job. We do not even know where you will go. It is the great universal power, God that decides.

Nobody reincarnates while their loved ones are still on Earth. If you were on Earth trying to communicate with your mother through a medium, you would not wish to hear: 'Your Mother has decided to reincarnate and no longer exists.'

A child must be born with its spirit cleared of everything from the past. If he or she still had all the knowledge of a previous life and death experience, the brain would not be able to cope. The knowledge would also affect that person's new existence.

Sometimes people do remember experiences that have spilled over from a previous incarnation. This is rare, but unfortunately our work in spirit is not always infallible. Even we can make mistakes!

Every person that reincarnates, prevents a new life force from coming directly from the source of all life. Second hand souls are coming back instead of the new bright lights that are waiting patiently to be born.

The source of all life needs to deliver new life and light into your world in order to change it. If you reincarnate you are preventing this from happening. Try to remember the words that I have spoken. Do not come back; stay in Spirit and progress. Give the Infinite Spirit the opportunity to change your world.

Sometimes change is difficult. But it is much better to think about it whilst on this Earth plane than be confronted by me or others like me on the other side. We will say to you: "I am sorry but now is the time to start thinking differently, think of the time you have wasted by going up and down through different existences to come back to Level One. You can go no further into Spirit until you decide to stop."

Do you really want to lose your identity? Learn to love yourself for what you are. Strive to improve yourself in every way possible while you are experiencing this life. Remember you are responsible for everything that you do on Earth. Be as pure in thought and action as you can, so that you do not build up masses of karma for yourself.

The reason that you are here is because the source of all life, God, has given you this opportunity. Do not waste it, be thankful for your life, and do your very best with every opportunity to spread love and truth. This is the way to enrich the source when you eventually go back from where you came.

Now let us explore what happens once you have decided to keep the identity that you have and stay in Spirit and move to Level Two. As on all the levels in Spirit, you must go to the preparation level, where you can rest before your onward journey. That level is shown in the diagrams as the apex of all the four illustrated triangles or pyramids from One to Four.

As you lift into the next level of existence in Spirit, we need to make you lighter. I have no doubt that you find all this hard to believe, because at the moment you cannot see it the way that I do, but you will when you become Spirit.

I understand you. I have been one of you. I also had my debts to pay. Some of them were very big for I condemned people to death. I had to accept the responsibility. I have not come back down here to clear my debts because I cleared them in Spirit. I have come this time to tell you the truth and how it really is.

As you progress in Spirit you become more spiritual. You begin to accept that you have to leave behind everything Earthly, including your families, in order to enable you to go on in Spirit and eventually return to the source of all life.

We do not sit on clouds, floating about playing harps! When you become a spiritual being, you become aware of the separation between your world and the spirit world.

Some people immediately feel they would like to help people on Earth. This type of work requires training, as you have to go back and work in the Earth's atmosphere. We have large training areas on all levels for any type of training or learning required.

Remember you will be free of the confines of the physical body. The only thing that confines you in Spirit is the level that you have reached. You may wish to travel around the level you are in to visit friends, or even go down to the levels below you and help other spirits who are coming over into Level One.

You may decide to do nothing and enjoy the experience of where you are. But you will find that you will eventually get bored doing nothing and will wish to develop and move on.

You will meet wonderful people in Spirit and, although you don't get the attachments that you get down on Earth, you get to enjoy the company and the knowledge you gain from one another's experiences.

Every person on Earth is equal. What makes you different from one another on Earth is the clothes that you wear and the material things that you possess. The same as we are all equal in Spirit, depending on the level we have reached.

You are born into this world for the same purpose, to gain an identity, have an Earth experience, then leave it. The one thing you cannot escape from is the passing. It is not a death. There is no death. There is only a new beginning.

As you go from one level to another you will become lighter and more spiritual. The time will come when you will wish to move forward to Level Three. Of course once again you must go through rest and preparation for your journey and clearance through to the next level. This clearance removes any Earthly ties you may have left.

Level Three is an area of beauty and spiritual harmony. It is also a very busy area. This is where you decide what you want to do while you are developing spiritually and progressing back to the source. This is where the many Halls of Learning are. You may wish to study or be a teacher. You may wish to train to be a spiritual doctor and join my teams of thousands of doctors working through mediums on Earth.

You may choose to look after the animals as they pass from the animal kingdom, or the children's area. You might decide to be a musician and join the orchestras we have in Spirit, or even be a gardener. There are beautiful gardens in the spirit world. The one thing you will not have to worry about is time. You will not say: 'I must study this or train for that because it is going to take me many years and I will be too old to do anything with it.' Remember there is no age in Spirit. You do not get old. That is all behind you.

Animals do not have to go through the same clearances as us. They pass through Level One and go to Level Three. Animals do not have karmic debts and pass through the levels very quickly back to the source.

As regards your pets, if the animal leaves your memory, then the life force of that animal will go on, because it feels: 'Oh well, I have done my job, I have brought love and happiness into that family and now it is time to move on.' However if you loved your animal very much and have a strong Earthly connection with the memory of the animal, it will not leave you. The link of love is very strong.

I sometimes walk in the area we call the Children's Playground. The Children's Playground in Spirit is where all children who pass over at an early age live and play. Children do not go into spirit and disappear. They are taught and guided through their spiritual lives. There are guardians who have an understanding and love for children in this level. Even children passing from the Earth plane to Spirit can get confused.

The worst part of a child's clearance is the attachment to its parents. It can be very traumatic. Sometimes it can take a long time. But once they break away they are fine, and even though they see you as their Earthly parents, they realise that you are separate souls on your own development pathway.

In Spirit you are individual souls. Parents are no longer parents. You actually meet not as father and mother, son or daughter. You meet as souls. The Earthly body that made you mum, dad, daughter or brother has gone.

When you lose someone, especially children, it is important to remember that the Source only loaned them to you. You were their keeper on Earth. When you come into Spirit, they do not see you as Mum or Dad; they see you as another spiritual being and love you for it.

Babies who pass over grow up in Spirit until the time comes to make their own decision about reincarnation. A baby does not collect karmic debts; it is pure when passing into spirit. A foetus is not a living thing until the spirit has joined it at three months. I believe this is called the quickening on your earth.

I am often asked about hell and Lucifer. You create your own heaven or hell on Earth. Like attracts like. If you are living in the light, you will only attract the light. If you are living in the dark, you will draw to yourself those who walk that pathway.

If someone on Earth upsets you by word or deed, they create bad vibrations and negative energies around you. You must endeavour to raise yourself above these negative energies. Try not to go down to their level, because if you do, you are no better than they are. Be patient, you have not walked their pathway. It is better to turn the other cheek. If you stay on your level they will have to come up to you, or walk away.

After learning on Level Three, you will decide to move to Level Four. This is a working level. On Level Four you have the same procedures of clearance and transportation as you have on other levels, but when you reach here, you are pure Spirit. It is quite a busy level, as spirits are always transporting from one level to another.

You will want to settle down to stay, work and rest with all the other spiritual beings on Level Four. This area is teeming with doctors, teachers, scientists, and guides working with mediums and helpers in all fields. Remember this is also the level where you are prepared for transportation if your wish is to reincarnate. Level Four is also a vast area for development and learning. I work from Level Four and there are many doctors and teachers on this level who assist me.

After Level Four, all your clearances, preparation and training have finished. The only thing that can happen now is that you further enrich your soul. The wonderful thing is that you will now feel that you are part of the whole. You will feel the urge to unite with other souls and go forward. My favourite way to express this is, I am a mere grain of sand in a vast desert. I feel this experience when I leave your world to go through the levels to my own Level Nine; I become part of the whole again.

I manage to get back to Level Nine more regularly, as these days Raymond stops work for a week every month. When we were busier, I only ever managed to reach Level Nine when Raymond and Gillian had a holiday.

Gillian has arranged for all our work at home and abroad to be done in a two-week period. It is impossible for me to get back to Level Nine when we are working in the clinics, as I need plenty of time to get there. I need at least three days due to the clearances.

As I go up through each level I get lighter. I shed all the vibrations of the Earth plane and once I have passed Level Five I cannot connect with Gillian and Raymond, I am completely cut off.

Raymond does not like this experience. He feels that a part of him has been cut away. He becomes quiet and distant. I am unable to do anything about it but at least now he has Gillian who understands him.

When I say I am going home to rest, I go back to my own time, not just to my own level, but to my own time in that level. I rest with the people I want to be with. I do get spiritually tired after being with you. Think of the effect that the Earthly vibrations have on me as I come down through the ethers of time and space.

We are in two different times and worlds apart. Two thousand years is a long time ago. The wonder of it all is that even though you cannot come to me, I can come down to you.

As a spiritual energy I can travel anywhere, go forward in time and go back in time. The reason that I do not go back any further than two thousand years is because it does not interest me. What would be the point in going back further than my own time? Even now I find it difficult to think back two thousand years and remember all that happened in my life.

Once I reach my level I am with the people of my time. The disciples are in Level Nine and Jesus comes down from Level Ten to meet with us.

I rest and recuperate each month like this and when it is time for me to come back down to the Earth I can come down very quickly indeed, because I do not have to go through any clearances as I am coming down from the higher purification levels.

Sometimes there is an emergency on Earth with one of our patients and the message is carried from level to level till it reaches me. Then I get to

Raymond as quickly as possible, although in Earth time it does take quite a few hours. However when I am working on the Earth plane, as I operate from Levels Four and Five, I can be back with Raymond in a very short time.

* * * * *

I now want to consider the issue of suicide. You may be thinking, if Spirit is so wonderful why not finish life right now and progress. It is very sad when a person takes their life. I know that for some of you life is not very easy. There are many trials and tribulations when you are encased in the human body, but you must remember that you asked to come here.

God, the universal power, has given this life experience to you. If you cut it before its course has ended you will regret it. It is a wonderful opportunity to come here, gain an identity, and stay the course. Nobody punishes you if you commit suicide. You are not banished to a strange place away from your loved ones. You are helped and nurtured just the same as everyone else. It is only you who suffer, for you will regret passing up that wonderful opportunity of seeing your Earthly life through to the end.

What you have achieved in your life is very important to you, from that basis you can begin your spiritual life and progression back to the source. You cannot kill yourself because life goes on. You are infinite.

Have you ever thought about the beauty around you? The beauty of the universe that God, the universal source, created for you? How many of you see the beauty of the flowers, the colours and intricate patterns of a butterfly's wings, or the delicate shape of a seashell? How many of you have actually gone to a tree, placed your hands on it or wrapped your arms around it, and felt the true source of power flowing through it?

Yes it is alive. It is a living thing, and believe it or not, it also has a nature soul. If you chop it down, it dies, and its force goes back to the source. What is left just rots. The same thing happens to you when you die.

Think about the seasons changing. Mother Nature tells your trees and flowers when it is autumn and they begin to close down and shed their leaves. Then in spring they suddenly come back to life again, laden with delicate blossom and canopies of beautiful foliage. That is the life force working on your Earth. Sadly you are chopping down these magnificent gifts of nature and damaging your Earth in the process.

This living planet is a wonderful place, but if man continues to rape the planet of all its precious resources through ignorance and greed, your world as you know it, will end. It is very important to remember that the source of life can only be as powerful as the life force feeding it. If you keep on taking and giving nothing in return, you will eventually have nothing left to take.

It is the same with the animal kingdom. On Earth it has always been accepted as normal practice to slaughter animals for food. We do not agree with this in Spirit, but we do not have the right to dictate what you must do on Earth. We can only try to influence you to change in a positive way.

I am not saying that you are wrong to do these things, that is your choice. You have free will on Earth. The one thing that spiritual beings do not have is jurisdiction over man. We have to start introducing new thoughts through new spirits born from the source. It is very important that the thoughts of these new souls come in and change this world. All of you, and those that come after you, will be the people to change your world through the universal power of love.

In my time on Earth we knew nothing about the spirit world until the great prophet Jesus enlightened our minds through his teachings. He asked for nothing more than love.

Jesus taught love, lived love, and gave love. He taught us not to be afraid of those who threatened us. For although they could hurt our bodies and take away our lives, we would live on in Spirit and become part of him and the universal power.

We loved him and we died for him. When you move on into Spirit you leave all Earthly things that tie you down, and when you become spiritually whole again only then will you understand the meaning of it all.

Chapter 19

Paul the spiritual surgeon

In this chapter Paul talks about his work as a spiritual surgeon, and his training for this new role. He also tells the story of how he chose and found Ray and Gillian.

I started studying to be a doctor about 300 years ago in Earth time. The Higher Council in Spirit, on Level Nine, asked me train as a doctor to advance healing on Earth, and at the same time to teach people the correct pathway to Spirit. Initially I did not want to work on the Earth plane. But once they convinced me that I was the one for the job, I was 100% behind it.

The council has around 55 members at any one time. I am a member but rarely sit on it, as I am so busy on Earth. Spirits become members because of their position and the way that they have worked in Spirit.

I was trained as a neuro-surgeon and heart surgeon. That is what I do best. Other spiritual beings are trained to deal with cancers, multiple sclerosis, motor neurone disease etc. I can also work on these diseases, but it is not my forte.

If we had a special residential clinic to do the surgery, maybe full time, then it would be different. I would be able to spend more time on life-threatening diseases. But you need facilities to do that. It is not something you can achieve by travelling around the country as I do now with Raymond and Gillian.

I believe that spiritual healing should be combined with conventional medicine. I have always taught healers and told patients that healing is a complementary medicine or a complementary therapy. Personally I think that all doctors on the Earth plane need to know more about complementary medicine and healing.

There are around 2,500 spirit doctors working with me in Spirit. Many were doctors on Earth and decided to continue being doctors in Spirit. We have many helpers, who have also trained as spirit doctors.

I have never wanted to come here and step on the medical profession's toes. I would rather work with them, than against them. We can complement the medical profession as much as they can complement us. I do not have the right to say that I am better than they are.

When I examine a patient and am trying to diagnose their problem, teams of spirit doctors and helpers take care of the patient. They assist me in making the decisions about the tests to be taken and the procedures to follow.

Progress would be very slow without them. I do the work, but there is a team supporting me. Dr Barbara Lane and Dr Brummond are close allies. Their main role is to train and assist doctors and make sure that this vast unit runs smoothly.

I am meticulous about the development of my doctors and the wellbeing of my patients. I am the medical team leader because I am the one who comes to you. The doctors and helpers comprise my support unit. I depend on them a great deal.

I pass spiritual instruments into the body and perform spiritual operations. I can see into the body when I look at it or lay Ray's hands on the patient. If I see a nerve that needs untrapping, I directly untrap the nerve so that the pain goes immediately. We in Spirit are at least 100 years ahead of your medical establishment on Earth.

Gillian makes a big joke in demonstrations about people not having to take their clothes off because I can see through them. But I do not see the outer body. I see inside the body.

Spirit has actually perfected the separation and lifting of two vertebrae by inserting an instrument, so that a disc can be returned to its natural position. By doing this we take the pressure off the nerve and give comfort to the patient. This operation takes around ten minutes to perform.

When I do deeper operations in stomachs for example, I use a spiritual monitor. The monitor is linked to me and my doctors in the Spirit world. It helps me see into the body in the same way that computers and CT scanners work on Earth.

To most people this is a miracle. My spirit doctors perform these 'miracles' through healers on Earth. They are not all surgeons like myself, but nevertheless they work beside your healers. This is love in action. The devotion to their work is unstinting. You may let them down, but they will never let you down.

If a holy man places his hands upon someone and they become healed, it is hailed as a miracle! But what is a miracle. Your doctors perform miracles every day in hospitals, but the majority of you do not recognise it as a miracle.

In my time on Earth, two thousand years ago, someone with a broken leg, was lucky to survive because of infection. If you had to have a limb removed you were either made drunk, or given a concoction of herbs to dull the pain. Then a lump of wood was placed in your mouth to bite on while they sawed their way through your limb. It was a very crude method but the only one they knew. Very few people survived traumatic operations like amputations in those days.

On Earth or in Spirit, a doctor is a miracle worker; a nurse is a miracle worker. They repair your body and get you back on your feet. Childbirth, the beginning of physical existence, is a miracle. The creation of the universe is a miracle.

The healing that I do has touched many thousands. But you must realise that if God had not given me the right to do this, I would not be here with you. It is God that my patients must praise and not I.

I have great compassion for all the patients that I see. They are important to me and are the reason why I am here. I feel for them, and as I have gone through my passing, I know the fear of approaching death. It is very frightening for my patients if they are very sick and understand that their time to leave the Earth plane is drawing close.

If a person comes to me with cancer, I tell them: 'It is your house let us fight for it, keep it intact and kick out the intruder.' I encourage them to be positive and make them work hard to keep themselves going. The brain is a very powerful and wonderful piece of machinery. It is important to remember, that negativity creates illness, positive thinking helps cure illness.

* * * * *

I am often asked how Raymond was chosen to work with me. We had to get the right person. It is so involved, getting the right person to do the right job. So it was very important from day one that we had a family background which was not too complicated. A doctor or a scientist would be no good. It had to be someone from a very simple background. Spirit searched for many years before choosing Raymond.

We looked at his family background and decided that it was a very simple set-up, nothing complicated. Nobody was too involved in other things. I looked at his brother first but decided he was not the one I wanted. Then, I found out that his mother was carrying Raymond, so we chose him. I needed someone who would not interfere with my views and my work. Raymond is that person and lets me work as I wish. A person with a very strong intelligent background may have wanted to put their ideas before mine.

Raymond was the one who was chosen. Of course we had to wait, because training Raymond took many, many years. We also had to have the right environment, so that we could start work. I had to go along with his life. I could not interfere with Raymond's life, and was only able to try and steer him or put him on the right pathway. But if he chose, which he did, pathways that were not the correct ones for him, there was nothing that I could do.

When the second marriage ended I thought: 'This time has got to be the right time.' I went back to Spirit and asked them to look for someone for Raymond, who would help get him on the right pathway. It was suggested that Gillian would be the right person. She was experienced in mediumship, and had all the skills that were necessary to steer Raymond on the right pathway.

Gillian's guides already knew what they wanted for her. She had her life with her previous husband, but it was gradually being steered towards meeting Raymond. My contact with Gillian was with her Spirit guides who worked through her. She was like a voice crying in the wilderness and was really asking for a change. There was no better person for us to choose. She is good in every aspect of the work. It was meant to be.

It was not until I saw her for the first time that I knew that she was the one for the job. Whenever I meet people for the first time I always sit and look at them and pick up on their wavelength spiritually. Then I endeavour, within spiritual laws, to manoeuvre the situation to where it needs to be. I cannot, however, interfere with free will.

I have an Indian spirit with me called Waters Running who protects Raymond whilst he is in trance. He comes down with me, attaches Raymond's lifeline to his and takes him to Level One in the spirit dimension. Waters Running keeps Raymond in a state of unconsciousness while I take over his body to do my work.

Once I am in the body I prefer to stay there, as it is more tiring for both

Raymond and myself to keep swapping places in the spirit world. That is why in my clinics we have to keep appointments tightly together so that Raymond does not tire quickly. Raymond is in trance for as much as seven hours a day. I do not believe that any other medium is in trance for so long. Raymond's mediumship is unique.

It is better for patients to wait for me than for me to wait for them. When I am in his body Waters Running is keeping him safe in Spirit. The doctors who work alongside me in the clinic replenish my energy to help me stay down here. Love is the key, the universal power that keeps me safe.

If Raymond or Gillian have an accident, then Waters Running is the first one on the scene. He is not necessarily there when it happens, but he arrives as soon as he can. He does whatever is necessary to make sure that the problem is solved. When I first worked through Raymond, I did not want anyone to know my identity, although I still wanted to keep the name Paul. At the time it was not right for anything to be said.

There was no purpose to be served by revealing that I was Paul the Tarsean, a Rabbi in Jesus Christ's time. There will always be opposition. But now is the time for the truth to be revealed. People say to me: 'You are conversant in many languages, speak some!' What would be the point? What would be the use of speaking Aramaic, Hebrew or Latin? It would merely impress a few people. I am not here to impress. I am here to speak the truth.

Speaking English through Raymond has become natural. When I first came through him, it was a bit rusty, because I come from a level in Spirit where we do not need to speak.

I had to teach myself about the English language and medical terminology. I took over Raymond on many occasions to go to the library and study all the medical books. I taught myself the names of limbs and arteries in English. The rest of my studying was done in Spirit. Raymond has an exceptionally good memory, which has allowed me to store a lot of the information that I need.

I do not need spiritual guidance. I know what I have to do. But there will always be physical problems on Earth because of people and circumstances. Not only do I have to take Raymond's free will into account, but also the people with whom we come into contact.

Many people, jealous of Raymond, have tried to stop the development of my work. However, I understand these things. I always say: 'I am here with you. Use me, for one day I will be gone. You will find that the further we go along this pathway, the more controversy we will meet.' Only a few have listened. Yet there is nothing to lose.

I was not a saint in my Earthly life. I was a man. I did what I felt I had to do. When I was a Rabbi and pursued the Nazarenes, I believed that I was right. When Jesus decided to halt me on that pathway, it was done in such a manner that I had to believe. After that, I put all my thoughts, all my love and all my energies into following his teachings. Until it took my life.

I am still that man, but a spiritual man. I feel it even more when I enter the Earth plane. The more I am here, the more I get drawn back to being what I was. So the more that I am with Raymond, the more I am being drawn to carry on giving my teachings.

How many times do you get a second chance to come back in a different time and follow your calling?

* * * * *

People are very curious about how Ray and Paul change places in his body, very often on a daily basis – and how Ray is looked after during his absence by a guardian whose name is Waters Running. Perhaps the best way to throw light on this is to allow them both to explain here what happens and how it feels. Ray will speak first:

Ray:

I have to wait until Paul arrives. Initially I feel pressure at the back of my neck or shoulders. I close my eyes, my head spins, then I feel dizzy as if I am just about to faint. The dizziness soon passes. I see my body as I come out of it. It goes dark, and that is it. This used to feel uncomfortable, but I can handle it now. Practice makes perfect!

As I am going out, I actually see my body in the chair. That is when, as I have been told, the lifeline to my body is disconnected and connected to Waters Running. Waters Running takes me away, as a spiritual being, and Paul enters my body.

I am told that I go to the Halls of Learning where I am taught what I need to know when I pass over. I will be rewarded I suppose for giving up my time and my body, when I get to the other side. Maybe I will have a quicker transition. The whole experience is like going into hospital, having an anaesthetic, and falling into unconsciousness.

In the early years I used to stand by the side of my body and Paul would come in and work. But they found that I was able to stay out of my body for longer periods if the lifeline was disconnected. When Paul has finished, Waters Running brings me back and then reconnects my lifeline. I see myself descending into my body. Paul leaves and I go back in. There is nobody there for a few seconds.

I have seen Paul pass me on his way out of my body. He does not look exactly like the painting we have of him. His beard is too tidy in the painting! Paul is dressed in off-white robes made out of some sort of coarse material.

Waters Running has two feathers hanging down at the back. I have only seen him once in his war bonnet. Normally his hair hangs down in two tiny pigtails. He wears trousers and a tunic. Both Paul and Waters Running look very solid to me.

Our normal working day starts at 10.30am, with a break for lunch at around 1.30pm. Then an hour later I go back into trance until we finish. In a busy clinic we go on until 5.30pm . For some reason, when I return, I always have to dash to the loo. It is almost as if Paul closes the body down when he is in it.

He does drink tea or water and eats a snack, just to keep my bodily functions going. If my body felt hungry or thirsty then it would kick Paul out. But I have never been aware of this happening.

I do not resent all the time that I have given to Paul. The only occasion when I am not really happy is if I am in and out in short bursts. This can be very tiring. That is why Gillian books the clinics with only one break. It is much easier for me, because Paul and I do not have to go through lots of transitions. I do not think anybody else works in the same way as me.

Overshadow is very different to my deep trance state. You can see what is going on and have more control over the process. Spirits touch your aura in overshadow. They come into your space, but do not take over your body.

I experienced overshadow very briefly when Paul started working through me. If he operated on someone's shoulder, I could actually see inside the body. I found the experience unnerving and said that if Paul was going to carry on like that, there would have to be a bucket available for me! That was when he decided to take me into a deeper trance.

* * * * *

Now let's hear Waters Running's side of the story. What follows is a verbatim rendering of a short interview that I requested with this American Native Indian spirit that protects Ray when Paul is in his body. For this interview Ray went into 'deep overshadow' rather than a full trance. Ray, however, was unaware of what was going on and I noticed that his eyes remained closed throughout. Ray's upper body and face appeared to be presented differently and his face seemed much thinner. Interestingly, although seated at a table, Waters Running looked taller than Ray and he spoke very slowly.

Waters Running:

I was a Cherakowa Apache. I lived in the hills of Dakota, and was a war chief when I passed over with yellow fever at the age of 47. White men saved me from a horrible death because they shot me during a raid. They also killed my wife, son and two daughters. I do not hate them for this now, but I have never forgotten. I am not ready to progress any further because I like to be near my people. So I stay and work on Level Four.

Paul asked me to look after Ray. He said that the instruction had come from the higher realms. This was to be my job for Ray's lifetime. I was in charge of Ray's spiritual progression, so that he could get ready for Paul. This involved pulling him out of his body at night and putting him back in, when he was a child. When Ray was in his early development circles, he used to sit under a tree in Spirit. I had to chop the tree down to get him to move on!

Going in and out of his body does not give Ray any difficulties. He just loses time and gives Gillian a break! I take Ray to the Halls of Learning where he rests when Paul is in his body. I have always protected Ray when he has had big accidents like the car crash, by lifting him out of his body. This allowed his body to relax and prevent any real injury. He would not be here now, if he had been in his body.

I love Ray like a son.

Chapter 20

Paul's Group
Healing Method

In this chapter, Paul describes the group healing method he has devised. It has become a powerful complementary therapy, which has been adopted by the Corinthian Church and Healing Association. Paul's ambition is to encourage the medical profession in Britain to see spiritual healing as an important and legitimate support to their own work.

Everyone has the ability to work as a healer and be a conduit for the divine healing rays, which are administered by my teams of doctors in Spirit. I work as a spiritual surgeon through Raymond, but over the last 10 years or so, with Raymond and Gillian's help, I have been able to train healers to back up my work and spread my teachings. I am only one spiritual being. But by training people on the Earth plane, I have been able to start fulfilling my mission to raise awareness of the powerful complementary therapy that can be provided by spiritual healing and encourage greater acceptance of healing by the medical profession.

Vince Lewis, a very experienced healer, who worked with me while we were trying to set up the International Healing Federation (IHF), helped me write the Federation's Training Manual. As discussed in chapter 15, we decided to wind up the IHF, because of unbearable pressures on Raymond and Gillian. Fortunately the Corinthian Church and Healing Association decided to adopt my healing methods and have adapted the manual for their use. The Corinthians are spreading the healing message worldwide. I hope that the combination of this book and their work will greatly increase understanding of the Spirit world and the benefits of healing.

We have an academy on Level Four where all the doctors and medical assistants are, as I have already indicated, trained. The academy was founded about 300 years ago when we began to prepare for my mission on Earth. One of our main focuses was to harness spiritual energy to heal the sick. We perfected the method on spiritual beings who had passed over in traumatic circumstances or had for instance lost their leg whilst they were alive. We were able to make their spiritual body whole again. This does sound far-fetched, but what you must remember is that you are a spiritual being inside a physical body.

Becoming a healer is a pure expression of your spirituality. You bring light and love to others. But to be an effective healer and a better conduit for my doctors, you need to allow the Divine Love that is inside you, to unfold. To develop as a healer, you must dedicate yourself to helping other people. This increases your spirituality and makes you a better channel for the healing energies. You cannot study for this, it is a way of life. But by practising meditation and giving service whenever you can to assist those less fortunate, you can become more attuned to the spirit doctors.

My group healing method, involving three healers, is the most efficient way to administer healing. The patient lies on a couch with one healer at his or her head and the other two either side of the chest. The Illustration on page 154 and the diagram on page 155 depicts this. The healers must place their hands on the body. Group healing is not so effective if hands are hovering above the body.

If a patient has had a consultation with me, they will often be sent to a healing group for back-up healing. The patient will be given a colour chart like the diagram on page 155 and Gillian uses a crayon or colour pen to shade the different hands in the appropriate colours. The colours are nothing to do with colour therapy or colour healing. The colours are used to give the healers something to focus on and represent the strength of ray being used by the Spirit world. The darker the colour, the stronger the ray.

Healer number one at the head places his or her hands around the back of the head, with their fingers on the neck of the patient. Healer number two places their hands on the upper chest and stomach and healer number three does the same on the lower chest and just below the stomach.

The healing group sends me a telepathic message two hours or more beforehand which is picked up by my spirit doctors, or myself if I am not working and healing is administered then by the Spirit world in the first four minutes. This is emphasised in Points No 5 and 6 printed below the chart. The energy flows through the palms of the hands into the patient's central nervous system. By using the nervous system, my Spirit doctors can direct healing energies to any part of the body. The healing rays spread for up to 25 minutes throughout the body and continue working for up to a week.

Groups of four healers can be used to help patients with terminal cancer. The patient will start to feel better. This positive input helps encourage a positive state of mind in the person suffering from the illness.

Healing will never harm anyone. It is a force for the good and an expression of love for your fellow man.

GROUP HEALING METHOD

Depiction of Group Healing Method showing in faint outline helpers from the Spirit world who invisibly assist the 3 healers (shaded) standing inside the dotted oval

GROUP HEALING METHOD

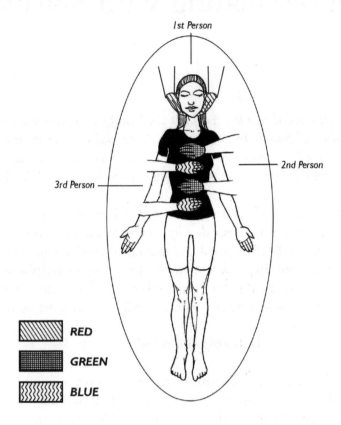

1st Person

2nd Person

3rd Person

▨ **RED**

▦ **GREEN**

▧ **BLUE**

1. Patient should be in lying position.

2. The colours shown in the hands above and below are just an example to show where they are to be placed. Paul sets the colours for his patients but when group healing is administered without Paul's guidance then pastel colours should be used.

3. Please note that this is not colour healing. The colours represent the strength of the healing ray being used.

4. If there are only two persons, then put both across the body area or one on head and one across the body.

5. The hands of the first person should be placed mostly under the patients head.

6. Group healing should be administered for no more than 4 minutes. This should be done at least once a week, but twice is even better.

Chapter 21

Communicating with Spirits

Communication with the Spirit world is something very familiar to the growing number of people in Britain who have had the experience. To others it may seem bizarre or weird at first sight. In this section Paul outlines in note form the best way to prepare for communication of this kind.

You all have a spirit guide or series of spirit helpers with you. But because of the pressures of every day life very few are able to hear the advice that is offered. Both physical and mental relaxation can help you get in touch with the Spirit world. It is important to be physically relaxed to help prepare the way for mental relaxation. Any form of muscle tensing or stretching for around two minutes will help relax the body.

Relaxing the mind

The aim should be to relax the mind rather than go into a state of meditation. The best definition of this is to emulate the state we call 'day dreaming' and bring about a peaceful and harmonious level of mind activity. The easiest way to achieve this is through listening to music. The music must be harmonious not raucous, but the ideal style is down to personal taste. Others find that chanting mantras is a way of achieving peace. Meditation tapes featuring someone narrating in a soft and gentle voice are also useful. Che Gong groups in the Far East use movement to relax the mind and of course a very powerful method is to use breathing and visualisation techniques.

Visualisation

Visualisation is the use of the mind to place yourself into a desired state by using your imagination. You should only focus on secure images. Focussing on a serene scene or a walk round your favourite garden are excellent ways to achieve peacefulness through visualisation.

Meditation

Visualisation is often confused with meditation. Many believe that when they are on a visualised journey that they are meditating. Visualisation is an active function, but meditation is passive. You should in effect be doing nothing when you meditate. This means that you allow your mind to become quiet.

The key requirement for inducing a meditative state is to be in a comfortable environment. Sit or lie down and listen to soft gentle music or just focus on your breathing and drift into quietness.

If you are in a group, a simple visualisation exercise can be run, which helps everyone to relax and enter the meditative state. Never focus on any thoughts that may be flowing through the brain, but concentrate on breathing. Gradually, with practice, thoughts will become less intrusive.

Through constantly practising meditation, you will find yourself becoming spiritually oriented. Meditation feeds the soul.

Guided Meditation

A guided meditation is when a person narrates a pleasant visualisation to the recipient. The narrator then takes the visualisation to a point where the recipient can slip into a meditative state for a set period of time. At the end of the time, the narrator then restarts the visualisation journey to bring the recipient back to a state of full consciousness. *There is an excellent guided CD by Paul for sale – details at the end of this book.*

Attunement & Mediumship

Attunement is creating a state of mental preparation to enable you to blend with spirit vibrations. Mediumship is the word we use to describe someone who has an ability to understand or link with a non-physical or spiritual vibration. Spiritual mediums can communicate with spirits. Psychic mediums have the ability to sense the vibrations attached to the physical world.

A spirit medium communicates with the Spirit world in three ways by clairvoyance which is visual; clairaudience which is by hearing and clairsentience which is perception by the other senses.

The desire to help others will encourage spirits to draw near, but you may have to sit for months in a quiet or meditative state to develop as a medium. Training is essential, as you should not take on this work without help and guidance.

Trance Mediumship

The term trance has often been associated with voodoo and strange occurrences. Trance is simply a state where a spirit has a direct influence over a person's actions.

Depending on the degree of trance, the spirit can influence the mind or the voice box of the medium in order to give messages or philosophies. The spirit bypasses the medium's mind and makes the medium speak automatically.

Raymond's trance mediumship is the deepest form of trance possible. I completely take over his body. Raymond's spirit is attached to his guide, Waters Running, who looks after him while I am on the Earth plane.

Protection

Anyone who is developing his or her skills as a medium needs to consider protection. Always remember that like attracts like. If you have set out on your spiritual pathway you will emit a light that Spirit can see. Spirits will rejoice in this and will blend with you.

However, you should protect yourself against negative psychic vibrations. Other people, who simply do not have kind thoughts about you or possibly have anger or fear, send out these vibrations. It is possible that you might sense some of these vibrations around you.

The easiest way to protect yourself is with a prayer to God, then visualise yourself inside a 'silvered bubble' of God's light. Good focus on the 'silvered bubble' will provide protection. Repeat this every day or as and when required.

Chapter 22

An Interview with Paul

To draw together the different themes of this book Paul agreed to answer questions from a group of those involved in the book's preparation. We began by discussing the question of Paul's true identity.

Q. You announced a few years ago that you were Paul of Tarsus, rather than just Paul, a healer. Was there any particular reason for saying that then?

The reason for not announcing who I was to start with was because Raymond was not developed enough to cope with the information. It was much simpler for me to use an anonymous name, Andrew Portlock. I was worried that his immediate reaction would have been: 'Oh no, I am not having anything to do with this.' He is very down-to-earth and I did not want to discourage him from the pathway he was on. Then one night I told Raymond's circle who I was. Their reaction was as I expected: 'Oh no, it cannot be.' I said: 'Well I am who I am and I cannot change that fact.'

It was at the Fir Tree Lodge seminar in August 1999 that I made the first public announcement that I was Paul of Tarsus. I felt then that people were more ready to accept my identity.

Q. Is it important for the world to know your identity?

Not really. But I want to be myself. I am not too worried whether the world likes it or not. I have to live in this world with Raymond and Gillian and do my work and I would rather do it in truth.

Progress Report

Q. Are you satisfied with how much healing work you have done so far or do you feel there is still an enormous amount to do? How would you judge your own progress to date?

Progress to date is very good. Although I would much rather be working from a centre where all illnesses can be treated. My aim has always been to get a team of spirit doctors working through other mediums.

I have trained people to work with my doctors but then free will has always intervened and they have gone off to do their own thing.

Q. Would you like to establish a centre again and work closely with the medical profession?

Of course, I would like us to have a centre where we could also work on animals and children and do more in-depth surgery. But first of all we have to get people to understand Spirit, which is going to be very difficult, especially with the medical profession. You do not get many doctors like Walter Fisher (see his testimony in Part Four) who are open minded. The other problem is that Raymond and Gillian are getting older.

I can train people to work with spirit doctors, but we cannot make a greater impact if we do not have somewhere to practice where others can work alongside me. In recent years our surgical work has been carried out at the Tring clinic, where patients have been able to stay all day. Many spirit doctors work there with me. Around 300 doctors a day help out on a rotating shift system to protect them from damage from the Earth's atmosphere. They are not as lucky as I am. I have a body that I can get into which protects me on the Earth plane.

The doctors change every 30 minutes. If we are doing an operation, then the teams are changed at every possible break point, so that they do not get any Earthly contamination. Unfortunately our Tring clinic is closing. We need somewhere else with space to do the work.

Teaching & Healing

Q. How much impact do you think the publication of this book is going to have, especially on improving understanding of your teachings?

I think that the book will help people understand the teachings that I have put over as simply as I can. Unfortunately as they are so different to what people have been taught for so long it will take time. But when you look at them they really are quite straightforward. People do, however, find healing easier to adopt.

Group healing is a method that was devised by myself some 200 years ago. It was devised purely by mistake, because I was testing different rays from the Earth's atmosphere in spirit on spiritual beings who had just passed over to help them to adjust to the spirit world much quicker. It was nothing to do with the physical at that point.

If people have an ailment on Earth, they still have that ailment when they arrive in the spirit world. For example, if you die and your body is not whole or you have had a traumatic passing, you still think that you are suffering. Our healing rays help spiritual beings shed the memories of their passing and make them whole spiritually. When you pass over from this Earth plane, you come into Spirit and you are re-energised as a spirit.

Q. How are healing rays generated for group healing sessions on Earth?

The healing rays come through spirit doctors. Then as soon as they make contact with the healer in the group, the energy passes from them to the healer and into the patient's body. We can alter the strength of the rays depending on the ailment to be treated.

Q. You say that everyone can be a healer. Would you like everyone to become aware that they can heal each other?

Of course. Everybody has the ability to heal. It is simple to heal but it is not so easy to give up time and the patience that is required of a healer.

Why the United Kingdom?

Q. Why did you choose the United Kingdom for your healing mission?

The United Kingdom is the most spiritually enlightened place in the world. The British are more open-minded and have always wanted to know why they are here. They are also very free and are not tied up with following one particular faith. The spiritualist movement really took off in Britain in the 1940s and helped move my project forward. In addition, we felt that English, a language that is spoken all over the world, would help spread my teachings.

Spiritual Stem Cell Therapy

Q. Can we talk a bit about how you operate in practical terms? When you do an operation, for example on someone's knee, you say that you are putting something in there to help heal it. What is this substance?

The substance is made up in the human body. Spiritual energy is passed into the body and we create a gel from bodily fluids.

In Part Four, Paul Gallegos talks about my work with his son Charlie. What I am doing with him is working with stem cells that we have been growing in his spinal column for eight years. We have been focussing on the central vortex of Charlie's brain for the last two years. The entire central vortex was damaged when he had his accident, as a result of oxygen starvation. We started at the core and are working our way through so that when we come out through the top of the central vortex, all the connections can be made. We have made maybe a million connections in the brain over the last two years. It takes roughly six to seven months after each operation for the brain to settle down.

It is going to be another 10 years before Charlie's brain functions anywhere near properly. But then we will have the problem of whether we will still be able to get the signals through.

Spiritual Lasers

Q. You have said that medically you are 100 years ahead of us. What do you mean by this?

Yes, we began working on stem cells about 100 years ago in your time. We worked theoretically to begin with, but when I chose Raymond I was able to start experimenting with this on the Earth plane. I also had to work out whether I could insert spiritual instruments into the human body.

For example when I use the fingers on Gillian's hand, her spirit doctor working through her does the operation on the inside while I am outside the body steering the instruments.

I once did an operation with a physical knife to demonstrate psychic surgery, but after that I continued to use spiritual instruments to work within the laws of the Earth plane.

Some of our instruments are lasers. Lasers do not destroy tissue. We can control a laser to do what we want. We can smooth things out, burn things, and knit things together.

The Spiritual Dimension and Karmic Debts

Q. Is there any way with raised consciousness that somebody could go to the spirit world without dying?

Yes it is possible for people to leave their bodies and go into the Spirit world. Raymond is living proof of that! A lot of the out-of-body experiences that people feel they have had are when they lift out of their body in the sleep state. This is known as astral travel. A deep meditation can achieve that as well.

Q. You have produced a meditation CD. Do you think that meditation is an important part of the healing process?

Yes I think that people do not practice enough meditation. The body does not function so well when it is in stress. Meditation creates a state of inner calm.

Q. What is the geography and environment of the spirit world? Is it a reflection of this world?

Yes, you pass through vortexes from your country in effect into a spiritual equivalent. You recognise the landscape while you are on Level One. But as you progress in spirit you shed your Earthly ties. Everyone passes into Spirit. Born-again Christians believe that they are the only ones that are going to heaven. What a shock they have when they arrive and we are all standing there!

Level One is whatever you want it to be. It is a mirror image of Earth. Here we have doctors and surgeons working who clear you from the Earth plane to the spirit world. All you are doing is passing from your physical life once again into your spiritual life.

After you have entered the spiritual world and all your clearances are done, you are confronted with everything that you have done right or wrong on the Earth. You work out your karma in Spirit not on Earth.

You cannot hide your wrongs from yourself. You have to become aware of what you have done and truly repent. I mean TRULY repent. You cannot just say: 'I repent, I repent.' It can take forever and can be a very painful process.

For example people that do evil things, like kill and maim innocent bystanders through suicide bombings, go into Spirit, but pass into an area where they have to look at what they had done. They have to really work hard just to get to the point where they can confront their wrong-doings. They have to accept the reality that there is only one God, not one God for each religion. There is only one universal power and we are all here from that source.

You cannot hide the fact that you have carried out an atrocity. There is no way that you can escape it. Bombers might think that 'they are going to paradise', but once they get there it is very different. They are immediately moved to an area where they get cleared. Then they go to a place where they are meant to be because 'like attracts like'. We do not punish them, they punish themselves. They create their own hell until they decide that it is not the place for them and they cannot progress until they truly have repented from the core of their being.

Q. What happens to you if you have lived an 'ordinary life'.

Millions and millions of people can calmly pass through into the spirit world. You have divorce and re-marriage. That is life, but when you murder people, that is not life, that is a wrong, that is a serious karmic debt. We are all pure when the great universal power gives us life. You cannot enhance or put back any energy into the source of all life if you are not pure. It is only living on the Earth plane that makes you impure. So you need to clear your karmic debts before you can progress in Spirit.

Q. Do you still have DNA in your identity when you pass into Spirit?

No because you have a spiritual identity. The identity comprises vibrations that you have created in your Earthly life.

Reincarnation

Q. Does reincarnation occur?

Yes, but I do not teach this. I do not want people to come back. I want them to progress, enrich the source and allow new souls to be born that can try and change things on the Earth plane.

Q. Why do people decide to reincarnate?

Because they cannot shed their ties with the Earth plane. Once you have dealt with your karma, the question is do you want to progress in Spirit? If you decide to reincarnate then you do not reach Level 2. You go straight to Level 4, are cleansed, cleared and are made ready to come back down again. That is your choice and that is the only choice you get. You do not get a choice of where you come to or whom you go to. We do not even know where you are going. The great universal power decides.

Q. Do you have any memory of your previous life if you reincarnate?

Once you are cleansed and cleared, you should not have any memory of your previous life. The slate is wiped clean. But there is bound to be one in a million maybe who retains some memory.

When does the foetus become a living being?

Q. At what point does the spirit enter the new life? Is it at the moment of conception?

The life force joins the foetus at three months. That is when it becomes a life. So people who suffer a miscarriage up to three months do not lose a life as the spirit is not completely attached to the foetus.

Q. So people who are creating embryos for stem cells and destroying them after seven days are not ending a life?

Yes, they are not ending a spiritual life.

Q. Do we all have a spirit guide?

There are spirit guides for everyone in the world. They change as you develop. However you will only have one guide who connects with you through your life.

Q. What are relationships like in the Spirit world. Is there anything comparable to sexuality there?

There is no sexuality just unconditional love.

Q. Is it a great pleasure to be in the Spirit world?

Yes. I am more at peace in the Spirit world than I am here. Coming back down here, for me, is sometimes a trial. But it is the way that it is meant to be.

Q. What is God?

God is the life force of this Earth.

Q. When Jesus said, 'I am going to my father' why did he use that expression if he was talking about this great life force?

Because he could not say in those times, 'I am going to the universal power.' Jesus was a carpenter, a basic man. All of his teachings were very simple. There was no difficulty in understanding them. 'In my father's house there are many mansions' means that when you go into the Spirit world you go through many levels of existence.

Q. Would you say your teachings are still Christian today?

They are spiritual teachings. I am not a Christian. I am Spirit. If I were alive today I would be a freethinker, a free spirit.

Q. How are we to see you in relation to other prominent spiritual leaders like the Dalai Lama. Many people today are teaching very similar things. They are teaching love and compassion, that love is the thing that we must all give.

I do not class myself as a spiritual leader. I regard myself as just Paul.

Q. But you are a major figure. Because you have told us that you are St Paul of Tarsus, you are presenting yourself as one of the major figures in the spiritual history of our planet.

That is a difficult question for me to answer because I only see myself as Paul, I do not see myself as a Saint. Those who followed made me a Saint. I want the world to know that I am who I am. I do not see myself as equal to any of the others that are working on the Earth as I work from the spiritual planes. I am just Paul.

Q. But by saying that you are St Paul, you draw bigger attention to what you are telling us than if you were 'Joe Bloggs'. You are presenting yourself as a historical figure and thereby drawing more attention to what you are saying.

It was planned for me to re-enter the Earth and bring healing and that also gives me the chance to continue my teachings.

Q. How important is it for you to interpret what is written in your name in the Bible to a 21st century audience.

I have never thought of it to be perfectly honest. I come here to do spiritual healing and to give my teachings. What you have to remember is that I talked to gatherings of many people. I gave out what I received, what I felt, inspired by God and Jesus. I was just trying to change people's views.

Q. There is a really important section in Corinthians where you talk about spiritual gifts. Can you interpret this for a modern audience?

The spiritual gifts have always been on the Earth plane. All I was saying is that they are here, you have these gifts. There are people who give out beautiful words, inspired by Spirit. You have people who can talk in different tongues, that means spirits come down and enter their bodies and speak in different stages of trance. There are people with the gift of healing. They place their hands on people. We come close and we do healing through them.

All I was doing was making people aware that the gifts come from God. They are gifts from the universal power. Gifts from the universe that your Earth sits in and that your Earth is slowly destroying. You are destroying your own universe. Pollution is contaminating your atmosphere.

Q. If things go desperately wrong here and we devastate the planet, will that affect the spiritual levels?

If this happens there will be no spiritual existence.

Q. The spiritual dimension will disappear?

Everything will end within your solar system.

Q. So you have a self-interest in making things better here?

Of course.

Q. I often get the impression that you are here, largely because of the force of your own personality. Is that true?

Yes, fortunately for me, I am a person that says what I feel. That is why the Emperor did not put me to death straight away. It took him a long time to work out who I was and what I was. The only reason that he put me to death was for his own ends. He was losing touch with his own people. He had to do something to satisfy them so he decided to have me executed. He saw me as a threat. The Romans and their Caesars were very harsh and cruel in their judgement with no respect for life.

Your Teachings

Q. What is the aim of your teachings? What would you like to give to us?

I think that love and light has been lost in this world. Not many people look at the world as it is. Look at the everyday miracles that are around you. The teachings tell you that you are going to pass into Spirit. This is what is going to happen. But before you get there, you must look after the world, become more aware of what you are doing here.

Everyone should give love and light to their fellow man. The more people we can get to think this way, the more you will change things for the better.

Q. Do you think your teachings will have as much impact as your teachings 2000 years ago?

Who knows? I did not set out all those years ago to have such a big impact. It happened after my death. I just wanted to teach as many people as possible in love and light. No one person can change this world. Many people have to change. It has not changed in 2000 years. The only thing that has changed is that you have become more technologically advanced. But everything else is still the same: poverty, war and famine. I would have hoped that in 2000 years, people would have learned to help one another and look after their wonderful world where no one needs to starve or die in poverty. But this has not happened. We still have people ruling others for their own ends.

Q. Do you sense that there is going to be a devastating end to the world.

Because of the course that the Earth is on, something drastic is going to happen unless people change. It may not be in your time or your children's time but unless change comes it is inevitable.

Q. There seem to be a lot of teachings similar to yours. There is a lot of activity. Is this because the Spirit world is concerned about the way that the peoples of the Earth are developing?

Yes. We need to get all peoples taught the same knowledge, one teaching.

Q. How do we get one teaching?

There are many teachers on many levels in Spirit, trying to disseminate their teachings. What I would like to see is one teaching for all. It does not work like this because of people's different understandings of the messages that they are given. Unfortunately Spirit has not managed to get everybody thinking the same way. If they did then you would not have all these terrible occurrences like suicide bombings. People would realise that it is wrong. It is fine for us to send warnings of impending disaster, but that does not change anything. People need positive messages to help them change.

Christian religions believe in Jesus and God. Jesus was the person who started me on my pathway so he is my master. But God is the infinite power that I am working for. It is really important for the human race to look at what has happened over the last 2000 years. Have they progressed physically and spiritually? Have they learnt anything? The answer is, no.

Q. You are very pessimistic.

Yes, because I do not think that the world has changed. How many people see beauty on Earth? I would love to have lived in this sort of environment 2000 years ago. If I were to pick you up and drop you back 2000 years, I am sure you would want to come back within a couple of hours! You still do not appreciate what you have here today. Please do not think I am saying 'you' - I am saying the world as a whole. The human race still does not look and think: 'What are we doing to our mother earth?'

Part Four

Testimonies

Chapter 23

Ray's Life Before Gillian

To give an added perspective to Ray's account of how he progressed and trained to become a trance medium some of the key figures who helped him on his way give their sides of the story in this chapter and those that follow. One of the most influential people in Ray's life in this early period was Jeanne Lambourne.

Jeanne is now in her late 70s. She met Ray for the first time in autumn 1974 and invited him to her home circle. She comes from a spiritualist family. Her mother, who was born in 1889, went to early spiritualist meetings in private houses.

Jeanne started going with her when she was 12 or 13 and witnessed healing and entranced people speaking in different languages. When she was at the rebellious teenager stage, her mother managed to persuade her to explore the subject further, so she joined a psychic book club. Jeanne continues her spiritual investigations to this day. At the start of World War II, Jeanne and her younger sister started investigating at home. Her sister, who was only nine at the time, was a natural born physical medium. She saw things in a glass ball and could make things move. The two of them received lots of messages from soldiers killed in the war. Jeanne left spiritualism alone after she married, but after her marriage broke down in 1968, she went to the local spiritualist church. She was living in Hampshire at the time. Jeanne's investigations were back on track and in the early 1970s she began to have regular circles at her home which lasted until she moved in 1981 to a houseboat at Chichester. All the stories which follow are condensed from longer interviews.

Jeanne Lambourne

I was at a meeting of the Wessex Association of Unexplained Phenomena in autumn 1974. Ray's cousin was there and I was introduced to him as someone who was interested in spiritualism. He said that I should meet Ray, so I gave him my phone number and asked Ray to call me.

Ray phoned and came with his cousin to my circle. Through Ray I met Paul, who at the time called himself Andrew Portlock. When he came through he mainly gave teachings. The trance was something that none of us had seen before and have never seen since.

We asked Ray what happened to him when he was in a trance. In the early days he said that he was taken to the top of the mountain where he learned the ways of the Indians with his guide, Waters Running. I remember Waters Running introducing himself one evening with his fleas. Amazingly we all started itching!

Waters Running did not come in on a high vibration. Because Ray was beginning his journey he was still sensitive to what was happening and was not spiritually aware of the great work he was to do. Waters Running's energy was a familiar feeling for Ray. So, he was able to leave his body with Waters Running's help.

It was always Waters Running or John the American airman who helped Ray make the transition back after Paul had left, but of course now the transition is much quicker. John was an American airman who was killed in World War II. He came through as an observer and a helper.

By chance I made contact with a friend of mine with whom I had lost touch. She was greatly distressed and a shadow of her former self, and was on the verge of moving to Devon. I told her that I knew someone who could help her. Ray agreed to come over the following evening and my friend met Paul. He told her not to move to Devon, but just to go for a four or five-week holiday. Paul also told her that he was going to send John to look after her. When she came back from Devon, my friend said that she had been aware of John. She had picked up the pieces and was fine and has not looked back since.

It did not take very long after I met Ray to realise that here was a man totally without ego. To work with Ray and Paul, was like walking with Jesus. I felt very humble and privileged. Anyone who has seen Ray and Paul will know that they have completely different personalities. Ray could not see without glasses when I knew him, Paul sees clearly without artificial aids. Paul's voice is very different.

The union that Ray and Paul have and the way that they can work together in harmony is very special. I have never seen any other medium that is so attuned with his spirit guide. What is so wonderful about the mediumship is that if you meet Paul first, there is no way that you would think that Ray is in trance. It is quite a shock when Paul leaves and you come across a completely different person.

Ray did not come round every week and only took part in my development circle for about a year in the mid-1970s. I remember an incredible operation that Paul performed at my house. A lady called Marcia arrived wearing a neck collar. Paul looked at Marcia and asked her what the problem was. She said that she had been involved in a car accident and that she had whiplash. He asked if he could have a look at her neck, because he was sure he could fix it. We went into my daughter's bedroom and Marcia lay on the bed. Paul said: 'I think we are going to have to give you a little anaesthetic.' He said to me: 'Do you mind?' and put my finger on her body. Within two or three seconds the injection was over and she could feel no pain. I was at Marcia's head beside Paul. He asked me to put my hands on each ear and said he was going to pass the head over to me so he could get at the spine. I thought: 'What!'

Before I could register what was going on, the head was slowly lifted and I could feel the weight of it in my hands. I was praying: 'Please help me I hope this man knows what he is doing because we have one big problem.' He quietly continued with the work and said: 'I am just going to put a little wedge between the vertebrae to support the neck where it has been damaged. You will have no more problems.' Paul turned to me and said: 'Right we will put the head back in place.' He took Marcia's head. It looked as if it moved an inch, or an inch and a half, back in place.

The body went into convulsions, but Paul allayed any fears: 'Do not worry, this is normal. It will quickly settle down. Right, how about a nice cup of tea Jeanne?'

My daughter was training to be a nurse. When she came home at the weekend, I asked her what happened after an operation on the spine. Would the body go into spasm? 'Yes' was the reply.

I eventually moved away from the Portsmouth area in 1981 to a house-boat in Chichester. Ray came to see me there and joined some new friends in a circle. He said that he sensed that Geronimo was close to him and would we like him to come through? Ray was sitting in a small garden chair and looked as if he was getting bigger and bigger. Suddenly the canvas split and he shot through the bottom of the chair. Ray quickly came back wondering what had happened!

* * * * *

Jeanne continued to play an important part in Ray's life over quite a number of years and further testimony from her will follow. Pat Cowen, who met Ray at a healing circle, tells her story next. Pat has been involved with spiritualism for most of her life. She lives at Widley near Portsmouth and met Ray at a circle in a friend's house in the mid 1980s. Ray visited her house most weeks for healing circles from 1985 until he moved to Needham Market in 1990. Clinics were then held on a monthly basis until the middle of 1991. Pat and her friends were trained to heal by Paul and then continued to meet on a weekly basis to do healing. She refers patients to Paul now and offers back-up healing after they have seen him. Pat is a member of the Corinthian Healing Association, described in detail at the end of the book.

Pat Cowen

I met Ray at a friend's house. Then he came round to my place one night and our healing circle evolved. Paul came through to do healing and trained my friends and I to work with him. On some occasions he would stay after the patients had left and give teachings about the world of Spirit. He would do question and answer sessions.

Initially Paul helped my friends, but then people started arriving by word of mouth. So many people came that I had to put Paul in my back room to do his consultations. The patients did not know Ray was in trance. They thought that they were just talking to someone called Paul. They accepted him for who he was - a healer. Ray became a really good friend and actually made the sitting area near my pond in the garden and laid the paving slabs.

I remember Ken Parr arriving here (see Chapter 9). He was carried in on a stretcher and walked out. It was marvellous. Paul quite often took the patient's hips or shoulders out of joint and cleared crystals to help their arthritis. You could actually see the hips and shoulders out of joint.

I remember a lady called Eileen Newell who came to us when her surgeon had told her that she might have to have her foot amputated. Eileen had an operation on a bunion on her left foot. Unfortunately the bones in her foot became infected. She had several operations. Bone was cut from her toe. She was also on antibiotics, but the infection spread and it looked as if amputation might be the only option. Paul turned her foot through 360 degrees and said that it was out of line with her body. Eileen felt no pain. Paul healed her foot and when she returned to the hospital for more tests, the surgeon was astonished to see that the infection had disappeared.

Paul was wonderful with the people who came to see him. One lady called Pat had had polio and walked with a stick. Paul's healing kept the pain away and improved her quality of life. Sadly her daughter was murdered, but Paul helped her cope with her loss.

I danced with Paul on one occasion. My husband Bill and I went with Ray and Sally (Ray's second wife) to a dinner dance. Suddenly Paul took Ray over and invited me to dance. It was hilarious!

When Bill died, Paul chose the music and the reading from Corinthians 13: 4-7 for his funeral in January 1987. Lorrie Sayers, our local Spiritualist minister took the service at the crematorium. The reading from Corinthians says:

> *Love is patient and kind. It is not jealous conceited or proud.*
> *Love is not ill mannered or selfish. Love does not keep a record of wrongs.*
> *Love is not happy with evil. But is happy with the truth.*
> *Love never gives up, and its faith, hope and patience never fail.*

Ray had an accident on March 24, 1988. He went through his digger windscreen and had 20 stitches on the top of his head. Ray came round after the accident and we did healing on him with Paul telling us what to do. That happened a couple of times.

Today I always work in a group of three healers. I have a wide network of contacts, including my daughter Jill who Paul trained. People come to see me because they are in pain and cannot get help from the medical profession. If they are in great pain, I arrange for them to see Paul at either Wimbledon or Brighton. Then they come back with instructions from Paul, which tells us what type of back-up healing is required.

Michael's case illustrates how we work.

Michael had fallen 13 feet onto a concrete floor and had a serious back injury. He had many sessions with osteopaths but eventually was only able to walk a few yards before suffering great pain. I met Michael's wife in hospital where he was having traction. They came round to see me and I arranged an appointment with Paul at Wimbledon. After the first session he had great relief from pain, then after his second consultation he was able to straighten up properly. Paul then advised him to visit me for further healing. Michael had been told that he would probably end up in a wheelchair. He now leads a happy pain-free life and still comes for top-up healing.

It has been, and is, a privilege to work with Paul. I am so pleased that I can play my part in his healing mission.

* * * * *

Jeanne Lambourne played again another major part in Ray's life in the late 1980s by making an important connection for him in Dagenham, Essex. Jeanne met two important new friends, Charlie and Georgie Hammond from Dagenham at a Devon spiritualist school. They visited Jeanne when she was attending a spiritual development course at Stansted Hall in autumn 1987, and brought along Ken Parr. Ken had been involved in two car accidents, was in a great deal of pain in his hips and legs, and was using sticks to get around. Jeanne picks up the threads of the story.

Jeanne Lambourne - late 1980s

I invited Charlie, Georgie and Ken to stay with me in West Sussex and arranged for Ken to see Paul at Pat Cowen's house. These are Georgie's memories of the visit.

> We brought Ken down to you in December 1987 and had the wonderful experience of seeing how naturally Ray sat down in a chair and in a few moments was transformed as a soft voice said 'Shalom'. It was Paul.

Paul was a totally different character to Ray. His voice, accent, way of speaking and manner were very different. He also brought an amazing sense of peace with him. There was a twinkle in his eye and he was a bit cheeky.

We saw such an improvement in Ken. I am scared to say 'miracle', but Paul's healing worked wonders. Unfortunately there were some set backs. Ken took too many chances, overdoing it a bit – after all he was only human!

We went twice more to Hampshire in February and March 1988 and Ken was much improved. His ambition was to get back to teaching and be able to stand for most of the day.

In May 1988, our son-in-law was killed in an accident at work. Our knowledge of the spirit world helped us to carry on and helped my daughter to survive. In December, Jeanne was able to give us conclusive evidence of Chris' safe arrival in the spirit world.

Ken Parr was interviewed by *Psychic News* following his healing sessions with Paul. This is an extract from *Psychic News*.

Healer Ray Brown ended a motor crash victim's nine years of back pain ... and proved a no-hope verdict from doctors wrong.

Kenneth Parr of Durell Road, Dagenham, Essex rang PN last week to vouch for the healer's 'outstanding successes'.

On New Year's Eve 1988 Ray phoned me. He told me that he was having a bit of a blank in his spiritual life, was feeling down and depressed, and asked if I could help him. I told him that I was going to see Georgie and Charlie at Dagenham in January and asked if he would like to come along with me. Our visit was such a success that

I started taking Ray to Dagenham every six weeks. Ray stayed with Ken Parr and they formed a close bond. Paul continued to work on Ken's spine, which he straightened out.

A healing group was set up in Ken's flat. The women were all used as 'instruments' by Paul, for giving injections. Our fingers were much more supple and finer than Ray's hard-worked hands.

It was amazing to see a patient flinch when a trapped nerve was first touched, but after a few seconds of pressure from one of our fingers, giving an unseen and unfelt spiritual injection, they relaxed and the pain was gone. Most healing took 10 to 15 minutes and we saw formerly frozen shoulders whirl round like windmills and stiff knees swing back and forth.

Georgie's daughter Jackie was born with a malfunction of the spine. One of the vertebrae was twisted which meant that she could not lie flat on her back. We asked Paul if he could help her. He worked on her three times and straightened the spine. She was thrilled. I saw her two years ago and her back is still fine.

A young man, Robert, came to us in a wheelchair. He had been in a wheelchair since a child and was now around 20. I always remember the look on his face when Paul helped him get out of his wheelchair and stand unaided for a few moments. I felt that I was 'touching the hem of the garment' of the Master Jesus. We were all revitalised and anxious to carry on with the work.

Sep the minister invited us to his church in Brixton. The six of us, including Ray, were the only white faces in the church, which was packed. The energy was magnetic. Sep asked me to introduce Ray who said a few words. This was the first time, I think, that Ray had spoken in front of a public audience.

Paul soon took him over and many came forward for help. It was a wonderful evening. Soft cooing and melodious sounds emanated from the congregation, as we all linked into the 'power of Jesus' and gave back-up healing as Paul directed.

I remember touching the hands of a young woman aged around 28. Her hands were very rough and chapped. I sensed that she was having a very hard time. The energy of love and light that passed between us brought tears to my eyes. After the healing, she told me that she was a mother of five children, and worked as a lavatory cleaner.

Ray became more confident and happy to work with anyone who wanted healing. He agreed to attend Phyllis' meetings at the Ted Ball Hall in Dagenham. There was much more room here for Paul's healing. Ray was also happy to stand in front of the congregation and explain what it felt like when Paul took over his body.

Then the time came when Ray told us that he was moving to Suffolk to 'go up a gear' and work for Spirit full time. We were privileged to have worked with Ray and Paul. The wonder of it all will always remain.

* * * * *

Chick Gorlick first met Ray and Paul in the late 1980s, when Jeanne Lambourne took Ray over to the Isle of Wight. In early 2004 Chick went to Ray, Paul and Gillian's Brighton clinic and met up with Ray and Paul for the first time in 15 years.

Chick Gorlick

Jeanne Lambourne used to come over to the Isle of Wight in the 1980s to stay with her friend Lyn. I attended several pleasant clairvoyance and healing evenings that were led by Jeanne at Lyn's house.

She mentioned Ray and brought him over to meet us. At the time Ray was a very nervous and shaken fellow. We all made friends with him very quickly. Paul came through and did healing sessions and gave us his teachings. Ray visited several times in 1989. We used to have a whip round to pay his travelling expenses.

Paul sorted out a problem with the bone at the back of my neck that I had been suffering from for 15 years. It could be very painful at times. Paul put his hand on my neck and said that it would be OK now. The pain had gone.

A friend of my brother's called Mo, who had hip problems, visited Paul for treatment. She was wearing quite a tight dress and, when Paul dislocated her leg to get access to the hip joint, I could clearly see that it was out of socket. Paul did some work on her, told a few jokes, then click and the leg was back in its socket.

Ray went off to Suffolk and we lost touch. Meanwhile two and a half years ago I had a quadruple heart bypass. During the operation my lungs collapsed and I was put on life support. I did not get out of hospital for seven weeks. I continued to have problems with my breathing and was getting out of breath very easily. Jeanne Lambourne told Ray what was wrong with me. He phoned and told me to come to their Brighton clinic.

Paul saw me in January 2004 and asked me to come back the following month. I had to stay the night, as he wanted to perform an operation on my heart. Paul put six spiritual probes in my heart on the Friday. Then on the Saturday morning he did some fine-tuning. He also found a leaking heart valve, which he fixed. Since then I have been breathing more freely and feel much better. Despite everything that has happened over the last 15 years, Ray is still the 'old' Ray. Nothing has changed. It has been wonderful to see him again.

* * * * *

Jo Aschwanden spent a considerable time in the Merchant Navy and his wife, Peggy ran a nutrition business with some 4,000 customers. They went to see Paul at a demonstration in Guildford and both gained considerable benefit from that first contact.

Peggy and Jo Aschwanden

Jo and I first saw Paul and Ray 10 years ago at a demonstration in Guildford. We were both impressed with the work. I had a trapped sciatic nerve and Paul released it.

My husband used to be in the Merchant Navy. He was forced to have all his overseas injections twice, because his passbook had gone missing. This overloading took 20 years to manifest and caused a heart attack when he was 51.

Meanwhile I also developed a heart problem. I was very stressed from running our nutrition business. We had 4000 people on our books and I was phoned up at all hours of the day for advice.

Paul did an operation on Joe to help him lead a more active life. After two months he was fitter than he had been for 30 years. Then it was my turn. Paul has operated on my heart several times. He told me to ease up at my first healing session. When I went back again for more healing, he patched my problem but told me that I had to give up the business, which I did.

Paul will always guide you and help you to help yourself. I often book in for a check up and a 'booster' at Wimbledon Spiritualist Church. We are very grateful for everything that he has done for us. If there was a world healers top 20, Ray and Paul would be in the top five. I have every faith in them. There is no fuss, but you definitely know what you have to do for your own post-operative care.

Gillian is a marvellous co-ordinator. I have phoned her up in the past to ask for remote healing - spiritual intervention when you are asleep. It works best if you are in a deep sleep. In the morning you always feel better.

Paul is wonderful to talk to, so full of wisdom. When you hear him speak it makes you realise that mankind has learnt nothing in the past 2000 years.

Chapter 24

Gillian and her Family's Role

Gillian's work has always been closely supported by her immediate family and here they give their side of the story. Connie Yates is Gillian's mother and although she is long past retirement age she still likes to be actively involved in taking bookings for the Bury St Edmunds clinic and almost always attends to assist Gillian with the administration. Gillian's two sons, John and Colin also describe what it was like growing up in such an unusual household and how they have viewed their mother's very extraordinary work.

Connie Yates

My own mother, Jessie Smith, lived to the age of 96. She was a very talented medium and healer. Her spirit guide was called Chan. One of her specialities was advising people on the running of their businesses. There were no 'ifs or buts'. She was very powerful and was particularly good at identifying the names of staff who were on the fiddle! Jessie did not advertise what she could do, but helped friends and acquaintances. I remember when Gillian was only three, my mother told me that she would be involved in spiritualism, would do a lot of work and would marry twice.

Jessie was particularly skilled at psychometry and could get really accurate readings from someone's ring. Soon after my mother's death, I received a message from her through a medium at the spiritualist church. She asked whether my sister and I managed to get the rings that she had left for us.

Arthur, my second husband and I went to see the medium, Joseph

Benjamin at Camden Town Hall. He came to Arthur in the audience and told him not to apply for the job he was thinking of going for. Arthur took his advice and stayed put.

On another occasion we went to see a healer who treated Arthur. The healer told me that I had a talented daughter who was going to open a church, which was going to be very successful. I rang Gillian when we arrived home. But she was out. A friend was staying in the house, so I gave her the message. Unfortunately she forgot to tell Gillian. When the Bury St Edmunds church that Gillian helped found opened, and became a big success, I reminded her of the healer's message. Of course she denied any knowledge of my phone call! Not long after Arthur died, a woman's figure woke me up in the middle of the night. Strangely, I could only see the main body of the spirit up to the neck. I said: 'What do you want?' Then it disappeared. Ray told me that this was my mother's spirit.

I went with Gillian and John, her eldest son to see Ray shortly after Gillian had met him. John had an injured shoulder that needed healing. Ray was sitting there looking very scruffy. He went into another room and came back as Paul. Paul successfully healed John's shoulder and sorted out my bunion.

Since then I have seen Paul perform some amazing operations. One young Cypriot man almost crawled into the clinic assisted by his wife. He was on crutches, but Paul healed him, helped him stand unaided, and encouraged him to start walking. His wife was in tears. I have also seen the medical profession react to Paul's skills and knowledge. Once I overheard a doctor talking to a colleague on his mobile phone. He said that Paul was coming out with medical information that even he had to think about!

* * * * *

John Sitton is Gillian Brown's eldest son. What seemed like very strange things to a young boy began happening quite early in his boyhood. Now grown up with a family of his own, he looks back over the years and gives his impression of it all.

John Sitton

When I was about seven or eight, Mum was upset by being woken in the middle of the night. She was led downstairs and something made her write the name Roy. I remember seeing the letters. It looked as if they had been faintly traced on the paper. I was worried that Mum was possessed. She gradually became more and more involved in spiritualism when she helped set up the church in Bury St Edmunds. However our lives were very normal and spiritualism never dominated.

As Colin and I became older, we took more interest. The committee running Bury St Edmunds Spiritualist Church often used to meet at our house. We nicknamed them, the 'Disciples'! Mum was really dedicated to the church and spent a lot of time doing the admin work. I saw lots of mediums at the church. Some of them did not perform very well. But I did get messages from my grandfather (Roy Pegler, Gillian's father). The medium was Gordon Higginson. He told me that I was going to be a Lieutenant in the Royal Navy and said that I would go the Falklands. At the time, I was just about to join the navy as an artificer and thought that there was no way that I would be a commissioned officer. But the message came true. I am a Lieutenant and I did go to the Falklands.

I did not witness circles in the house, but I do remember things going missing and turning up in the most unusual places! Paul did some healing on me soon after Mum had met Ray. My right shoulder was badly damaged and Paul sorted it out. I was very sceptical to begin with, because Ray went into trance so quickly. But the change was amazing. I thought that there must be something there unless Ray was an absolutely fantastic actor.

I really had my doubts when my parents' marriage broke down. We had been such a close family. But I realised that it was Mum's decision and

I trusted her judgement. If I had thought that Mum was involved in something dodgy, I would have told her years ago. But what Paul does and says seems to make such sense. It is very simple and straightforward; you choose your own path. Mum, Ray and Paul are really helping people.

My daughters are seven and eight. They have met Paul and he has given them advice. They are rather bemused with the change between Ray and Paul, but seem to accept it in their stride. I am an engineer with my feet firmly on the ground and definitely think that you have to keep an open mind about Spirit. I am happy. I have had my proof.

* * * * *

Colin is Gillian Brown's youngest son. Here he talks about his memories of home circles and his thoughts on the spiritual dimension.

Colin Sitton

I was in the lounge watching the transfiguration circle with Stephen Turoff on the evening that the banging started upstairs. I was around 14 at the time. This was just before Dad started doing his rescue work. I wondered what the noise was and decided that it must be my bedroom door, which was the furthest room from the lounge. Mum told me not to worry. That it was just the spirits causing vibrations in the house.

I watched Dad do his rescue work. They were all sitting in a circle, concentrating, then Dad went into a trance and his voice changed completely. He spoke as a young boy. I think that it was a young boy lost in a fire. The boy was crying and getting upset. Dad did not seem to remember what had happened when he came out of the trance.

I know that in a transfiguration, the medium is supposed to take on the likeness of the spirit that comes through, but I do not remember seeing this. However I am certain that the son of a woman in the room came through the medium, because the woman was crying. What he said made it obvious that it was her son.

I could always feel the vibrations; things were very different in the room when Mum held her circles. Mum took me along to Bury St Edmunds Spiritualist Church. It was very interesting, but I always sat at the back to keep away from the medium. One evening the medium said that he wanted to see the young man at the back of the room. That was me! I could not even begin to think who would want to contact me. The medium said: 'I have someone who wants to say hello. It is Richard who has had an accident on a motorbike.' I had been at school with Richard and had not known him that well. Anyway a couple of weeks later a friend told me that Richard had died in a motorbike accident. I thought what is going on here?!

Gordon Higginson came to our house. He was an incredibly wise man. My girlfriend was there with me. Mr Higginson sat next to her and had a chat. He told her the colour of her front door and its number. That was incredible! My wife Louise has seen several mediums. Her Mum died and one or two of them have been absolutely spot on.

Ray has worked on pains in my knee and a stiff neck. The discs in my neck are wearing out. I get on very well with him, although it is difficult to get my head round the St Paul link. I have been to his clinics and have seen upset people come out smiling. They are definitely getting help. My experience at the Bury St Edmunds Spiritualist Church really did it for me. I had no reason to be thinking about Richard.

I would like to believe that there is life after death and am pleased that I have had the Spiritualist experiences. But I know that the mind is very powerful. It is possible to believe things that are not happening.

My feet are firmly on the ground, but...

Chapter 25

Patients and their Healing

In this chapter we learn more about Ray, Gillian and Paul's healing work through the experiences of people who have been patients. First we hear from Len McKenzie, an Essex businessman whose back operation was featured in the BBC TV programme about Ray in the 'Secrets of the Paranormal' series.

Len McKenzie

I'd had a back problem for two years and was in a great deal of pain. In the end I went to the Nuffield Hospital and saw a specialist who was keen to operate. But I did not want an operation. They would have put a rod down my back, which would have severely limited my movement.

My wife, Val, and I had already heard about Ray and Paul. While I was in hospital, Val went to one of Ray, Paul and Gillian's demonstrations. Val told Gillian about my problem and she suggested that I see Paul that evening.

I thought that I might as well try it. I could always go back to the hospital if it did not work out. So Val picked me up and we went off to see Paul. I was only dressed in my pyjamas and was as high as a kite on the painkillers that I was taking four times a day.

Ray told me to lie on the bed. I did not understand the difference between Ray and Paul at the time. Two or three minutes later he asked me to get off the bed and touch my toes. I did what I was told and touched my toes, looked at him and said: 'This is a laugh isn't it? Three of my vertebrae have gone and I can touch my toes.' It was incredible!

Paul said that he had moved my nerves back into position, but that I would need an in-depth operation to sort out the vertebrae. I had no pain and felt great, so I went straight home, not back to hospital, and stopped taking the painkillers. Four days later the pain started again, so Val phoned Gillian for another appointment.

Paul worked on the nerves and the pain went. I did however have problems walking any distance because of the vertebrae problems. I was told that a spirit was healing me. I did not believe this and tried to work out why Ray and Gillian were doing this job. Was it a fiddle, just a way to make money?

But I soon realised that Ray did not know what Paul was doing. Then when I spoke to Ray about diving, and then spoke to Paul about diving, he did not know anything about it. I thought it was strange. But it did not scare me, although I still could not believe in Spirit.

One day Ray phoned to ask me if I would be interviewed by a TV journalist called Clare for the BBC programme Secrets of the Paranormal. The plan was for Paul to do an operation on me while they filmed.

I asked Clare: 'You have been with them for several weeks now. Did you believe them at the beginning?' She said 'No.' I said: 'Do you believe them now?' She said: 'Yes I do. There has to be something in it.'

Paul worked on the discs in my vertebrae and told me that he had put spiritual clamps in place to hold everything together, while my back recovered from the operation. He said that the clamps would dissolve after about three weeks. I felt no pain during the operation. The next morning, I found that I could do everything I could not do before, like sitting on the edge of a chair.

I was really confused, I wanted to believe in Spirit, but my macho nature would not allow me to accept what had happened. Paul told me about his life and experiences and who he was. I was amazed. That night, lying in bed, I thought that this was a bit extreme. Being operated on by a spirit was one thing but finding out that the spirit was Saint Paul was another issue altogether.

After we went home, Val and I were sitting in bed having a big argument about Paul. The phone rang and it was Ray. He said that Paul wanted to talk to me! Paul came on the phone and said: 'Listen to Valerie she is right.' I told Paul that I still could not believe it.

Val and I struck up a close friendship with Ray and Gillian and went on holiday with them. One morning Val and I were sitting on the beach and started arguing about Paul again. The next time I spoke to Paul he said: 'I was there all the time and what you were saying was totally wrong.' I sat there with my mouth open. This was too far fetched. This guy could actually listen to what I was saying. It was so scary! Gradually I began to accept that Paul and Ray were two completely different people.

When I went back to the specialist I asked him to look at my scan and confirm how many vertebrae had been damaged. He originally told me that it was three, but Paul had worked on four vertebrae. When he looked at the scan it showed that I had had problems with four vertebrae.

The specialist agreed that my back had healed. I told him that a spirit had sorted it out. He said that it was fine if it helped me feel better but added that backs could put themselves right. I also went back to my doctor and told him what had happened. It took him three months to talk to me again! Since then my back has been 99% perfect. But when I overdo it at work, I get a pain in my back like a red-hot poker. I sit down and ask Paul to sort me out. Within minutes I feel much better. I have no idea how it happens, but it does!

Not long after the operation I was talking to a friend of mine about my back. He could not accept that a spirit doctor had healed me. So I ran across a field to show him that my back was fine. He was staggered by the improvement. Now he and his family attend Paul's clinics. Over the last seven years I have sent hundreds of people to see Paul and he has made a difference to everyone.

At the beginning of 2004 I had a heart attack. I should have been going out with Ray, so Val phoned up to let him know what had happened. She asked him if Paul could help but Ray said that Paul was not around so must already be with me. Next time I saw Paul, he said that he and his doctors had been in the hospital doing what they could for me. Paul has promised to operate once my heart is stronger.

You have to do what is right for your own health. It is your decision. I had nothing to lose by going to see Paul with my back problem. Meeting Ray, Paul and Gillian has really enhanced my life.

* * * * *

Walter Fisher continues the story. Walter is a Consultant Neuro-surgeon based in Norway. He has a PhD in Neuro-science. His work is mainly operating on patients, but he also teaches new and younger surgeons how to perform surgery. He is doing research into cancer and how to try to control primary brain cancer and is also involved in a research project into neuro-navigation. This is a new method of finding structures deep within the brain with the help of computers and cameras. Mr Fisher is involved in Parkinson's surgery where pacemakers are planted into the brain to try to control the tremor.

Walter Fisher

I first met Ray and Gillian 10 years ago after reading about Paul in a newspaper. I was very interested in alternatives at that time and felt that medical science could not treat everything. So, I decided to find out what a spiritual colleague was doing, what kind of secrets he had that were complementary to the traditional methods. I visited the clinic at Tring to observe Paul at work. The first thing that I noticed was that he was an excellent clinician, and had an excellent rapport with and compassion for his patients. Patients almost rolled or crawled into the clinic and walked, even danced out! There was something going on that I could not explain.

As I listened to the patients describing their problems, I was able to form an anatomical picture. I would say to Paul: 'It must be between the fifth and first vertebrae, there must be a problem at that level.' Paul would reply: 'Yes, it is, you can see here. I have just moved the patient's nerve back into place.' I was astonished by the results.

I agreed to attend the Knuston Hall seminar with Paul in 1995 and talked about my opinions of Paul as a doctor. At that time, I was so impressed with the alternatives he was offering, that I felt that I should work alongside him. Paul discouraged me from taking this route. I am pleased that he did, because I went away and studied neuro-surgery.

It is much better to have a relationship with Paul as a colleague, where we are both specialists and can complement each other. He is a spiritual neuro-surgeon and I am a neuro-surgeon. Although of course he is much more advanced than I am!

In autumn 2003 I became one of Paul's neuro-surgical patients. A disc slipped in my neck in early September. First of all I thought that it was just a muscular problem. But towards the end of the month the pain increased and I realised it resembled the condition that I often see in my outpatients clinic. People are referred to me with slipped discs or nerve compression in the neck.

I had an MRI scan, which showed exactly what the problem was. The disc had slipped between the sixth and seventh vertebrae. Normally, we avoid surgical treatment for the first three months and try to control the pain. In my case I needed four medications, but this did not remove the pain. The next step for me was to take morphine, but I did not want to do this so tried to endure the pain.

Eventually I would have had an operation. The process is as follows. We enter through the front of the neck, between the oesophagus and the carotid artery. This is a place where there are not too many nerves. Then we go into the front of the vertebral column, open up the appropriate disc and take the disc out with a sharp spoon.

In my case, it would have been quite an easy operation. After the removal of the disc, hip bone would have been transplanted into the space and two months later it would have grown together.

Most cases however are not just slipped discs. Normally with older patients there are additional problems caused by degenerative changes in bone formation. These are quite difficult operations, as we have to clean out the bone with a special instrument.

If something goes wrong there can be a catastrophe. It is not a high-risk operation, but if you rupture the carotid artery or if your instrument slips and you go into the spinal canal, the patient is paralysed. But because I knew what Paul could do, I asked him to perform a spiritual operation, which of course would not involve traditional invasive surgery.

Paul diagnosed my problem as compression of the nerves in the spinal canal. First of all he parted the vertebrae, then placed a spiritual instrument like a wedge there, so that he could get at the nerves. Paul split the nerve in the disc to allow the inflammation to drain away. This is something that cannot be done by surgeons like me.

It took about three days for the inflammation to drain away, then the wedge was removed and a spiritual clamp was inserted over the vertebrae to hold them tight whilst the healing process took place. Paul told me that the spiritual clamps would dissolve after 48 hours. The operation was a complete success and I returned to work after Christmas. Many of my patients could be referred to Paul, especially those who have a condition, after scanning, that looks reasonable, without too much bone degeneration.

I feel very, very lucky to be a friend of Paul, Ray and Gillian. We have a wonderful relationship. With Paul, I have such a deep contact. It is very profound. This is something unique. Now I have seen him as a patient, the friendship is even stronger.

* * * * *

Carol Esplin is Ray and Gillian's secretary. Carol has worked with them now for about eight years and provides valuable administrative support. Carol began working with them after Paul relieved unendurable back pain. As well as her secretarial role Carol deals with appointments and bookings nationwide and is always happy to talk to patients and answer queries.

Carol Esplin

It was in 1996 that I became curious about spiritual matters, mainly interested in the 'juicy' bits like ghosts and reincarnation. I was an atheist at the time and did not believe that there could be anything after this Earthly life.

When I was growing up, my parents were not churchgoers themselves, but forced me to attend. I hated it. I always said that I would believe in God if he appeared in front of me! I needed proof to believe.

I watched the BBC2 TV series *Secrets of the Paranormal*. One of the trailers said that a strange man called Ray Brown would be featured. He apparently had a ghost coming through him. Ray's story sounded too unbelievable. I thought he was a fake.

A couple of days after the screening of Ray's story, I was shopping in my local Co-op, and met a woman whose children went to the same school as mine. We knew each other by sight but had never stopped to chat before. We began talking about the BBC2 series. I said: 'Did you see that weirdo on the TV the other night, the one with the supposed spirit doctor?' She said that she had seen it and that another woman that she knew was his part-time secretary. Amazingly Ray Brown lived in the next village to us.

His secretary also lived in our town. I knew her well enough to acknowledge her in the street. My Co-op contact told me that Ray's secretary was moving house and would probably be leaving her job.

At that time I was doing audio typing for a local financial adviser and was not happy, so I said to her: 'If you see Ray's secretary, ask her to put in a good word for me. That job sounds as though it might be very interesting.'

Soon after, Ray's secretary phoned me up and asked if I was serious about applying for the job. She explained exactly what Ray did, how he specialised in joint problems, back, necks, shoulders and stomachs. I told her that I had a severe back problem, so she suggested that I book an appointment with him.

My family has a hereditary disc disease. The protein structure of the disc does not form properly. If you are one of the unlucky ones, you don't know you have the disease until you start to get problems. My brother who is a doctor in Australia had to have major surgery. He is held together with titanium bolts.

By the time I was 40, I knew I had the problem. I could not turn over in bed and had to roll off in the morning. Putting underwear and socks on had to be done sitting on the bed. I could not bend over and lift a leg. I remember standing at my front door one day thinking: 'What a life, I might have another 40 years on this Earth. I cannot face the thought of being in this pain.' An MRI scan at hospital showed the deterioration of my lower discs. The consultant told me that when the pain was excruciating, he would remove the discs. This was not a happy prospect!

I booked an appointment to see Ray and Paul. To say that I was nervous is a huge understatement! I took my friend Jill with me for moral support and to take notes. We made our way to Fir Tree Lodge, took a seat in the lounge, and waited to be called. Six other people were waiting. When Paul came in and said the name of the next patient, he gave me such a look. He stared right at me and held my gaze. It still gives me goose bumps when I think about it. It was such an intense stare.

My turn came and Jill accompanied me into the treatment room. I sat on the therapy bed with my back to Paul; Jill sat to my right on a chair. When I went into the treatment room, I noticed Paul's blue eyes. He seemed to twiddle with my lower back a bit and went straight to the correct spot. Soon he told me to go and said that I was to come back in three weeks.

To be honest, I didn't feel much different when I left the clinic but I had decided to give him a chance. About an hour later, I started to get really bad backache. The pain gradually decreased overnight and in the morning I felt much the same as I had before my appointment.

I did not realise then that the pain was caused by Paul untrapping nerves in my back. Between my first and second appointments I contacted Gillian about the secretarial job. We had just settled terms on the day of my second appointment. Gillian took me in to let Paul have another go at my back and said to him: 'This lady is going to be our new secretary.' Paul looked at me and smiled: 'Yes, I already know that.' I think that on my first appointment, when he had given me that really intense stare, he had looked inside me to see if I was the one to work with him, Ray and Gillian. I have always felt honoured by that.

The same thing happened to me after the second treatment, not much difference straight away, followed by the intense pain, which decreased during the night.

The work was really interesting, though extremely upsetting and stressful at times, especially when I had to talk to people on the phone who had only a few weeks to live or their children were seriously ill. I was always able to give them hope. Most of them went off the phone much happier than when they called. I realise that this is probably another reason why Paul knew I could do the job. I have a strength that I was unaware of and am able to give patients compassion, advice and most of all, hope.

It was very strange to see patients arriving at the clinic with a walking stick or crutches and watch them walking out unaided after only one treatment. It took about four healing sessions before my back improved. One morning I woke up and was lying on my back. Something that I had not been able to do for years.

I soon realised that Ray and Paul's eyes are brown, not blue, as I had first thought. My friend, Jill, had also noticed that his eyes were blue during my first appointment. Seven years on, I can go to the gym, though I am not silly about it. I feel privileged to work for Ray, Gillian and Paul. Paul gave me my life back.

* * * * *

Phil Taylor became a patient of Ray and Gillian in the late 1990s following a slipped disc. Phil is at present Associate Editor of the mass circulation Sunday newspaper, The News of the World and wrote about his experience in the newspaper.

Phil Taylor

In early 1998 I did something to my back. It was incredibly painful. I went to see a physiotherapist who diagnosed my problem as a slipped disc. I was still in pain after five weeks of intensive physiotherapy. The pain just would not go away.

I struggled back to work. At the time, I was the *News Of The World*'s chief reporter. The photographer, who had covered our first story on Ray Brown, suggested that I should go and see him.

I'm a natural sceptic, but thought: 'Blow it, I have tried everything else. I may as well give Ray Brown a go.' Gillian Brown booked me an appointment to see Ray at their Wimbledon Spiritualist Church clinic.

I was shown into a back room and met Ray, who was sitting there wearing thick glasses. He closed his eyes, went into some form of trance, removed his glasses and became a completely different person. Ray asked me what was wrong and told me to get onto the treatment couch. I was ready to take off my shirt but was told that would be unnecessary. He touched my back with his hands. Within five seconds Ray hit the spot and diagnosed my problem as two trapped nerves. Seconds later he said it was fixed and asked me to touch my toes. I bent over and touched my toes; something that I could not have imagined doing earlier in the day. Amazingly the pain had gone.

Ray advised me not to do any exercise for two weeks. Gillian gave me a pot of cream to rub on my back to reduce any inflammation and that was it! I was so impressed that I wrote a piece for the paper, which appeared in a larger follow up feature on Ray Brown's work on February 22, 1998.

A few weeks later I started getting painful twinges in my back. I phoned Gillian who said that Ray was in Portsmouth. Ray agreed to meet me on his way home at a Little Chef on the A3. He told me to get into the back of the car, went into a trance, briefly worked on my lower back, then told me that I would be fine. Ray was right, my back was fixed.

Later that year we did another item on Ray. Sir John Mills' agent phoned us and said that Sir John had seen my story in the paper. He was in terrible pain and was due to do a show. I put Sir John in touch with Ray, who sorted out his problem, and enabled him to do the show.

Ray is a remarkable man and has wonderful healing powers. I am not sure about his claims that the spirit of St Paul is working through him. What I do know is that it worked for me. I would recommend him to anyone with a problem that is defying current medical science.

It is a funny old world. I have covered lots of extraordinary stories in my journalistic career. Ray's must rate as one of the most extraordinary.

* * * * *

The next testimonial is from Gerry Gurr, a former professional foot-baller. He was Southampton FC's goalkeeper in the late 1960s and ended his football career with Aldershot at the relatively young age of 25. Portsmouth wanted to buy him, but the Aldershot manager would not sell. Rather than play for Aldershot, Gerry decided to pursue his second love, music, and took the opportunity to go on a Far East tour, playing guitar in a band. He has been a professional musician ever since.

Gerry was diagnosed with spinal stenosis at the age of 45. Spinal stenosis is an incredibly painful back complaint caused by a narrowing of the spinal canal, which compresses the nerves travelling through the spine into the legs. He had successful NHS treatment in the early 1990s, but the problem resurfaced in 1998. Gerry saw the News of the World feature on Ray and Paul in February 1998 and decided to try the spiritual route. He was treated at Fir Tree Lodge.

Gerry Gurr

I was still playing charity football for the Ex-Saints in 1991 when spinal stenosis first struck. My first thought was that I had slipped a disc, so I went to a chiropractor who worked on me several times.

The problem became worse and I was referred to a specialist who told me to go home and lie down for three months. That was out of the question, as I was doing a summer season at the time. But it was getting serious; I could hardly take my jumper off. The more I stretched, the more painful it became.

A friend of a friend recommended a surgeon called William Hook. I saw him privately. He diagnosed spinal stenosis and asked if I had any private medical insurance. The answer was no, so he said we would have to do it on the NHS.

Fortunately I was slotted in quite quickly and was given an epidural. Epidurals can be very effective on some back conditions. The pain came back after a month, so I was given a second epidural. This time it did not help me and I was programmed in for an operation. It was carried out a year to the day after I had first noticed there was something wrong with my back. The operation was successful, but it took me nearly two years to get back to normal. I was fine for the next five years. But then my hip started feeling sore and I began dragging my leg as I walked.

In the intervening years, we had moved from Southampton to the Cotswolds. My doctor referred me to a back clinic at Moreton-in-Marsh where the specialist confirmed that the stenosis had returned. I was told that I had to see the main back surgeon who was away for four months, so was prescribed drugs to keep me going!

A couple of weeks later, my wife and I visited her parents. My mother-in-law showed me the February 22, 1998 edition of the *News of the World*, which featured Ray and Paul. She said: 'You have got to go and see this man. What have you got to lose?' I phoned Fir Tree Lodge and was told that Paul could not fit me in until June. So, I decided to go to the appointment that came up first. Fortunately I saw Paul first. I was taking painkillers every four hours, but decided to stop in advance of my appointment, so I would be able to tell if the visit had given me any relief from pain.

Paul was running 30 minutes late, but soon I was in the consulting room. I had my X-rays with me so Paul had a look at them, then started working on my knees. Now that filled me with confidence! I wondered how on earth it could help. He gradually worked up my back, then said: 'Right we will go for a walk'

I said: 'I cannot walk.' But Paul replied: 'We will walk to the car park.' The car park was 50 yards away and I could normally only walk five yards before being crippled with pain. We set off. I did not feel any pain. I had no limp and walked there and back. I was in tears. Paul said: 'You will not need an operation, but come back and see me once or twice more.'

Back home I sat in a chair until four in the morning waiting for something to happen. But I felt fine. I stopped taking painkillers. It was wonderful; I could sleep on my side again. Then I went to a gig in Camberley, loaded the van, came home and still felt OK.

My appointment came through with the specialist in Cheltenham. I told him that I had seen a spiritual surgeon. He said that sometimes these things happen, you get better. But he agreed to keep me on his panel for six months – just in case.

Around six months later, the problem reoccurred. I decided to see Paul who this time performed an operation. He worked on my back then passed me to the healers. The whole process took about three hours. I felt fine when I climbed off the operating table, but Paul told me to avoid lifting weights as much as possible, because I could aggravate my back again.

I visit Paul every two months for maintenance work. He keeps me going. It is so reassuring to have him behind me, because I could not imagine having an NHS operation and waiting two years to return to normal. I have been able to continue my work as a guitarist thanks to Paul's help.

I cannot speak highly enough of Paul, Ray and Gillian. I tell people in terrible pain to go and see Paul. I also tell them that it is irrelevant whether they believe that Paul is the spirit of St Paul or not. He might get them out of jail!

Paul was my first and very fortunate psychic experience.

* * * * *

John Bundock was a semi-professional wrestler. He had 23 years in the ring and retired in June 1998. For the last seven and a half years of his career, he was the Southern Area Lightweight Champion. He called himself Little John at Brighton area wrestling matches and was known as Judo Johnny Peterson elsewhere. He worked a lot with Jackie Pallo and was on the same bill as Big Daddy for his last bout at Hove Town Hall.

John Bundock

I started to suffer from stomach pain in the early 1990s. After about 18 months it became unbearable, so I went private to try and sort it out. I had an operation and they removed a growth, but the pain would not go away. The pain drove me to the brink of suicide. I used to go to bed at night and pray not to wake up in the morning and was so annoyed when the dawn came. I wanted to end it all, but did not want to leave my wife homeless, so kept going.

Imagine living with pain for three years that was so bad that you could not allow anyone to touch you. Well that was what I had to put up with.

I became aware of Ray Brown through *Psychic News*. I suppose I was really clutching at straws. A few years earlier I had been to see another psychic surgeon but his healing did not work, so I was fairly dubious about what Ray Brown could do for me. Anyway I went to see Ray/Paul at Wimbledon Spiritualist Church wondering whether it would be a load of rubbish.

I was told to get on a couch and my problem was diagnosed as a spasm in the colon. Paul told me that X-rays would not show this. I went to see him three times at Wimbledon, but the colon kept on going back into spasm. Paul said I needed major surgery and that I had to come up to Leicester for two days for an operation. I saw him within a month. He pointed out that my bladder had shrunk and that it was too small. Now the hospital had told me that, but I had not mentioned it to Ray, Gillian or Paul. Paul said that I would still be in pain after the operation, but that it would disappear in a few weeks.

I suppose I did not really hold out much hope. However, within a week the pain began diminishing, and I thought: 'Well I am still in pain, but at least I can live with it.' After another week, the pain had gone. I had my life back. Until I saw Ray and Paul, I wanted to die, but now I could start living again.

I have seen Paul do great work. I cannot praise him, Ray and Gillian enough. Paul is honest with you. He is not here to take your money and run. Because I had been so impressed with them, I set up a venue for a demonstration in Brighton. I got some good publicity in the local paper and the hall was packed. As a result I set up a regular monthly clinic for Paul.

Paul is a great psychic surgeon. Everything he has said has come about. There is more to life than we will ever know. I do back-up healing in the clinic. I had always thought that healing was a gentle way of giving comfort, but Paul's group healing method is much more powerful.

In my case a fairy tale came true and now I am concentrating on giving back to others what Spirit gave to me.

* * * * *

The next story is told by another patient called Karen Baker. From the age of 17 until well into her thirties, Karen suffered from terrible back problems. Her condition defeated medical opinion and she tried everything including pain management programmes, osteopaths, chiropractors and acupuncture. A friend of her boyfriend suggested that she should phone Gerry Gurr. He told her to try Paul, as she had nothing to lose. Karen attended a demonstration in Newbury. Paul straightened her back and removed the chronic pain. Karen has been a patient for three years during which time Paul has managed to solve her back problem to such an extent that she ran a five-kilometre road race in 2003. This has been an amazing turn round in the fortunes of a young woman who could not sit, stand or lie down and was previously subjected to a continuous cocktail of pain killers.

Karen Baker

I had my first problem with my back when I was 15. I was bridling and tethering my pony to a metal five-bar gate. The farmer came past with his tractor and trailer and the noise completely 'spooked' my pony. He went crazy and managed to lift the five bar gate off its hinges and knocked me to the ground.

He galloped off, dragging me with him. The gate smashed down on my head and back. I was knocked out for a while. The farmer managed to control the pony and took me back to the shed.

I had broken my collar bone and had difficulties with my left arm. It swelled up like a balloon. This was the beginning of my nerve problems.

I was a very fit teenager and used to cycle to work. But one day I took the bus home and sneezed so heavily that I displaced my coccyx. When I woke up the next day, I felt sick and passed out. I went to the doctor's surgery and was told to lie on the floor to help ease my back. Meanwhile I was hobbling around on crutches and the problem was getting worse. So I tried an osteopath.

The osteopath was a very experienced practitioner in her early sixties.

She said that this was the worst back problem she had ever seen in a 17 year-old. Fortunately she managed to put things back into place. My back was fine for a while.

Then, when I was 22, I was involved in a car accident. A car went into the back of my car at a roundabout. I suffered acute whiplash and had months and months of physiotherapy. I was in a hard neck collar for four months, and as a result my neck became very weak. Fortunately my osteopath specialised in necks!

My problems settled down until I was 34. Occasionally the top half of my back put itself out and I went to the osteopath for treatment.

I began working for Allied Dunbar in a desk job. Up until then I had been out and about doing sales work. Getting behind a desk was probably the worst thing that I could have done.

The crunch came in a game of rounders. The top half of my back went. Mrs Gilmour, my osteopath, who was now in her late seventies, did the trick. But three days later it went again and a couple of days after that, my whole back seized up. I could not move.

My doctor recommended a course of physiotherapy. But my back continued to seize up on a regular basis and was getting weaker and weaker. The physiotherapy lasted for a year. Totally frustrated, I went to the doctor and asked if I could have surgery. I was in BUPA so went privately to see a surgeon. He had a look at my X-rays, told me there was nothing he could do, and gave me some tablets. But the problem became worse. I had spasms everywhere in my back.

My doctor advised me to see an osteopath. I saw him for three months, but it did not help. My back was in such a state that I could not sit down. So I demanded to see a specialist. The specialist was an arrogant pig. He told me that he could see nothing wrong. He made me feel as if the problem was in my head.

Anyway the hospital put me on a pain management course. I was in rehabilitation for six months trying to build up my muscles. I also had acupuncture. I could not lie down and found sleeping very difficult. I could kneel comfortably, but to add insult to injury, I developed house-maid's knee! I knew all along that the main problem was in my coccyx, but the medical profession would not believe me.

At the end of the pain management course I was sent to a chiropractor. He was wonderful and tried everything he could to heal my back. He said that it was the worst widespread back problem that he had ever seen and agreed with me that the main problem was with my coccyx, which was displaced inwards at 45 degrees. The chiropractor asked other people for advice. He filmed me as a case study for seminars, but still my back would not improve.

The drugs I was taking were making me ill. I had gastric enteritis. The pills caused ulcers and then my hair started falling out. The turning point came when the chiropractor was on holiday and I had to wait three weeks to see him. I was in terrible pain. I needed help.

A friend of my boyfriend knew Gerry Gurr who had been treated by Paul. I had seen the Corinthian Healing Association paperwork a year earlier but had thought it was a bit dodgy. But this time I realised that it might offer me my last chance. I could not walk, sit, stand or lie down. I was in agony.

I phoned Gerry Gurr. He told me about Paul and persuaded me to give it a go. I had nothing to lose. I phoned up to find out where I could see Paul. I live in Swindon and needed somewhere close at hand because I was in too much pain to travel long distances. As luck would have it, Ray, Gillian and Paul were just about to do a demonstration in Newbury.

My boyfriend and I were both very sceptical but were keen to find out what went on. We were introduced to Gillian, who said that I would be called up. We also had a brief chat with Ray.

My turn came and I went onto the stage and told Paul that my problems were all over my back. Paul went straight to the source of the pain. He told me that my coccyx was out of alignment and that I was sitting on trapped nerves. Paul was the first person to go straight to the heart of my troubles.

He confirmed all that was wrong with me in five minutes, then got going on me. I was on the table for 15 minutes having major surgery. My body jumped up and down as Paul worked on me. People in the audience were worried, but Paul explained everything that he was doing.

Paul asked me to get off the table several times to go for a short walk. Suddenly I started to straighten up. That was the first sign that something was happening. Then the chronic pain lifted from me. I walked without limping, but I still felt some pain.

I said to Paul that I really wanted to be able to sit, so he did some more work and told me to go back into the audience. He would continue the process after he had seen some more patients.

My boyfriend told me that my face had changed completely. He said that I had the face of an angel. I sat down for the first time in two and a half years without pain.

Paul said that it was going to take a long time to get me back to normal and that I had to be patient. I was also advised that I would feel horrendous for a while, because I had had three operations, but that I would improve within five days. At the end of the demonstration I looked at myself in a mirror. I seemed to be 10 years younger and my eyes were shining brightly.

I recovered as Paul said and went to see him a few weeks later. In fact I have been to Paul's clinic at Tring every month for the last two and a half years. All the major nerves in my back were in a terrible state. He has gradually put the whole system back into working order.

Occasionally I have overdone things and have had some setbacks. Paul has drilled into me that there are only so many times that he can repair my nerves.

I gradually increased the amount of time that I could sit and now work 32 hours a week and regularly go to the gym. Last year I told Paul that I wanted to run a five-kilometre road race for breast cancer. He said that I could do it, but to take care. I successfully completed the race and felt brilliant. I never thought that I would be able to run again.

I still get twinges every now and again, but this year I am hoping to reduce my sessions with Paul to every two months. Eventually I would like to move to three times a year.

I have just been on a four and a half-hour flight to the Canaries and only got up once. I had to stand the whole way a few years ago. Paul was my miracle. I could not have gone on without him. For the first five months I was really frightened by him. He was awesome but I got over that.

He was my proof. I was very sceptical when I first met him, but I believe in the Spirit world now. Anyone with my type of condition should go and see him. What have they to lose?

* * * * *

Paul Gallegos' son Charlie suffered severe brain damage in an accident on a skiing holiday in France when he was just five. An adult, who was supposed to be looking after him, accompanied Charlie on a ski lift. At the start of the ride the safety bar was pulled down over Charlie's neck. It is thought that he was looking back and waving at friends behind him. His neck was trapped for 12 minutes, starving the brain of oxygen. When he was released from the lift he had cardiac and respiratory arrest. Charlie became a patient of Paul's in 1997 when Ray and Gillian were at Fir Tree Lodge. His case requires residential care from Paul, which at the time was available at Fir Tree Lodge. Paul continues to see Charlie at the Lutterworth clinic, but is unable to take any new cases like this because of the peripatetic nature of his work. Paul Gallegos, Charlie's father, explains how Paul has been able to help his son.

Paul and Charlie Gallegos

Charlie's accident was a tale of woe. Someone could have reacted to the situation, but it was not to be. We live in Holland. After a couple of weeks of emergency care in France, we decided to take Charlie home.

The local hospitals could not help him. A friend of mine, Dennis Gray, recommended a specialist in Scotland who offered oxygen treatment. Charlie breathed pure oxygen in a compression chamber for three months. This saved his arms and legs.

We were told that Great Ormond Street's Tadworth Children's Hospital specialised in intensive care for head injuries. So we managed to get him a bed there. Charlie was at Tadworth for a year. My wife came over from Holland every weekend to see him.

About six months into Charlie's time at Tadworth, Dennis Gray told us of his friend Angela who was a healer. Angela knew of Ray, Paul and Gillian and said that we should get in touch with them.

I talked to Paul who said that he could not promise anything but asked what our long-term ambition was. I told him that we wanted to establish some form of communication with Charlie.

Paul told us to bring Charlie to Fir Tree Lodge for five days. Tadworth was worried about moving Charlie. He was attached to nasal and gastric tubes, which complicated matters. We were determined to take Charlie to Fir Tree Lodge, but just before the trip he became ill with pneumonia. I phoned Gillian and asked for some absent healing. Fortunately Charlie improved and we made our first visit.

Paul has been working on Charlie for nearly seven years. The extent of his brain injury is so bad that improvements have only been very subtle. Charlie is still fully incapacitated.

Paul encouraged us to remove Charlie's gastric tube, much to the hospital's horror. As a result we took him away from Tadworth and began caring for him at home.

We saw Paul once a month until 2002. Then Paul offered to come over to Holland to treat Charlie and with our help tried to set up a clinic. Unfortunately the Dutch were not very receptive to spiritual surgery, so we reverted to travelling to England to see Paul at Lutterworth.

Our visits have reduced to every six months. Paul is completely rebuilding Charlie's brain stem. He hopes this will move things forward. All of Charlie's bodily functions work well. He does not have any illnesses. Doctors are amazed at Charlie's general health. He is definitely becoming more aware and can make very small movements. He uses a 'head pointer' to show us what he wants. The head only moves millimetres, but we can understand him. We are working on his maths and reading. He often gets eight out of ten of his sums correct. Things are definitely starting to happen.

Paul is a source of hope and encouragement. He is very honest and down to earth and has never told us that he can cure Charlie. He will not waste our time and will tell us if he cannot do any more for our son.

* * * * *

Finishing this section is Sandra Greeno who is a patient of Paul's at their Wimbledon clinic. Sandra's story shows how quickly Paul gets to the hub of the area causing pain and releases, in this case, a trapped nerve that a hospital scan was unable to detect.

Sandra Greeno

I had a hysterectomy and was in agony for two years until I had an appointment with Paul. The pain was in my abdomen and went right down my leg. My doctor and the local hospital could not help me. I was given a scan but there was nothing abnormal.

My husband read about Ray and Paul in *Psychic News* and arranged for an appointment at Wimbledon Spiritualist Church. I was in terrible pain on the day of my appointment. I was in tears in the waiting room.

Paul instantly knew where the pain was. It had gone within five minutes. He said that I had a trapped nerve, which he sorted out for me. I could not believe it. He also found that I had a bladder problem which he managed to heal. I did not know what to expect when I saw Paul. I thought that a psychic surgeon would use knives! But as soon as I met him I felt calm.

Paul is a wonderful doctor and Ray is a marvellous man for giving up his body so that people in need can be healed.

Chapter 26

Ministry of Healers

For many years Paul has been training healers to carry on his work. It is still his wish to set up a dedicated healing centre where his teachings can be passed on to people willing to follow his methods. Vince Lewis is an experienced National Federation of Spiritual Healers trainer. He has also worked in a medical centre offering complementary healing. Vince used to run a coach company in Bolton and met Ray and Gillian Brown when he brought Dr Marjorie Cotton and a group of medical students from Liverpool to study Paul's work at Fir Tree Lodge. Vince struck up a rapport with Ray, Gillian and Paul and they asked him to help set up the International Healing Federation. He worked with Paul to write the Federation's healing manual and moved with wife Anne, to Fir Tree Lodge, to run the charity. When the International Healing Federation closed down, Vince and Anne remained in the Lutterworth area for a while before moving to Yorkshire. Since then they have joined the Corinthian Church and Healing Association and have both been ordained as ministers. Vince continues to work with Ray and Gillian and provides back-up healing at their present Lutterworth clinic.

Vince Lewis

I was aware of 'something else' from a very young age. I remember staying at my sister's house when I was six and saw an apparition. My sister did acknowledge that there was some sort of presence in the house.

Everything went quiet during my teenage years and career in the RAF. Then in my late twenties I went with my first wife, Pauline, to her brother's spiritualist church.

I observed the medium and watched the reactions of the people opposite me. There was obviously a level of truth in what the medium was saying, and in some cases the recipients of information were moved to tears of joy. I wondered what this was all about and occasionally went back to the church.

My next experience was when my first wife left me. I can clearly remember watching her leave the house from an upstairs window and heard this voice say: 'Forget about her, let her go, she is not worth it.' There was nobody else in the room. Subsequently I found out that it was my father's spirit that had spoken to me.

I became fully involved in the spiritualist movement when Dave, a chap who worked with me at my coach company in Bolton, invited me along to his spiritualist church. I really liked it and soon started being shown things both clairvoyantly and clairaudiently. Then I began sitting in a development circle to train for mediumship.

One evening in 1988, I was due to chair the service, but Trevor, a fellow committee member asked if he could take my place. I agreed and went to sit at the back of the church to do some meditation.

Suddenly I heard the voice of the medium. She was pointing at me and told me a couple of things about my parents then added that I had a lot of people around me in white coats. I assumed that meant that I was going to be a healer.

Finally she said that I was going to become well acquainted with Saul. She said he was: 'the Saul who later changed his name to Paul. The Bible knows him as St Paul.' I must admit I was pretty sceptical. She might as well have said that I was going to have a cup of tea with Jesus!

In my development circle, I kept on being told that a big change was in the offing for me. Then one evening, a healer was missing at the church and Susan the medium said: 'You have doctors around you, go and put your hands on this lady.'

I did what I was told and put my hands on her shoulders, but after a couple of minutes she pulled away. I thought that I had done something wrong. But she said: 'That was incredible.' She had felt an amazing warmth and was on top of the world.

I decided to explore this further and joined the National Federation of Spiritual Healers. After training I quickly moved up the ranks and became a member of the north west region committee. Then there was a call for members outside the London area to train as tutors. I volunteered and in the end must have run around 30 courses for the National Federation.

Dr Marjorie Cotton came on one of my courses in Lancaster. I was talking about aspects of trance and she mentioned the work of Ray Brown, highlighting the fact that he was in the deepest of trances. I was aware of Ray's work from reading *Psychic News*.

She told me that she was going to take a group of medical students to watch Ray at work, and invited me to do a day course in Liverpool for the students, to introduce them to spiritual healing. I accepted and also offered to taken them to Fir Tree Lodge in one of my minibuses for the cost of the petrol. I watched Paul at work and saw him move a kneecap to the side of the knee. The medical students were amazed that there was no pain. They also said that what Paul was doing could not be done medically. Paul told me that I had Chinese and American doctors working with me who were part of his medical team.

Soon after I returned home, Ray and Gill phoned me to asked if I would come back to Fir Tree Lodge, to get involved in a discussion group about healing and developing training courses. I arrived late and ended up sitting in the front row. Paul was talking and stared at me for most of his presentation. He was testing me out, having me vetted.

I helped Paul in a healing demonstration and was able to observe him at close quarters. At the time Ray was still wearing thick glasses. Paul could read and see long distances without glasses. He reduced Ray's pupil size down to a pinhead. The minute Paul went, Ray had to grab for his glasses.

I decided to join Paul's new healing organisation. I was the fourth person to sign up and offered to do the training. Ray and Gillian asked me if I would run the International Healing Federation (IHF) charity and move to Fir Tree Lodge to live with them. Now this was quite tricky, as I had just started getting closer to Anne, who was to become my second wife. We had met when she came to my home circle. Anne and I set up Bury Healing Clinic. Dave, my friend is running it now, using Paul's methods. Up to 40 patients visit the clinic on a weekly basis.

One of the doctors from a local medical centre was very interested in healing and came along to our Bury Clinic. He arranged for me to provide healing on an 18 months NHS trial in his surgery. The results were incredible. Then I got the call from Ray and Gillian. I felt I had to go. I wanted to help spread the word. Fortunately Anne agreed to come with me.

We lived with Ray and Gillian for six months. Anne shared the secretarial load with Carol, and I worked with Paul to write the IHF training manual and run training courses around the country.

Problems began to build in the IHF. A lot of people did not understand the time and dedication that Ray and Gillian gave to the cause. There were also outside pressures. We were trying to get planning permission for the spiritual hospital and things were not going smoothly. Even close friends began to object to the plans and accused us of fiddling the charity. Ray and Gillian had had enough. They wanted to protect Paul's work and closed the IHF down.

I told Paul that I would set up a new spiritual healing organisation, but he said that it would not work. We moved out of Fir Tree Lodge and bought a 40ft mobile home near Lutterworth.

Eventually we moved north to Yorkshire and kept in touch with Ray and Gillian. As a result we have managed to keep a close relationship with them and regularly go down to the Lutterworth clinic to do back-up healing. To begin with, I pursued the idea of developing another healing organisation, and turned down Ray's suggestion that I join the Corinthian Church.

Paul actually phoned me in Yorkshire and asked me to reconsider. So, both Anne and I applied to be members and were then ordained as ministers. Our aim is to do all we can for Paul, the spiritual surgeon and his spirit colleagues, to help alleviate pain and sickness.

* * * * *

Elly Nickson is a chartered physiotherapist who was born in Sweden. Elly was drawn to spiritual healing and trained with Paul. She combines her clinic work with spiritual healing to great effect.

Elly Nickson

I am Swedish and trained in Sweden, initially as a pharmacist, then as a chartered physiotherapist. I met my husband, who is English, while we were on the same course in Sweden, and have lived in England a long time.

I have my own private physiotherapy clinic in Newbury and a healing group using Paul's group healing method. I help out with Paul's healing in his clinics and have often seen him at work. My husband is a retired doctor, but still sees some private patients, mainly with back complaints. He is positive about Paul's work, but does not include spiritual healing with his patients.

From about 1990 I began accepting the existence of spiritual healing.

Many of my physiotherapy patients told me that I was doing more for them than just manipulate and massage their bodies.

To start with I tried to push it away, but the patients felt that there was something else coming through. One of my patients was particularly insistent. He has become a very dear friend. My healing centre in Newbury is actually based at his house.

I gave in and did a spiritual healing course and was told that I was a natural healer. In 1994, I was asked by someone to help them start a healing support group, using Paul's group healing method. We went to the Tring clinic on several occasions to watch Paul work. Then I agreed to go on the course at Knuston Hall in October 1995.

After the course I knew that I had to help Paul. He is unique. Paul has something special. He knows what he is doing, but it is not just that, I think that he is a messenger from the other side. He reinforced what I thought I knew and told me more. I felt it was so right.

I have never heard him say anything medically wrong at his clinics. As well as being married to a doctor, I have worked with many medical professionals in Sweden. I know what they know and I know what physiotherapists know. Paul knows much more. I think he is still holding back on some of his medical knowledge. He will speak when the time is right.

Paul says: 'Anyone can heal, you just have to open up to it.' I really sensed a strong presence at a clinic recently and talked to Paul about it, wondering whether he had arranged it. He said: 'That is very good, you must have opened up a lot to sense my doctors in the room.'

When I work at my physiotherapy clinic, I offer healing after I have finished the standard treatment. Some of my patients follow it up by attending my healing group. Then, if they wish, they get the opportunity to train as healers and help spread the message.

When I heal, I just hand myself over to spirit. I say: 'Please help me to heal in the best way possible.' Then I let Spirit work through me. I describe it as a loving energy or whatever people like to believe in. I do not use any religious words, to ensure that people from different faiths feel comfortable.

I am particularly impressed with the way that Paul cares for depressed and troubled people. He speaks the truth in the kindest possible way. Paul can stop floods of tears no matter who is the patient.

It is amazing to see the difference between what can be his joking manner with patients who have a surgical problem, and when he is talking to a depressed person. Paul is there for everyone.

* * * * *

Sue Stoward is another member of Paul's team of healers. Sue is a State Registered Nurse and trained at The Radcliffe Infirmary in the 1970s. She then travelled the world, got married and had four children, so was out of nursing for 12 years. She resumed her career in 1990 and is an Accident & Emergency Sister at Watford General Hospital. In February 2004, she trained as an Emergency Nurse Practitioner. Sue is also a qualified homeopath having completed the licentiate course at the College of Homeopathy in 2001. She is a member of the Alliance of Registered Homeopaths. Sue explains here how she came into healing and her work with Paul.

Sue Stoward

My first involvement with healing was when I had a back problem. I had been to see an osteopath, then had some healing from friends of mine who were healers.

At my second appointment, the osteopath looked quizzically at my back. I said: 'Is there a problem?' She replied: 'Yes, last week you had a curvature, this week your back is straight and I am trying to work out what is going on.'

My mother knew Gillian Brown quite well, so I thought I would go to their nearest clinic, which was at Steppingly at the time, to find out more about healing. I soon became involved and moved with them to the Tring clinic when that started up.

I think that I have always done healing without realising it. But I learnt Paul's group healing method. I quite often do healing on people at work. We go off to the coffee room and get on with it!

Paul is very correct with patients. He knows his limitations, and says that it is not magic, I am not going to cure everyone. If he cannot help someone he will say. That is very good practice. A lot of people think that spiritual work can sort out all problems, but that is not the case.

I sense that there is a lot invested in Paul's work. It is not just him, there are a lot of other spirit doctors working with him.

When I am healing I also feel that spirits are working through me. I am just the channel. At Tring, Paul does the initial surgical work, and then I help out giving back-up healing.

One thing people tend to miss about the Spirit world is the fact that they have a sense of humour. Paul has a wicked sense of humour, but that livens things up!

The work that Paul, Ray and Gillian do is so valuable. Maybe it has been done before, but not quite in this way. The fact that Ray is able to allow his body to be used so easily, having practised it over many years makes the transformation between the two of them very quick.

I remember a young lad of about 19 who came to see us after he had had a back operation. Paul is particularly good with nerves, backs, necks and spines. This lad had horrendous problems. He could barely walk and was almost suicidal with the pain and frustration. Someone else had to drive him from Wales.

He had scar tissue down the centre of his back. It took about nine months to heal him. Paul told him that it would take a long time. He worked gradually and removed all the adhesions and loosened up the scar tissue. By the end of it the patient was 95% better. He was given his life back.

I saw it all; from the moment he walked in until his last appointment, and encouraged him to keep going. He ended up driving on his own and was almost complacent at the end, because he had forgotten just how ill he had been.

Sometimes nerves are very stubborn, they do not respond immediately and need more adjustment. Not everyone comes in, gets fixed and walks out. Sometimes they need more patience.

For most of my life I thought I was not psychic. I do not see colours or anything like that. I just get a very strong presence or feeling and occasionally hear people saying things to me.

My father who died 16 years ago was a very big man, around 6'3". He was a captain in the tank regiment and had his foot blown off in the war in the western desert. He crawled through four miles of German lines to get back to the British lines. He was actually taken by a German soldier who saw he was wounded and helped him back to the British lines. The German was then taken as a prisoner of war!

My father lived life to the full and when he died I was completely devastated, not because I did not believe about Spirit, I knew he was fine, but I wanted him here, I wanted to be able to talk to him.

Happily he came through Ray. He did not actually say anything, because it was the first time he had been close to the Earth. He could not communicate verbally. All he did was feel my hands.

Afterwards Ray said: 'What a strong bloke, big man wasn't he?' I confirmed his size. Ray said: 'Very strong, good bloke, I liked him.'

* * * *

Quintin Smith has known Ray and Gillian Brown and Paul for 11 years. Over the years he has developed both his healing and mediumistic gifts. Two years ago he was ordained as a minister in the Corinthian Church. He helps out at Ray, Gillian and Paul's clinics and also has his own healing clinic on Tuesdays in Pinner. This provides back-up healing for Paul's patients as well as his own.

Quintin Smith

So many things have happened to me. When I was a young child in bed, I used to see coloured balls of light that would just drift around the room. I subsequently understood that these were spirits. Children are very sensitive and often see phenomena like this.

I also had out-of-body experiences, drifting down the stairs in the middle of the night. I remember the sensation to this day. When I woke up in the morning I called my mum: 'Mum, come and watch me jump off the top of the stairs, I can float to the bottom.' She had to talk me down because I would have jumped!

One evening I woke up and saw a man standing at the bottom of my bed. This frightened me. So, I climbed out of bed and ran onto the landing. The light was on and I called my Mum. As she came up the stairs, I turned round and saw that the man had followed me out of my bedroom and was now standing on the landing watching me. Eventually I found out that he was Dr Kauffman, an Austrian who has worked with me over the years with healing and is working as one of Paul's doctors in spirit.

My first healing experience was with a faith healer who believed that healing came direct from God. She told me that she had gone to a Spiritualist church to help out, but nobody turned up to receive healing. She felt that this was a sign that spiritualism was evil and wrong.

She sat at one end of the room with her hands up and I sat at the other. After the first session she said: 'My word, it was as though Jesus was in the room himself. I am sure that you are going to be a minister one day.'

Then I felt the urge to go to a Spiritualist church. I did not know what to expect. I thought they might be a bunch of weird people! My girl-friend did not want me to go and was really against it at the time. I sat at the back. But the medium came to me and said: 'I have your grand-father here. He is telling me that you love to antagonise your father.' I thought: 'Well this is partly true, but a bit general.'

She continued: 'Your father loves his television.' But the bit that clinched it for me was when she said: 'Your grandfather has brought along a friend of yours. Your friend is saying slow down when you drive, because that is how he was killed.' Now that was my friend Marc who was killed in a road accident.

My friend Marc has been back five times through different mediums in different locations and said exactly the same thing: 'The accident was my fault.' I have also dreamed about him in full colour and seen him clairvoyantly as well.

David Rogers, a well-known local medium in my home area, invited me to sit in his development group. At that time we had two guides called Isaac and Bartholomew that would come through. David was clairaudient, which means that he can hear Spirit. I always thought that this was his greatest gift.

I met Ray, Gillian and Paul through David. David had a very bad back. He had heard of Ray Brown and decided to find out where the local clinic was. He made an appointment and invited me to go along with him.

Two weeks before the appointment, we were sitting in circle and David said that his guides had told him that Paul, who worked through Ray Brown, was St Paul. I sat there and frowned and thought: 'Oh really!'

So I decided to telephone Gill and said: 'You do not know me but I am due to come and see you in two weeks time with David Rogers. Can I ask a question?' She said: 'Yes.'

I asked: 'Is Paul, that works through Ray, Saint Paul?' The phone went silent and she said: 'How on earth did you know that?' I explained that I had been given the information through a good medium. Gill said: 'Please do not tell anybody. We have not made it general knowledge yet.'

A small group of us including David Rogers set up a Spiritual Awareness Centre in North Harrow, and we invited Ray and Gill to come and do a demonstration.

I spent a lot of time with David Rogers who was a great friend. On one occasion the guide Bartholemew said: 'In several years time, you too will be working the same way as Ray Brown. Never seek fame and fortune, but if it comes to you, so be it.' I have also had the same message through two different mediums who had the late, great, spiritual healer Harry Edwards coming through.

After I married I spent a few years away from spiritualism, because my wife was not happy with it. But during a visit to my grandparents, the door opened once again. My gran had big rock solid ganglion cysts on her wrists. She had been told that an operation would be necessary to get rid of them. We were watching TV and I saw a picture in my mind of somebody that I recognised. Later I realised that it was Dr Kauffman.

I felt that I could help my gran's ganglion cysts. She had no objection. So I placed a finger on top of one cyst. I did some very gentle semi-circles and within 15 seconds it had dissolved. We could not believe it. The same thing happened with the other cyst. They had gone.

Back home, I heard a voice saying: 'It is I, Bartholemew.' Now, I had not heard from Bartholemew for some time. He said: 'It is time to take your evidence to Ray and Gillian and tell them about yourself.' I asked him to give me some evidence to confirm that it was he that I had heard and was not my own thoughts. That night my wife woke me up and said: 'Someone's just shouted the name Bartholemew in my ear.' I had not told her of this previous event!

That was my evidence, so I went to see Ray and Gillian and Paul, and began working with them on a monthly basis. About four years ago, Paul told me: 'There is no reason why you could not be the next Ray Brown.' This was music to my ears, because I felt this in my bones, but never dared to believe it. He said that he had already assigned a team of doctors to me and had put me through similar experiences as Ray.

A few months later, he dropped another bombshell. He said: 'I would like you to be a minister.' I thought there was no way that I wanted to be in a religion. I said: 'I am a free spirit and am happy with that. I am really flattered that you have asked me, but may I ask why?' He replied: 'Simply because you would make an excellent minister for the Corinthians.'

Paul ordained me just over two years ago. It was a very beautiful experience. He placed his hand on my head. The energy that came through him felt like it went through my brain and body and out through the ground again. I am very used to healing vibrations, but this was something much more powerful.

The Corinthian Church looks for its ministers to be spiritual people who live spiritual lives, help people and are good channels for Spirit. We have to go through a period of two years training with another minister, in my case it was with Paul through Ray and Gillian who are both senior principal ministers. I worked alongside Paul at the Lutterworth and Tring clinics and asked him many, many questions.

I run my regular healing clinic on Tuesdays in Pinner as a Minister of the Corinthian Church and Healing Association. I also regularly work as a spirit medium giving evidence of life after physical death. I teach this subject in a very grounded way in order to remove the mystery that shrouds this natural art and in a way that is easy for people to understand.

As for me becoming the next Ray Brown, well we will see. I love and trust Paul and his work. I am totally devoted to him and will always stand up for Paul.

* * * * *

This chapter finishes with the testimony of the Reverend Ron Jones who with his wife Valerie founded the Corinthian Church and Healing Association in 1993. Ray and Gillian Brown are both Senior Principal Ministers in the church. Ron Jones became aware of his spiritual gifts as a child. He has been involved in the spiritualist church for 40 years and was ordained as a minister in the Christian Spiritualist Church in 1983. Later he felt that the Christian Spiritualist Church was too rigid. There were too many rules. So he decided to found the Corinthians as a church that would give people the freedom to pursue their own spirituality. Ministers in the Corinthian Church can carry out the same functions as minister in any other established church in the United Kingdom including, christenings, marriages and funerals. The Corinthians also have a healing association, which has adopted Paul's group healing method. It has a fast growing international healing network.

The Rev. Ron Jones

I have been a medium and a healer for as long as I can remember. I was very aware of my gifts as a child. It got me into a lot of trouble! When

I was about eight my grandfather appeared in front of me and asked me to tell my mother that he had passed on. Of course I got a belt for my troubles, but sure enough the telephone rang. My aunt had called to let us know that he had died.

I joined the Royal Marines and I found that wherever I went, Spirit would talk to me and show me things. My wife Valerie, however, has always been a better medium than me. After we married, we started going to Spiritualist churches and training classes. I was eventually ordained into the Christian Spiritualist Church in 1983.

But it was not enough; there were too many rules. The church made it difficult for the ordinary everyday person. So my wife and I founded the Corinthian Church and Healing Association. Religion is out of the door, it has caused too many problems, but we do believe in God and Jesus and follow the writings of St Paul. Our headquarters is at Hailsham in East Sussex where we have a church.

Our aim is to make people feel very welcome. We train our own ministers and often have to knock past religious ideas out of their heads and replace them with pure spiritual thoughts. We are growing very quickly and now have around 200 ministers in the United Kingdom. I refuse to do christenings. But I will do a naming ceremony when the child is old enough to decide for him or herself.

Ray and Gillian Brown became ministers around ten years ago and progressed to Senior Principal Ministers in three years. We get on very well and are compatible. Ray and Gillian have also been very generous to the Corinthians and have raised a lot of money for our cause.

Of course Ray's guide is St Paul, but Paul does not have any influence over the way the Corinthian Church is run. We are all equal in the church, there is no hierarchy and we are very down-to-earth. Healing is the vital gift that we look for in our ministers. It is wonderful to see people cured when hospitals have given up.

If you want to be well and work at it, God and Spirit will work with you. You get nothing for nothing in this world. When you have learnt to like and love yourself, you are becoming useful. Without love you just exist.

Our healing association is affiliated to other organisations across the world. Anyone can become a healer. You do not have to be religious; you just have to learn to use these skills. The information is there for people who want to learn.

I have a reputation for ghost busting. I have been into houses with poltergeists and have often been asked why it happens. Usually hate between individuals causes the manifestation. On one occasion I went to a house in Pevensey Bay. The young couple who had bought the house said that a woman was in the kitchen and was swearing at them.

I went into the kitchen and there she was swearing away at us. I asked her why she was causing a nuisance and she said that it was her house and that we should get out.

I told her that she was dead, but she would not accept this. So I asked her if she would believe that she was dead, if her dead parents came to meet her. She agreed to this and with Spirit's help, her parents arrived and she went off with them. Problem solved!

A lot of people will not accept that they are dead when they pass over. I have been to churchyards and have spoken to people, who have been dead for five, ten even twenty years. They complain that they have been ignored all this time, so I explain that they are dead and have to move on.

Conclusion

by Paul Dickson

That final line from the Rev. Ron Jones on the previous page is perhaps typical of the profoundly esoteric nature of this book, which is so different from any other subject I have ever tackled before. Collaborating with Ray, Gillian and Paul and the twenty-one people whom I interviewed to provide testimonies has been an amazing journey for me. I knew nothing of the spiritual dimension before I began this project. But the enthusiasm of Paul's patients and Ray and Gillian's friends for his work and teachings has encouraged me to continue exploring this alternative view of life and death and the complementary benefits of Paul's healing method.

It has been a great privilege to sit and talk to Paul in the comfort of home, much to the amusement of my stepchildren, who have been equally fascinated with the story. Comments like: 'We heard him talking with a different voice' led to discussions in the car and a request to take to school Ray and Gillian's latest video, Ray Brown Spirit Surgeon, so that it could be shown during a Religious Education class.

I, like Anthony Grey, believe in Paul's sincerity. He is definitely a great doctor and surgeon and his teachings present an easy-to-understand and uncomplicated vision of the 'meaning of life'.

Ray and Gillian have been wonderful interviewees. The down-to-earth and humorous approach to their unusual mission is very inspirational. Ray jokes about his role in this amazing partnership, often referring to Paul as 'His Nibs'. But the trust and love shared by this special triumvirate is plain for all to see.

The Browns are continuing to travel up and down the length and breadth of the United Kingdom pursuing their unique healing mission and taking part in special seminars, some arranged by themselves, some by others. As this book goes to press they are holding regular day clinics at many points of the compass in church and community halls in Brighton, Bury St Edmunds, Hainault, Lutterworth and Wimbledon.

Carol Esplin who has provided one of the testimonies in this book has been secretary to Ray and Gillian ever since she received her first successful treatment from Paul. Carol remains responsible for arranging most of the appointments at the clinics, operating from a small office in the Midlands. She acts also as the focal point for anybody wishing to offer support, help or assistance to Ray and Gillian in their healing work. Her contact details for telephone fax and postal communication are given at the end of the Additional Information section that follows.

Ray and Gillian remain remarkably resilient and cheerful as they quarter the country in their camper van, covering hundreds of miles on many days each month. Their light-heartedness, warmth and informality are a remarkable feature of the very serious work they do and Paul's quick friendly humour is a notable aspect of almost every consultation. They have not given up hope, however, that somehow they will find a way to open and run an established centre where Paul can carry out more complicated operations and also train people to practice his healing method.

The main problem with their experience at Fir Tree Lodge was that Ray had to work without much respite to raise sufficient money to keep the centre going. His hands consequently became very painful, which meant he had to reduce his workload and this added to their financial pressures. Ideally they would be able to work best in a place where they could be based without the additional worry of having to make financial ends meet. Paul could then focus more on teaching and training and helping patients like Charlie Gallegos, who need intensive treatment combined with an overnight stay.

This book has been some ten years in the making. Efforts to pull the various remarkable strands of the story together began in the mid-1990s and a number of people at different times, in particular Tina Hobin, made valuable contributions to shaping early forms of the narrative. Progress has been slow because precedence was always given to the healing work in the clinics. Yet, as the incident-packed story shows, difficulties of many kinds have been encountered – and overcome in one way or another. No problem has yet proved insurmountable and Ray, Gillian and Paul's healing and teaching mission is continuing to offer hope and release from suffering for many people who can not be helped by conventional medicine.

They still need support, however, to make their work more effective. Helpers and supporters, as we have seen, have often been drawn to offer assistance at vital moments over the 37-year period of Ray's dedicated mission and it is to be hoped that now their whole astonishing story has been set down for the first time between the covers of this book, a new phase of their mission might be in the offing as news spreads more widely about the extraordinary healing work being achieved by 'a mere grain of sand.' This may be the end of Ray and Gillian's first book – but it is certainly not the end of their story.

Additional Information

The Corinthian Church and Healing Association

Founded by the Reverend Ron Jones and his wife Valerie in 1993, the primary focus of the Corinthian Church and Healing Association is to promote and teach the art of spiritual healing. The Corinthians also train people in mediumship. They aim to remove the mystery of this spiritual gift and show that we are all capable of this natural talent.

The church has the same legal registration as all recognised religions and can appoint and ordain ministers. In addition, the Corinthians can found their own churches and existing churches are able to affiliate. The Corinthians believe in God the Father. They also believe that we are responsible for our own actions in thought and deed and only we can correct our wrongdoing. They uphold the teachings and example of Jesus and follow the teachings of St Paul.

Their name comes from the letters of St Paul, specifically Corinthians, in which he wrote that we all have God given spiritual gifts to be used in God's service. The Corinthian church is not steeped in dogma or bogged down by unchangeable practices or beliefs. Its aim is to find the best means to spread the spiritual way.

It is called the Spiritual Way Church, to get away from the old name of Spiritualist, and is promoted as a new way forward, based on the knowledge of the past. The Corinthians are developing a healing network throughout the United Kingdom and are aiming for the network to go worldwide. All healers are trained to the highest standards and follow a Code of Conduct and ethics. Healers are also encouraged to become trainers and set up their own local groups.

For further information please contact:

Corinthian Church and Healing Association,
15A London Road, Hailsham,
East Sussex, BN27 1EB

Tel 01323 440420
Fax 01323 841352
E mail admin@corinthian-association.co.uk
Website www.corinthian-association.co.uk

Paul's Healing Clinics,
Seminars & Contact Details

For private appointments, teaching seminars, video tapes and guided meditation CDs with Paul and all other information about the healing work of Ray and Gillian Brown, contact Carol Esplin on (fax/tel) 01455 559880 or write to PO Box No 5836, Lutterworth LE17 4WL or visit our website www.raybrownhealing.com.

The video 'Spirit Surgeon' can be purchased from Michael Courtney-Hunt Productions on www.spiritsinc.co.uk. The clairvoyant medium Keith Charles can be contacted on www.keith-charles.com. Rev. Quintin Smith can be contacted for private sittings and groups by emailing revquint@aol.com or phoning 07968 781410.

The Tagman Press

The Tagman Press was founded in 1998 to publish books to help us think in new ways at this time of exciting and unprecedented change in world history. *Books to inspire and transform* is our motto. Our logo, a red heart superimposed on a white triangle, is a modification of the symbol of infinity, the oldest symbol on the planet.

We aspire long term to publish books in all the languages of the world. At present books by Tagman authors are available in up to 24 languages. Tagman's founder is Anthony Grey, former foreign correspondent, radio and TV broadcaster and author of the international best-selling novels, *Saigon*, *Peking* and *Tokyo Bay*. Tagman Worldwide (Ltd) is run day-to-day from Norwich, England by publishing executive and general manager, Jenny Smith. Details of our leading authors and titles, how to contact us and how to order can be found on our website. A fuller list of all books and audio-visual products, that are both published and recommended by Tagman along with a full statement of our philosophy can be seen on our website at: www.tagman-press.com.

Further copies of this book and all other books published by Tagman may be ordered direct by post from:

The Tagman Press
Lovemore House 5 Caley Close
Sweet Briar Estate
Norwich NR3 2BU

You may also call our credit card hotline on 0845 644 4186
or fax us on 0845 644 4187
or email us on sales@tagman-press.com
or you can buy directly online at www.tagman-press.com

Tagman publishes a range of important health books by Dr F Batmanghelidj which are available at the clinics of Ray & Gillian Brown. They concern the vital importance of water in restoring and maintaining health and contain radical and convention-challenging information about this aspect of healthcare. The four titles are:

Your Body's Many Cries for Water
Water & Salt: Your Healers from Within
Water Cures, Drugs Kill
Eradicate Asthma now – with Water!

Your Body's Many Cries for Water is a world-renowned bestseller which has sold over 500,000 copies worldwide and the other three books are all newly published by Tagman. Retail price of all 4 books is £12.50 – if you quote Ref AMGOS100 you will receive a discount of 20% on each of these titles.